THE LOST SOUL OF
AMERICAN PROTESTANTISM

American Intellectual Culture

Series Editors: Jean Bethke Elshtain, University of Chicago,
Ted V. McAllister, Pepperdine University,
Wilfred M. McClay, University of Tennessee at Chattanooga

The books in the American Intellectual Culture series examine the place, identity, and public role of intellectuals and cultural elites in the United States, past, present, and future. Written by prominent historians, philosophers, and political theorists, these books examine the influence of intellectuals on American political, social, and cultural life, paying particular attention to the characteristic forms—and evolving possibilities—of democratic intellect. The books will place special, but not exclusive, emphasis on the relationship between intellectuals and American public life. Because the books are intended to shape and contribute to scholarly and public debates about their respective topics, they will be concise, accessible, and provocative.

When All the Gods Trembled: Darwinism, Scopes, and American Intellectuals
    by Paul K. Conkin
Heterophobia: Sexual Harassment and the Future of Feminism
    by Daphne Patai
Postmodernism Rightly Understood: The Return to Realism in American Thought
    by Peter Augustine Lawler
A Requiem for the American Village
    by Paul K. Conkin
A Pragmatist's Progress? Richard Rorty and American Intellectual History
    by John Pettegrew
The Next Religious Establishment
    by Eldon J. Eisenach
A World Made Safe for Differences: Cold War Intellectuals and the Politics of Identity
    by Christopher Shannon
Ralph Waldo Emerson: The Making of a Democratic Intellectual
    by Peter S. Field
Intellectuals and the American Presidency: Philosophers, Jesters, or Technicians?
    by Tevi Troy
In Search of the Higher Self: Feminism and the Birth of New Age Spirituality
    by Catherine Tumber
The Lost Soul of American Protestantism
    by D. G. Hart

THE LOST SOUL OF
AMERICAN PROTESTANTISM

D. G. HART

ROWMAN & LITTLEFIELD PUBLISHERS, INC.
Lanham • Boulder • New York • Oxford

ROWMAN & LITTLEFIELD PUBLISHERS, INC.

Published in the United States of America
by Rowman & Littlefield Publishers, Inc.
A Member of the Rowman & Littlefield Publishing Group
4720 Boston Way, Lanham, MD 20706
www.rowmanlittlefield.com

12 Hid's Copse Road
Cumnor Hill, Oxford OX2 9JJ, England

British Library Cataloguing in Publication Information Available

Library of Congress Cataloging-in-Publication Data

Hart, D. G. (Darryl G.)
    The Lost Soul of American Protestantism / D.G. Hart.
        p.   cm.
    Includes bibliographical references and index.
    ISBN 0-7425-0768-8 (alk. paper)
    1. Protestant churches—United States. 2. Evangelicalism and liturgical
churches—United States. I. Title.

BR515 .H375 2002
280'.4'0973—dc21   2002021997

Printed in the United States of America

♾™ The paper used in this publication meets the minimum requirements of American
National Standard for Information Sciences—Permanence of Paper for Printed Library
Materials, ANSI/NISO Z39.48-1992.

To Mark Noll

CONTENTS

Foreword   ix
R. Laurence Moore, Cornell University

Preface   xi

Introduction   xv

CHAPTER 1
The American Way of Faith   1

CHAPTER 2
Confessional Protestantism   29

CHAPTER 3
Defining Conservatism Down   57

CHAPTER 4
The Intolerance of Presbyterian Creeds   85

CHAPTER 5
The Sectarianism of Reformed Polity   113

CHAPTER 6
The Irrelevance of Lutheran Liturgy   141

CONCLUSION

Confessional Protestantism and the Making
of Hyphenated Americans   169

Index   187

About the Author   197

Foreword

R. LAURENCE MOORE, CORNELL UNIVERSITY

When I travel outside the United States, I am frequently asked, "Why are Americans so religious?" Darryl Hart's *The Lost Soul of American Protestantism* offers a novel response that I am eager to try out. Americans—at least American Protestants—are not, in fact, very religious. True, the great majority believes in God. Most say that religion is important to their lives. Compared with citizens of other highly industrialized countries, American Protestants go to church with astonishing regularity. Nonetheless, if being religious means an understanding of creed, a confessional loyalty that clearly separates worldly purposes from worship, and a refusal to try to make God's power "relevant," then most American Protestants have merely confused the sacred with their well-known devotion to practical results.

Hart is committed to what he calls confessional Protestantism—a neglected and almost defeated tradition in American religious history that he skillfully traces from "Old Line" Presbyterians of the eighteenth century to Missouri Synod Lutherans in the late twentieth century. It is grounded in Luther and Calvin and deeply tied to creeds, clergy, and liturgical ritual. What Hart finds powerful in this tradition is apparent throughout the book. Yet to learn from his analysis, readers need not share the particular religious concerns that prompted his opening question, "What is wrong with Protestantism in the United States?" His history aims to redefine the most important division in American Protestantism; in doing so, Hart brings an important and fresh perspective to many debates that rage today about religion in public life.

Hart rejects the standard "two-party" view that is fixed in most histories of American Protestantism—a view that pits liberal Modernists who seek to reform society against convert-seeking Fundamentalists who have, until recently, kept their religion private. Hart insists that both of these parties belong in a mainstream tradition of American Pietism, a tradition that gained the upper hand in American Protestant life through the engine of revivalism and that always has the concept of changing the world at its core. The God of American Pietism is one called upon to do public and private work that always touches on the secular. Pietists rouse God to lay low their enemies at home or abroad, support government and non-government crusades for a better society, fix a bad marriage, and help them lose weight. The important division is between this activist Pietism and Confessional Protestantism, a churchly tradition that challenges Pietism's emphasis on an individual's sense of direct experience with God. It makes worship a rigorously private affair among members of a church community bound together by creed.

American Pietists have never agreed on a platform that spells out exactly what God should do, hence the seeming divide between liberals and conservatives. But what the purported two parties of Pietism share is more important than their differences. They both believe in a public-minded deity who was yoked into partisan political service by Modernists as well as Fundamentalists long before the 1980s. Billy Sunday and Washington Gladden were brothers under the skin. And although Jerry Falwell and Martin Luther King, Jr., played quite different roles in American history, they had more in common with each other than either had with J. Gresham Machen. Hart's sympathies are with the latter, who tried to hold Americans to a radical separation of church and state that perhaps not even Thomas Jefferson had contemplated.

The Lost Soul of American Protestantism is controversial in the best sense of the term. Alert readers will find something to quarrel with on virtually every page. They may or may not be fully convinced by the way Hart unites Protestant liberals and Protestant evangelicals who have been happily fighting one another for years on end. Without question, however, Hart's "alternative" narrative of American Protestant history rescues a critical component of the subject and changes the nature of the discussion as few other recent books have managed to do. If Hart is correct, what went wrong with American Protestantism gave an important part of American culture a distinctive—and some would say unfortunate—cast.

Preface

This is a book about a subject that for many scholars of American religion does not seem to exist. It is about confessional Protestantism, a designation as easily misunderstood as it is hard to see. For those with roots in Roman Catholicism, confessional Protestantism might sound confusing because it connotes the confession of sin to priests, a practice that Protestants abandoned in the sixteenth century. For others confessional Protestantism suggests a variety of Christianity that stresses the importance and correctness of specific creeds or doctrinal summaries of the faith. Both of these connotations, however, miss the mark.

Ironically, the scholars for whom this designation makes the most sense are political historians of the ethnocultural school who use confessionalism interchangeably with liturgicalism to refer to Protestants whose piety is grounded in the ceremonies, officers, teachings, and worship of the church. According to this usage, confessionalism is a high-church expression of Protestantism in contrast to the low-church outlook of Protestants who thrive in revivalistic and parachurch settings. Some of these historians have argued that the differences between confessional and revivalist or pietist Protestants is significant for understanding the political debates and alignments of the nineteenth-century United States. This book attempts to apply the same point to twentieth-century American religion. It raises this question: "What does the history of twentieth-century American Protestantism look like if the tension between confessionalism and pietism is the central dynamic rather than the struggle between liberalism and evangelicalism?" Whether the answers that follow will convince readers is one way to judge this book's success. But another barometer of the book's merit is its ability to raise questions about whether the categories now applied to American Protestantism are adequate or in need of serious revision.

My reasons for raising questions about the usefulness and precision of the evangelical and liberal categories are professional and personal. Having studied evangelicalism, first in graduate school under the direction of Timothy L. Smith at Johns Hopkins University and then as director of the Institute for the Study of American Evangelicals at Wheaton College, all the while exploring the specific history of Presbyterianism in the United States in my dissertation on J. Gresham Machen and during my teaching at Westminster Seminary, I became increasingly aware that the stories of evangelicalism and Presbyterianism are substantially different. What has been especially frustrating has been to see how the labels "evangelical" and "liberal" fail to do justice to Presbyterian history. At the same time, my own convictions and practices as a Presbyterian, both as a church member and teacher at a Presbyterian seminary, have made it difficult for me to identify with either the so-called conservatism of evangelicalism or the social justice ecumenism of the mainline Protestant denominations. Yet, historians, sociologists, and theologians continue to serve up evangelical and liberal Protestantism as the only alternatives on religious surveys. If there is no box for "other," it is hard to know which one to check.

Attention to confessionalism as a genuine category in American religion may provide a way around the impasse in which the study and living of American Protestantism now exists. This is certainly my hope. Part of my aim in writing this book is to develop a way of evaluating American Protestantism in categories other than evangelical or liberal that will yield more nuanced scholarship and possibly even better Protestantism than now exists.

I am much indebted to Bill McClay, who initially raised the possibility of developing into a larger study thoughts I had written elsewhere. Without his invitation and encouragement, this book would still be at the stage of notes and lectures. I am also thankful for the sabbatical that the faculty and board of Westminster Theological Seminary in California granted to me during the fall of 2000, which made it possible to write an initial draft. My wife, Ann, offered good counsel and cleaned up bad prose along the way, thus dramatically improving the manuscript. Finally, the book is dedicated to Mark A. Noll, who has been a mentor and friend for almost twenty years and who introduced me to the idea that confessionalism is different from other varieties of Protestantism. Although he may not agree with all of the differences observed in the pages that follow, his insights and advice have been so helpful to me that this dedication can only be calculated as a partial payment of my intellectual debt to him.

Introduction

Whaat is wrong with Protestantism in the United States? For most scholars who study American religion, this question is not usually asked. Part of the reason is that by most measures the United States ranks as the most religious country of Western democracies, and Protestantism deserves much of the credit. According to the National Survey of Religious Identification (1990), for instance, 86 percent of Americans identified themselves as Christian, with the various Protestant denominational affiliations accounting for 49 percent of the U.S. population.[1] Furthermore, a recent study conducted by George P. Gallup Jr. demonstrates that America's religious vitality is unique among other Western nations with historical Protestant affiliations. On the religion index (e.g., a ranking of the importance of God in respondents' lives), the United States (67) comes in well ahead of West Germany (37), Norway (36), the Netherlands (36), Great Britain (36), and Denmark (21).[2] Of course, adherents of religious traditions other than Christianity might very well have a different perspective on such statistics. But a view from within the Protestant fold suggests that religion in the United States is flourishing.

To be sure, most scholars and church leaders will be among the first to admit that all is not well for American Protestants. A number of trouble spots continue to show that Protestantism in the United States is not a story of unhampered success. The most obvious problem in recent years is the gradual hemorrhaging of the mainline Protestant denominations. Over the last thirty years, to take mainstream Presbyterianism as one example, the Presbyterian Church in the United States has lost on average thirty thousand members a year.[3] Sociologists and historians have offered a number of explanations for such decline, but evaluations of America's spiritual health cannot easily ignore the significant loss of membership and resources among the nation's historical Protestant denominations.[4] On the other side of the Protestant divide, evangelical churches and organizations also show areas of concern. The most glaring in recent memory are the scandals associated with various televangelists and financial schemes. Another area recently highlighted in the detailed research of Christian Smith is a dynamic within evangelicalism whereby as a subculture it thrives, but as a "faith-based movement" to influence the larger society it "seems somewhat to falter."[5] Then, the way that evangelicals mix religion and politics is still another source of worry to some.[6] Nevertheless, despite these blemishes, American religion generally—and Protestantism specifically—displays a comely visage to most observers. In the words of the legal scholar, Stephen L. Carter, "the best evidence is that this deep religiosity has always been a facet of the American character" and that "religion, as a moral force and perhaps a political one too, is surging."[7]

As Carter's statement implies, one instance of Protestantism's vigor, readily on display in the 2000 presidential campaign, is the increasing acceptance of religion's presence in public life. Here, it is interesting to compare 1960, when many thought John Fitzgerald Kennedy's Catholicism should prevent him from being president, to the 2000 campaign, in which expectations forced all of the presidential and vice presidential candidates to manifest some kind of religious commitment.[8] This change over the last forty years indicates the degree to which religion has become a desirable part of public life. And this is not simply the conviction of the religious right. It is a view gaining ground in such heavily secular sectors as professional social and political science. According to political philosopher, Jean Bethke Elshtain, the American system at its best proliferated churches "as public institutions that, rather than challenging government routinely, instead reminded people of what membership in a body requires," thereby sustaining "civic habits" necessary to democracy.[9]

To be sure, those who advocate greater recognition of religion's positive contribution to significant areas of national interest also recognize limits to the intermingling of belief and legislation. For this reason, although the evangelical religious right since 1980 has led the charge in injecting religious concerns into political debates, many commentators conclude that the way the Moral Majority or the Christian Coalition apply religion into public life goes too far. Such figures as Pat Robertson and Jerry Falwell come off as more judgmental than compassionate. But as long as religion has a tolerant and inclusive manner, it is generally welcome. This is because religion is thought to promote virtue and character. It is also supposed to nurture empathy and care for the marginal and oppressed members of society. In sum, religion is inherently useful in solving social problems because it yields moral guidelines that inevitably generate both a concern for justice and the welfare of all people. As a recent story in the *Chronicle of Higher Education* on sociological studies of faith-based charities put it, scholars who research religious nonprofit organizations "believe that those groups provide what government cannot and secular non-profit groups will not: personal, moral transformation."[10]

Relevant or Trivial?

The argument of this book, as idiosyncratic as it may seem, is that the Protestant-inspired notion that faith produces compassion, virtue, and harmony—that is, that religion is a benign influence that affects everyday life positively—is what is wrong with American Protestantism. For secularists and atheists, the argument that follows will likely be agreeable since the presence of religion in public life, as in the case of prayer and Bible reading in public schools, is obviously objectionable to a certain portion of the population, thus proving that religion is not always a welcome presence but actually divisive and out of place in some settings. But the concern of this book is not simply with religion and politics or with how to keep the public sphere religiously neutral. Instead, what follows is an examination of what such a fundamentally utilitarian view of belief has done to religion itself, specifically Protestantism, which, for good or ill, has been the dominant faith in the United States. What happens to faith when its adherents fashion it to serve practical, whether personal or public, ends? Of course, if the founder of a specific religion intended to solve sundry personal and social problems, then the only legitimate question is whether his followers have applied their faith in him correctly. But this is the question that has been begged by the majority of American Protestants as well as students of Protestantism in the United States. The argument that follows is that the mainstream churches, both liberal and evangelical, abandoned large pieces of their Christian heritage by working so hard to make their faith practical and relevant to everything from the personal lives of ordinary citizens to the affairs of one of the most powerful nations in modern history. In a word, by trying to make religion relevant, American Protestants ended up trivializing Christianity.[11]

This point is probably most obvious when it comes to questions about the relationship between religion and politics. Aside from the damage that public religion may do to the balancing act required by America's commitment to governmental neutrality in religious matters, the act of applying religion to everyday concerns trivializes faith by taking something that many believers regard as profound and reduces it to the less majestic proportions of political maneuvering. This is a point made well in an editorial for the *New Republic* in response to then–Texas Governor George W. Bush's declaration of June 11, 2000, as Jesus Day, a time dedicated to Christ's example of "love, compassion, sacrifice, and service." These virtues, the writer insisted, were not the reason for Christians worshiping Jesus; instead, it was his status as the Son of God. Consequently, Bush "did not glorify Jesus, he cheapened Jesus," which is "the certain fate of religion in the public square."[12]

But the trivialization of religion by making it public was not only a problem for Republicans. Another writer for the *New Republic* spotted a similar pattern in the way the press covered the responses of 2000 Democratic vice presidential candidate and Orthodox Jew Joseph Lieberman to questions about the relationship between religious observance and public ethics. The problem with all of the effort to read religious significance into Lieberman's politics was that it missed an essential feature of modern Orthodox Judaism—namely, that all realms of life "do not submit equally to religious authority" and that Judaism need not "promise an answer for each of life's multitudinous questions." "Political questions," this writer added, "do not always have theological answers; on certain subjects, the OMB [Office of Management and Budget] can be more helpful than the Babylonian Talmud." In sum, "a healthy spiritual existence often depends on the rigorous separation of the sacred from the mundane."[13] But this assertion runs against the grain of the dominant expression of American Protestantism and the way that religious tradition has shaped American conceptions of the relationship between this world and the one to come.

Less obvious, but just as troubling, is the application of religion to everyday problems that are common to all people, both God fearing and atheist alike. Evangelical Protestants lead the way in this category. Christian bookstores offer guidance on everything from food to sex in a way that turns the ordinary aspects of human existence into acts in the cosmic drama of divine redemption. But evangelicals are not alone in this regard. Mainstream Protestants may have a different set of concerns that are less domestic and more global—*justice* is a word that is often heard among mainline leaders—but the practical dimensions of faith are no less evident.

The predominance of this way of understanding religion was a prominent feature of the study of individualism and commitment in American culture conducted by a research team that Robert N. Bellah headed. In the first volume of this project, *Habits of the Heart* (1985), evangelical and liberal Protestants helped the sociologists make the point that even if Americans accept the doctrine of the separation of church and state, they nonetheless believe, "as they always have, that religion has an important role to play in the public realm." This role was perhaps easier to see in the case of a "liberal" Presbyterian congregation in which church members participated "in a range of activities from environmental protection to fighting multinational corporations marketing infant formula in the Third World." In contrast, for an evangelical congregation examined in this study, "biblical Christianity provides an alternative to the utilitarian individualist values of this world." As such, the team of sociologists concluded that evangelicalism did not "go very far in helping [members] understand their connection to the world or the society in which they live." Unambiguous answers on murder and adultery reduced ethics to personal relationships, but it separated evangelicals "from attachment to the wider society."[14] Perhaps in 1985 such morality looked more privately than publicly oriented, but that would be a much harder point to prove after almost two decades of evangelical involvement in American electoral politics and a presidential scandal involving adultery. Bellah's team may not have thought evangelical morality capable of nuance and compromise, but that incapacity did not prevent it from becoming a significant factor in public life. And much of the reason for both mainline support for liberal causes and evangelical support for family values derives from a prior belief in religion's unique ability to transform the here and now.

In the second volume of their study, *The Good Society* (1991), these sociologists found greater overlap between evangelicals and liberals. They quoted one Methodist minister of a liberal inclination who said the fight with evangelicals was largely finished. "I see a lot of them recognizing the positive role of the church in social action besides soup kitchens and shelters . . . They're for peace and civil rights. . . . They're moving toward the center as they get smarter and better institutionalized." This growing convergence allowed the authors to conceive of both evangelicals and liberals contributing to a "public church," not in the sense of religious establishment, but rather from the perspective of participating in "the common discussion about the public good." Of course, there were still important differences between evangelical and liberal public theologies, but the team was more inclined to see both sides as contributing to the construction of a common social ethic. And none of the authors raised a single question about whether this was a desirable phenomenon. This is because they basically agreed with the sentiments expressed by one person in their study, who said that "the Bible can speak to us today only if we do the hard work of making sense of it and seeing how it applies to our current situation." Without this effort, they explained, "religion slowly evaporates into pious phrases that no one understands anymore."[15] Few evangelical and mainline Protestants would dissent from these statements, let alone prominent sociologists of religion.

Relevant or Holy?

Some readers may well wonder why anyone would reasonably take issue with these convictions. Protestant views on the relevance of faith to everyday life are really par for the course. What else is religion for, some might ask, if not to help people cope and live well? Furthermore, what if evangelicals are a little more tacky in their application than Protestants in the mainstream? No one ever promised that religious life in the United States, unencumbered as it is by political or ecclesiastical establishments, would be neat. Others might add that religion appears to be responsible for a lot of charity and welfare in America, let alone the sorts of movements that previous generations of believers carried out in the name of their faith, such as antislavery, women's rights, and even the eighteenth-century liberation of thirteen colonies in North America from the British Crown.

One response to these objections is simply the factual observation that not all believers see their faith as having this kind of relevance. For some

Protestants, the goal of applying the faith to all areas of life misconstrues the essence of the Christian message, which has far more to do with eternal rather than temporal realities. Yet, the Protestant expression of Christianity's transcendence has not been well understood thanks to the widespread acceptance of pietist Protestantism's assumption that religion makes a noticeable difference in common affairs. At the same time, the failure to recognize the sacredness of faith inevitably produces the sort of awkwardness that is so common in American society. On the one hand, inserting religion explicitly into nonreligious spheres can turn something that believers and nonbelievers share in common into a source of antagonism. Does faith, for instance, make a difference in medicine, and, if so, is there a Christian form of medicine, let alone a Baptist one? What is more, for every reform for which Protestantism gains credit such as the abolition of slavery, the advocates of faith's relevance do not readily acknowledge its failures such as Prohibition. Some Christians believe it would have been better to resolve the issues over slavery and alcohol without introducing religion, thereby keeping some forms of prejudice and self-righteousness as much as possible out of the equation. On the other hand, the application of Christianity to social and personal problems can hurt religion by leading believers to forget what makes their faith holy or sacred. As the editorial in the *New Republic* argued, "'In God We Trust' is on all our coins, but the ubiquity of the affirmation has not led to any sharpening of the soul or the moral sense. Instead, God is dropped into parking meters and vending machines throughout the land."[16] In sum, the application of religion to practical affairs sacralizes things that are common (e.g., exercise, eating, and politics) and trivializes things that are sacred (e.g., creed, sacraments, and pastoral ministry).

The point here is not that religion is without relevance to common life. But as social scientists have argued, religion has to do primarily with the holy and sacred rites and symbols.[17] In the words of H. L. Mencken, "Religion, if it is to retain any genuine significance, can never be reduced to a series of sweet attitudes, possible to anyone not actually in jail for felony." Instead, faith in God is "something far more deep-down-diving and mud-upbringing."[18] The stress on the relevance of religion, however, ignores this perspective so that the question most often addressed to religious traditions in the United States is whether they contribute to public life or instead exhibit a private or sectarian form of faith. As such, the quest for relevant religion obscures such categories as the profane, holy, secular, and sacred, designations that are crucial to Christianity at least. Such concepts as the holy or the sacred may encourage believers to withdraw from "the world," as if converts should not be involved in secular life. But in the United States, religious activism, not religious quietism, is a far more likely extreme where Protestants have turned even the most trivial of pursuits into holy endeavors. And even when those pursuits are not trivial, the introduction of faith can do much more harm than good, such as when believers identify their favorite candidate for public office with the will of God or their preferred system of economics with a biblical standard. If no middle ground exists for believers and nonbelievers to discuss government and business because these areas are so saturated with divine significance, then religion's relevance becomes downright destructive.

Some scholars have, in fact, detected the toll that relevance has exacted from American Protestantism. According to the literary critic Harold Bloom, it is odd that 88 percent of Americans are convinced "that God loves him or her" and that two out of three evangelicals believe that "God speaks to them directly." The dominance of this form of religious enthusiasm leads Bloom to conclude that "[r]eligion, in the ostensibly Protestant United States, is something subtly other than Christianity, though to say that we are a post-Christian country is misleading." The better term is "post-Protestant," which suggests that Americans live with such a "persuasive redefinition of Christianity" that they "refuse to admit that [they] have revised the traditional religion into a faith that better fits our national temperament, aspirations, and anxieties." Interestingly enough, Bloom asserts that the "American awareness of God, and of the relation between God and the self, is very different from that of European Christianity, and perhaps that of any Christianity the world has ever seen."[19] Whether Bloom has American Protestantism right is, of course, open to question. Nevertheless, his perception that the dominant features of American Protestantism are novel, and that these innovations depart from older forms of Christianity, is one that this book explores.

Pietism and Confessionalism

In the chapters that follow, the first tries to account for the high regard for practical Christianity among American Protestants specifically and within American society more generally by examining the influence of revivalism, an Anglo-American form of pietism. The sort of religion heralded by the revivals of the First Great Awakening is chiefly responsible for the triumph of a utilitarian view of faith. The itinerant evangelists of these revivals, as well as their successors, transformed Christianity from a churchly and routine affair into one that was intense and personal. The conversion experience marked the beginning of this new form of Christian faith. But it was only the start. True converts were expected to prove the authenticity of their faith through lives that were visibly different from nonbelievers. Indeed, the demand for a clear distinction between the ways of the faithful and those of the world not only propelled many of the social reforms associated with evangelicalism but also provided the foundation for viewing Christianity in practical categories. If faith was supposed to make a difference in all areas of life, not just on Sunday but on every day of the week, it is no wonder that the emphasis in Protestant circles shifted from churchly forms of devotion to ones that should be seen in personal affairs, community life, and national purpose. In other words, the cycle of revivals throughout American religious history, inaugurated by the First Great Awakening, secured the victory of pietism within American Protestantism. Like its European antecedents, American pietism dismissed church creeds, structures, and ceremonies as merely formal or external manifestations of religion that went only skin deep. In contrast, pietists have insisted that genuine faith was one that transformed individuals, starting with their heart and seeping into all walks of life.

The thrust of this book, however, is not a critique of pietist Protestantism or the tradition of revivalism that secured its victory, an aim that would be more theological than historical. Instead, it concerns the consequences of pietism's triumph for churchly or liturgical Protestant traditions in the United States, such as Lutheranism, the Reformed churches, Presbyterianism, and Anglicanism. For the sake of convenience, the label applied to these traditions throughout the book is confessional Protestantism. Unlike pietist Protestantism, which attaches great religious significance to public life and everyday affairs, confessionalism situates the things of greatest religious meaning in the sacred sphere of the church and its ministry. At the same time, it places those areas that believers share in common with nonbelievers in a different sphere, one that is not inherently profane, but neither is it holy. For the confessionalist, some endeavors are holy, such as the ministry of word and sacrament; some are common, such as baking and banking; and some are profane, such as prostitution and racketeering.

It is this expression of Protestantism, the one more reluctant to assert Christianity's relevance, that is the lost soul of American religion. On the one hand, as chapters 2 and 3 indicate, confessionalism is the Protestant form of devotion that suffered most when pietism became dominant within Protestant circles under the aegis of revivalism. The literature on American Protestantism typically identifies theological liberalism as the chief rival to evangelistically minded Protestantism. But this analysis ignores almost completely the opposition of traditionalist Protestants to the innovations of revivalism. Confessional Protestants resisted revivals in large part because the methods of evangelists and the piety expected of converts were generically Christian—sincerity, zeal, and a moral life. As a result, revivalism did not respect but in fact undermined the importance of creedal subscription, ordination, and liturgical order. In a word, confessionalists opposed revivalism because it spoke a different religious idiom, one that was individualistic, experiential, and perfectionistic, as opposed to the corporate, doctrinal, and liturgical idiom of historic Protestantism. Confessionalism is the lost soul of American Protestantism, then, in the sense that pietism, through revivalism, has largely routed it over the course of two and a half centuries.[20] One way to measure this defeat is to ask any American Protestant if the Apostles' Creed, the real presence of Christ in the Lord's Supper or the ministry of the local pastor is as important as personal times of prayer and Bible study, meeting with other Christians in small groups, witnessing to non-Christians, or volunteering at the local shelter for the homeless.

On the other hand, as the three remaining chapters of the book argue, confessionalism is the lost soul of American Protestantism in the sense that scholars of American religion have largely ignored it.[21] Of course, as the old chestnut has it, winners write the history. It is little wonder, then, that confessionalism has not been featured in the sociology or history of American religion. But part of the problem is not that the defeat for confessionalism has been so comprehensive. Rather, it is that the vital statistics of American Protestantism are deceiving. Many confessional Protestants still exist in various Lutheran, Episcopalian, Presbyterian, and Reformed denominations. But because confessionalists are either classified as part of the Protestant establishment or members of the evangelical movement, historians have not pursued confessionalism as a separate category in white American Protestantism. Even here, trends within the field do not bode well for confessionalists since the study of white, mostly male Protestants of European descent who also had a high view of their particular churchly tradition does not fit the recent expansion of scholarly interest in the faith of minority groups. Ironically, the recovery of confessionalism conforms well with the effort to give greater attention to America's religious diversity by highlighting the variety of Protestantism in the United States. In fact, without the triumph of pietism in American Protestantism, historians would be hard pressed to justify the way they lump believers of various confessional and churchly traditions together into blocks of evangelical and mainline Protestants. In other words, pietism, in the form primarily of revivalism, has worn away the confessional identity of Methodists, Baptists, Presbyterians, Episcopalians, Lutherans, and the Reformed. Confessionalism has been lost, then, not simply because of scholarly neglect but also because of pietism's role in the creation of a Protestant mainstream.

Reconfiguring the Two Parties

As much as the recovery of confessional Protestantism may contribute to the stress on America's religious diversity, it could also be a step backward for religious historians by generating more denominational history. Prior to 1970, according to the conventional view of American religious history, the largest Protestant denominations dominated the field. As such, American religious history was synonymous with church history, and it was written by scholars working at Protestant divinity schools. Within the last three decades of the twentieth century, religious historians abandoned this older style of scholarship partly because this form of parochialism appeared to be of little interest to scholars in history departments. In turn, religious history, as opposed to denominational history, blossomed after 1970 as historians and sociologists looked beyond the mainline denominations and began to study not merely non-Protestant groups but also the manifestation of religion in sectors outside the church such as the economy and politics. Giving more attention to confessionalism would seem to mean a partial retrenchment of the field to patterns dominant a generation or two ago.[22]

The problem with this trend in American religious history is that it has left the study of Protestantism virtually frozen in categories scholars used circa 1970. According to the older literature, white American Protestantism consists of two main groups, one liberal or mainline, the other evangelical or conservative, with a portion of the conservative party being fundamentalist. Thus, the labels commonly used in the 1960s are still in force—liberal, evangelical, and fundamentalist. To be sure, the study of evangelical Protestantism has exploded since 1970. But even this line of inquiry usually begins with the older categories that divide liberal and conservative Protestants. Many studies of conservative Protestantism use the term *evangelicalism* as a catch-all for Protestants, from Pentecostals to Lutherans, who have some belief in the necessity of conversion, a concept that has a long and controverted history within the history of Christian theology.[23] And because conversion is said to involve the work of the Holy Spirit, many scholars assume that born-again Protestants are supernaturalists—that is, people who affirm the possibility of miracles or immediate divine intervention into human affairs. As such, supernaturalism, especially in conceptions of conversion, is the category that historians typically employ to distinguish evangelical from mainline Protestants. The result is that study of American Protestantism is stuck in categories that since 1970 have been reified and only account for a period of Anglo-American Protestant history stretching from roughly 1920 to 1950. Older differences between Presbyterians and Lutherans, Baptists and Congregationalists, or Episcopalians and Methodists have all but vanished.[24]

In a recent essay, religious historians Douglas Jacobsen and William Vance Trollinger Jr. lament the effects of this paralysis on the study of American Protestantism. The "two-party paradigm" that divides Protestantism between the public-minded liberal churches on the left and convert-seeking evangelical denominations on the right "is more rhetoric than reality," according to these writers, and obscures a much more "complex and multifaceted" side of twentieth-century American Protestantism. Although they do not try to prove the inadequacies of this approach, these authors have shown its dominance of the field, especially in survey texts. From Martin E. Marty's *Righteous Empire* (1970) to Catherine Albanese's *America: Religions and Religion* (1992), Jacobsen and Trollinger argue that the two-party paradigm is alive and well, encompassing not only Protestantism but American culture in its "entirety."[25] Had they wanted to include narrower studies, Jacobsen and Trollinger could have found many articles and books on American Protestantism that work within the closely patrolled borders of the evangelical and liberal camps.

As good examples as any are two popular and well executed books by Randall Balmer, who teaches religious history at Barnard College. The first,

Mine Eyes Have Seen the Glory, which appeared in 1989 and has subsequently gone through one revision, is an ethnographic study of the American evangelical subculture. On a journey that took him from the beaches of southern California, to New York's Adirondack mountains, and back to Oregon's Greenspring Summit, Balmer shrewdly observed evangelicals in a variety of settings, from camp meetings in Florida to urban missions among African Americans in the Deep South. The second book was an effort, initiated by the mainline Protestant magazine of record, the *Christian Century*, to do for the mainstream denominations what Balmer had done for evangelicals. The result, *Grant Us Courage*, took him to twelve "great" congregations that the *Century* had featured in a 1950 series on the most important mainline churches. Balmer's task was to observe and assess what had come of these centers of mainline Protestant strength over the course of the last half of the twentieth century, a period that many regard as one of decline. Aside from Balmer's astutely made points about evangelical vigor and mainline atrophy, these books confirm the impression that Protestantism can be divided neatly in two, with born-again Christians who interpret the Bible literally and evangelize aggressively outdoing the underachieving ecumenical Protestants who built the wealthiest churches and acquired the most cultural clout by tailoring the Christian heritage to fit American trends. Thus, an ethnographic study conducted by the perceptive gaze of a prominent religious historian sees little change in American Protestantism since the rivalry initiated by conservatives and liberals during the 1920s.[26]

The pattern of dividing American Protestantism in two has also been the dominant motif among sociologists of American religion. Here the work of Princeton sociologist Robert Wuthnow is illustrative. In his book *The Struggle for America's Soul* (1989), Wuthnow identifies two major parties in American religion, one liberal, the other conservative. As crude as this formulation may be, and he concedes that the religious landscape is capable of much more fine-tuning, when asked most Americans place themselves in one camp or the other. Consequently, self-styled conservatives identify themselves as evangelicals, "believe in a literal interpretation of the Bible," "say they had had a 'born-again' conversion experience," "indicate that they had tried to convert others to their faith," and "hold conservative views on issues such as abortion and prayer in public schools." Conversely, liberals "were less likely . . . to attend church or synagogue regularly," regarded "the Bible as divinely inspired (but not to be taken literally)," and affirmed "liberal views on a variety of political and moral issues."[27] According to Wuthnow, this description is only a snapshot of the situation. The explanation involves a host of changes in American society after World War II. Under the strain of these developments, conservatives embraced preaching, high moral standards, and "above all the personally redemptive experience of salvation." Liberals, however, insisted on the need to change social institutions because they reflected values and behavior that prevented America from achieving its ideals.[28] So again, the view of American religion provided by sociologists finds that Protestants at the closing decades of the twentieth century were still occupying fronts from battles fought at the beginning of the century.[29]

Nevertheless, as insufficient as the two-party view of American Protestantism may be, worse is what it neglects. The two-party interpretation lacks nuance and so lumps together disparate Protestant communions on the basis of a slim set of criteria, such as conversion or social activism. Such a minimalist approach to the various denominations of Protestantism, in turn, ignores such historically important aspects of Christianity as liturgy, creeds, and catechesis, preaching, sacraments, ordination, and church government. Ironically, by overlooking these churchly dimensions, the standard approaches to American Protestantism miss what may in fact be a more significant division in United States religion—namely, between believers who distinguish the essence of Christianity from the external practices and observances of it (i.e., pietists) and those who refuse to make such a distinction (i.e., confessionalists). Another way of illustrating this difference is to notice which Protestants define their religious identity by looking to the routines of church life and the teaching and preaching of their minister, and which Protestants structure their religious observance around personal acts of devotion along with efforts to make their faith more influential through either evangelism or social activism.

What is important to notice about this distinction between pietists and confessionalists is how evangelicals and liberals, the alleged antagonists, actually occupy the same position in the history of American Protestantism. Evangelicalism and liberalism both discount the formal or churchly aspects of faith in favor of religious sincerity and moral uprightness. These traditions may vary over the necessity of conversion or about what constitutes a righteous society. But neither group shows great interest in the specifics of historic Protestantism, such as the teaching of a particular creed, the authority of ministers, or the effects of baptism on children. As such, they are at odds with confessional Protestantism, and the reason for this antagonism has much to do with evangelicalism and liberalism's roots in pietism.

The Relevance of Confessionalism

As defective as the evangelical/liberal dichotomy may be for understanding the depth and variety of Protestant expressions in the United States, establishing another historiographical paradigm is less the goal of *The Lost Soul of American Protestantism* than is recovering the history of confessional Protestantism and examining its significance for American religion and society. In fact, the primary aim of this book is to introduce confessional Protestantism as a way of conceiving certain forms of Protestant faith and to illustrate this outlook through different episodes in the histories of Lutherans, Reformed, and Presbyterians in the United States. In a way, *Lost Soul* is an attempt to do for historic Protestant traditions what R. Laurence Moore did in part for Mormons, African American Protestants, Fundamentalists, Roman Catholics, Jews, and Christian Scientists in his book, *Religious Outsiders and the Making of Americans.*[30] In other words, in this study confessional Protestants are treated as Protestant outsiders—that is, Protestants for whom the categories of mainline and evangelical are inadequate. To be sure, this study is more introductory than exhaustive. It only includes examples of confessional Protestants, such as eighteenth-century Presbyterians; nineteenth-century Lutherans; and twentieth-century Presbyterians, Reformed, and Lutherans. What is more, these cases by no means conform to an abstract definition of confessionalism, as if these Protestant communions have been immune to the symptoms of pietism. Nor is the point that predominantly pietist Protestants, such as evangelicals and mainliners, make no effort to hold on to parts of historic Protestantism. But by introducing the category of confessional Protestantism, *Lost Soul* offers a different perspective on American Protestantism and the way historians have told its story.

Consequently, a subordinate, though important, purpose of this book is to suggest a different master narrative for the unfolding of American Protestant history. Most accounts of American religion begin with the Puritans, turn to the modifications of British Calvinism introduced by the revivals of the eighteenth century, and finally document the formation of the evangelical mainstream as the back drop to the division between liberals and conservatives in the twentieth century. To be sure, parts of this narrative are accurate, thus helping explain its resilience. Yet, this way of looking at American Protestantism fails to notice just how novel the piety and practices of the evangelical mainstream were from the larger perspective of Christian history. Consequently, the assumption in much scholarship on American religion is that revivalistic Protestantism is a conservative form of Christianity, and departures from it must be, by definition, liberal. In other words, evangelical piety (i.e., conversion, small groups, moral discipline, and religious outreach) has become the norm for evaluating and categorizing Protestantism in the United States. Unfortunately, by ignoring the teaching and practice of historic Protestantism in Europe, this approach flattens Protestant history and neglects a genuine tension between confessionalism and pietism. In contrast, by giving greater attention to the antagonism between pietism and confessionalism in American Protestantism, *Lost Soul* may contribute to a richer understanding of the Protestantism mainstream in its evangelical and liberal forms. Furthermore, instead of starting with the triumph of evangelicalism as a given, stressing the conflict between confessionalism and pietism makes the formation of the Protestant mainstream a fairly remarkable phenomenon.

A final aim of this book is to highlight confessional Protestantism as an alternative to the most common ways of relating religion to public life and everyday affairs. Throughout the twentieth century, evangelical and mainline Protestants have assumed, thanks to their pietist heritage, that religion has immediate relevance to all walks of life. Such an assumption has often nurtured simplistic formulas for grappling with deep-rooted problems, or it has contributed to shrill national debates. In fact, much of the blame for the self-righteousness and moralism that has characterized American culture can be laid at the feet of a Protestant faith that looks for evidence of genuine religion more in the everyday affairs of citizens and national officials than in the religious observances of believers gathered as the body of Christ. Surprisingly, the legacy of pietism is a this-worldly form of devotion that, in words that David N. Livingstone wrote of fundamentalists but equally applies to their pietist parents, manifests "the passion to hammer down history, to touch the transcendental, to earth the supernatural in the mundane."[31]

Confessionalism's alternative to pietism's promise of relevance looks at first glance like the worst form of irrelevance or, even worse, irresponsibility. Indeed, confessional Protestantism so stresses the church, its creed, order, and liturgy, as the chief vehicles by which believers are sustained in this world for life in the next that, by pietist standards, it appears to be of no earthly good. In fact, one of the common complaints against confessionalism is the way it avoids the tempest of social justice by retreating into the safe harbor of liturgical and creedal certainties. Although confessionalism in its corporate dimensions may not match pietism's energetic activism (the activities of its individual adherents may be another matter), it possesses resources for careful reflection about personal and social affairs that avoid the pietist extremes of self-righteousness and moralism. Even so, confessionalism cannot produce immediate results the way pietism promises, through either the imminent inauguration of God's kingdom on Earth (the liberal Protestant preference) or the speedy end of human history in divine judgment (the evangelical hope). But confessionalism's longer perspective on the flow of human history, thanks to its understanding of the institutional church, often yields as much wisdom as pietism produces results. In the end, this book features confessional Protestantism not as much to criticize pietism but as a means of calling American Protestantism to its better and older self.

Notes

1. Barry A. Kosmin and Seymour P. Lachman, *One Nation under God: Religion in Contemporary American Society* (New York: Harmony Books, 1993), 1–4.

2. George Gallup Jr. and Jim Castelli, *The People's Religion: American Faith in the 90's* (New York: Macmillan, 1989), 47.

3. For assessments of Presbyterian decline, see Milton J. Coalter, John M. Mulder, and Louis B. Weeks, eds., *The Mainstream Protestant "Decline": The Presbyterian Pattern* (Louisville, Ky.: Westminster/John Knox, 1990).

4. See, for instance, Robert Wuthnow, *The Restructuring of American Religion* (Princeton, N.J.: Princeton University Press, 1988); and Dean R. Hoge, Benton Johnson, and Donald A. Luidens, *Vanishing Boundaries: The Religion of Mainline Protestant Baby Boomers* (Louisville, Ky.: Westminster/John Knox, 1994).

5. Christian Smith, with Michael Emerson et al., *American Evangelicalism: Embattled and Thriving* (Chicago: University of Chicago Press, 1998), 219.

6. See Steve Bruce, *The Rise and Fall of the New Christian Right: Conservative Protestant Politics in America, 1978–1988* (New York: Oxford University Press, 1988).

7. Stephen L. Carter, *The Culture of Disbelief: How American Law and Politics Trivialize Religious Devotion* (New York: Basic Books, 1993), 4.

8. On the election of 1960, see Martin E. Marty, *Modern American Religion, Volume 3: Under God, Indivisible, 1941–1960* (Chicago: University of Chicago Press, 1996), chap. 26.

9. Jean Bethke Elshtain, "The Bright Line: Liberalism & Religion," *The New Criterion* 17, no. 7 (March 1999): 8.

10. D. W. Miller, "Measuring the Role of 'the Faith Factor' in Social Change," *Chronicle of Higher Education*, November 26, 1999, A22.

11. Owing as much as my argument does to those arguments by R. Laurence Moore about the deficiencies of describing the Anglo-American Protestant denominations as "mainline" or "mainstream" because of these terms associations with normalcy—thus, leaving outsiders in the position of being abnormal—I do not want to be misunderstood in my usage. See R. Laurence Moore, *Religious Outsiders and the Making of Americans* (New York: Oxford University Press, 1986), especially 207–9. I refer to these denominations (i.e., Congregationalists, Baptists, Methodists, Presbyterians, and Episcopalians) as "mainstream" not to suggest that other Protestants are inherently bizarre. Instead, the word refers specifically the efforts of these Protestants to create a homogenous religious center that fostered cooperation and mutual sympathy for common endeavor and that implicitly marginalized those reluctant or refusing to join.

12. "Crevices," *New Republic* 4463 (July 24, 2000): 9.

13. Benjamin Soskis, "Washington Diarist: Walking the Walk," *New Republic* 4467 (August 28, 2000); 4468 (September 4, 2000): 50.

14. Robert N. Bellah, ed., *Habits of the Heart: Individualism and Commitment in American Life* (Berkeley: University of California Press, 1985), 219, 230, 231.

15. Robert N. Bellah and Richard Madsen, *The Good Society* (New York: Knopf, 1991), 179, 189, 219.

16. "Crevices," 9.

17. According to R. Laurence Moore, "Secularization: Religion and the Social Sciences," in *Between the Times: The Travail of the Protestant Establishment in America, 1900–1960*, ed. William R. Hutchison (New York: Cambridge University Press, 1989), 251, "anthropology, the most historically minded of the social sciences, has been influential in promoting the value of parts of the religious imagination in which Protestantism is most deficient—myth, symbol, ritual."

18. H. L. Mencken, "Doctor Fundamentalis," *Baltimore Evening Sun*, January 18, 1937.

19. Harold Bloom, *The American Religion: The Emergence of the Post-Christian Nation* (New York: Simon & Schuster, 1992), 45, 53, 54.

20. In chapter 1, it should become clearer what I mean by revivalism. In the broader sense in which I am using it, it refers to the constellation of practices and convictions that make up pietism, rather than simply a system of mass evangelistic crusades.

21. For some effort by American religious historians to account for confessionalism, see H. Shelton Smith et al., *American Christianity*, vol. 2 (New York: Scribner's, 1963), 66–118; Sydney E. Ahlstrom, ed., *Theology in America: The Major Protestant Voices from Puritanism to Neo-Orthodoxy* (Indianapolis: Bobbs-Merrill, 1967), 371–460; Robert Bruce Mullins, *Episcopal Vision/American Reality: High Church Theology and Social Thought in Evangelical America* (New Haven, Conn.: Yale University Press, 1986); and Mark A. Noll and Cassandra Niemczyk, "Evangelicals and the Self-Consciously Reformed," in *The Variety of American Evangelicalism*, ed. Donald W. Dayton and Robert K. Johnston (Knoxville: University of Tennessee Press, 1991), 204–21.

22. On trends within American religious history since 1950, see Henry F. May, "The Recovery of American Religious History," *American Historical Review* 70 (October 1964): 79–92; David W. Lotz, "A Changing Historiography: From Church History to Religious History," in *Altered Landscapes: Christianity in America, 1935–1985*, ed. David W. Lotz (Grand Rapids, Mich.: Eerdmans, 1989), 312–29; Russell E. Richey and Robert Bruce Mullin, introduction to *Reimagining Denominationalism: Interpretive Essays*, ed. Russell E. Richey and Robert Bruce Mullin (New York: Oxford University Press, 1994), 3–11; and D. G. Hart, "The Failure of American Religious History," *Journal of the Historical Society* I (2000): 1–26.

23. An older Protestant understanding of conversion from the seventeenth century regarded this state as synonymous with regeneration, the time of the soul's quickening by the work of the Holy Spirit. But regeneration was not necessarily instantaneous, as it came to be regarded in the eighteenth century during the First Great Awakening. Instead, it was gradual and occurred over the course of a life. See the *Canons of Dort*, III–IV, 11–13.

24. For historiographical examples of this tendency, see Christine Heyrman, *Southern Cross: The Beginnings of the Bible Belt* (New York: Knopf, 1997); Paul K. Conkin, *Uneasy Center: Reformed Christianity in Antebellum America* (Chapel Hill: University of North Carolina Press, 1995); and William R. Sutton, *Journeyman for Jesus: Evangelical Artisans Confront Capitalism in Jacksonian Baltimore* (University Park: Pennsylvania State University Press, 1998), all of which dissolve denominational differences into revivalist Protestantism.

25. Douglas Jacobsen and William Vance Trollinger Jr., "Historiography of American Protestantism: The Two-Party Paradigm," *Fides et Historia* 25 (1993): 11.

26. Recent books that divide American Protestantism relatively neatly between liberals and evangelicals include the following: George M. Marsden, *Fundamentalism and American Culture: The Shaping of Twentieth-Century Evangelicalism, 1875–1925* (New York: Oxford University Press, 1980); Joel A. Carpenter, *Revive Us Again: The Reawakening of American Fundamentalism* (New York: Oxford University Press, 1997);

William R. Hutchison, *The Modernist Impulse in American Protestantism* (Cambridge, Mass.: Harvard University Press, 1976); William R. Hutchison, ed., *Between the Times: The Travail of the Protestant Establishment in American, 1900–1960* (New York: Cambridge University Press, 1989); Heather A. Warren, *Theologians of a New World Order: Reinhold Niebuhr and the Christian Realists, 1920–1948* (New York: Oxford University Press, 1997); George Marsden, ed., *Evangelicalism and Modern America* (Grand Rapids, Mich.: Eerdmans, 1984); Douglas Sloan, *Faith and Knowledge: Mainline Protestantism and American Higher Education* (Louisville, Ky.: Westminster/John Knox, 1994); Thomas C. Reeves, *The Empty Church: Does Organized Religion Matter Anymore?* (New York: Touchstone, 1996); and Donald E. Miller, *Reinventing American Protestantism: Christianity in the New Millennium* (Berkeley: University of California Press, 1997).

27. Robert Wuthnow, *The Struggle for America's Soul: Evangelicals, Liberals, and Secularism* (Grand Rapids, Mich.: Eerdmans, 1989), 24.

28. Wuthnow, *The Struggle for America's Soul*, 34.

29. For other sociological literature that reinforces this bifurcation, see Christian Smith, *American Evangelicalism: Embattled and Thriving* (Chicago: University of Chicago Press, 1998) and *Christian America: What Evangelicals Really Want* (Berkeley: University of California Press, 2000); James Davison Hunter, *Culture Wars: The Struggle to Define America* (New York: Basic Books, 1991); Robert Wuthnow, *The Restructuring of American Religion: Society and Faith Since World War II* (Princeton, N.J.: Princeton University Press, 1988); Roger Finke and Rodney Stark, *The Churching of America: Winners and Losers in Our Religious Economy* (New Brunswick, N.J.: Rutgers University Press, 1992); Nancy T. Ammerman, *Bible Believers: Fundamentalists in the Modern World* (New Brunswick, N.J.: Rutgers University Press, 1987); Stephen R. Warner, *New Wine in Old Wineskins: Evangelicals and Liberals in a Small-Town Church* (Berkeley: University of California Press, 1988); Steve Bruce, *Religion in the Modern World: From Cathedrals to Cults* (New York: Oxford University Press, 1996); Dean R. Hoge, Benton Johnson, and Donald A. Luidens, *Vanishing Boundaries: The Religion of Mainline Protestant Baby Boomers* (Louisville, Ky.: Westminster/John Knox, 1994); and Robert S. Michaelsen and Wade Clark Roof, *Liberal Protestantism: Realities and Possibilities* (New York: Pilgrim, 1986).

30. R. Laurence Moore, *Religious Outsiders and the Making of Americans* (New York: Oxford University Press, 1986).

31. David N. Livingstone, "Introduction: Placing Evangelical Encounters with Science," in *Evangelicals and Science in Historical Perspective*, ed. David N. Livingstone, D. G. Hart, and Mark A. Noll (New York: Oxford University Press, 1999), 9.

The American Way of Faith I

Among the many noteworthy aspects of Billy Sunday's (1862–1935) career, none was more unusual than his midlife transformation from a major league baseball player to a Presbyterian evangelist. From 1883 until 1891, Sunday played right field for the Chicago White-stockings, using his exceptional foot speed to set several base-stealing records. Three years after moving from Nevada, Iowa, to Chicago, Sunday came under the influence of the Pacific Garden Mission, an evangelistic work to alcoholics and the homeless. At one of the meetings he heard songs that his mother, a devout Methodist, had sung at home; liked what the preacher said; and converted. It did not hurt that Sunday had fallen for a pious Presbyterian girl whose father disapproved of Sunday baseball games. By 1888, the ballplayer was a member of Chicago's Jefferson Park Presbyterian Church, holding down the duties of Sunday school superintendent. Three years later he left the big leagues and its $500 per month salary to work for a considerably smaller sum as assistant secretary for the YMCA. After serving as an apprentice to the evangelist, J. Wilbur Chapman, and then conducting a series of revivals on his own, in 1903 Sunday sought ordination in the Presbytery of Chicago where his track record of soul winning more than made up for his lack of theological training.[1]

What was remarkable about Sunday's change of vocation was not the relative ease with which he went from wearing a baseball glove and spikes to a business suit and spats. Dwight L. Moody had already broken down the barrier between a business career and a call to the ministry when he

I

switched from shoe sales to soul winning. Instead, Sunday's notoriety lay in his ability to speak in the idiom of the urban common man. Nor was he above using his athletic ability to perform stunts that drew crowds to listen to his simple gospel message laden with "slangy humor and florid rhetoric."[2] Sunday's folksy appeal undoubtedly stemmed as well from his boyhood experience with rural poverty, enhanced by his days hustling through the gritty neighborhoods that surrounded major league ballparks. Here is how the skeptical journalist, H. L. Mencken, described Sunday's allure:

> As for his extraordinary success in drawing crowds and in performing the hollow magic commonly called conversion, it should be easily explicable to anyone who has seen him in action. His impressiveness, to the vegetal mind, lies in two things, the first being the sheer clatter and ferocity of his style and the second being his utter lack of those transparent pretensions to intellectual superiority and other worldliness which mark the average evangelical divine. In other words, he does not preach down at his flock from the heights of an assumed moral superiority—i.e. inexperience of the common sorrows and temptations of the world—but discharges his message as man to man, reaching easily for buttonholes, jogging in the ribs, slapping on the back. The difference here noted is abysmal. Whatever the average man's respect for the cloth, he cannot rid himself of the feeling that the holy man in the pulpit is, in many important respects, a man unlike himself . . . ; his aura is a sort of psychic monastery; his advice is not that of a practical man, with the scars of combat on him, but that of a dreamer wrapped in aseptic cotton.[3]

Mencken's obvious disparagement of the clergy and Sunday's hearers should not obscure the journalist's perceptive explanation of the evangelist's effectiveness. Sunday's substitution of colloquial slang for the staid prose of Protestant theology, combined with his reduction of Christian teaching to practical advice, gave him immediate appeal to a swath of Americans alienated by the good taste and learned discourse of the institutional church. Mencken added:

> Even setting aside [Sunday's] painstaking avoidance of anything suggesting clerical garb and his indulgence in obviously unclerical gyration on his sacred stump, he comes down so palpably to the level of his audience, both in the matter and the manner of his discourse, that he quickly disarms the old suspicion of the holy clerk and gets the discussion going on the fa-

miliar and easy terms of a debate in a barroom. The raciness of his slang is not the whole story by any means; his attitude of mind lies behind it, and is more important. . . . It is marked, above all, by a contemptuous disregard of the theoretical and mystifying; an angry casting aside of what may be called the ecclesiastical mask, an eagerness to reduce all the abstrusities of Christian theology to a few and simple and (to the ingenuous) self-evident propositions, a violent determination to make of religion a practical, an imminent, an everyday concern.[4]

Sunday was not the first evangelist to demystify Christianity, but the popularity of his techniques along with his ordination by the Presbyterian Church marked the degree to which pietist Protestantism would continue to supplant historic forms of Christian faith and practice among mainstream American Protestants. As Mencken shrewdly observed, the formalities of regular clergy could not compete with the charisma and uplift of itinerant evangelists. Ever since the First Great Awakening, in fact, American Protestants had been eagerly downplaying the mysterious and ceremonial aspects of Christian devotion in order to make the gospel relevant to individuals, families, and society. To be sure, the tradition of revivalism in which Sunday stood appealed to converts by promising the rewards and threatening with the punishments of the world to come. But the overriding importance of figures like Billy Sunday and his forebears was to make Christianity so practical that any hint of religion's irrelevance was proof at best of its inferiority, if not a sign of infidelity. In sum, thanks to the influence of revivalism, by 1900 mainstream Protestantism had rid itself of most of Christianity's theoretical obstacles to become the practical solution to the everyday problems of average Americans.[5]

The Evangelical Mainstream

Until the 1920s, when fundamentalists and modernists squared off in some of America's largest denominations, the major wing of Anglo-American Protestantism was a remarkably cohesive entity. Protestant unity had, to be sure, gained momentum during the five decades after the Civil War thanks partly to Protestant fears about what would happen to the United States if groups such as the Roman Catholics settled and flourished. But an important bond among the several denominations that constituted the Protestant mainstream was the common identity of being evangelical. Since the 1920s, that word has taken on a more definite meaning, one that typically distinguishes conservative Protestants from their mainline or liberal cousins.[6] But until the 1920s, at least, in the eyes of many American church leaders, to be a Protestant of the right kind was to be evangelical. And that designation spoke volumes about the chief characteristics of mainstream American Protestantism.

One of the earliest historians of Christianity in the United States to use the word *evangelical* in reference to the Protestant mainstream was Robert Baird, who did so in *Religion in America* (1844). Baird was a Presbyterian, and his reading of American Protestant history could not hide his Calvinistic convictions. Nevertheless, when it came to accounting for the most significant differences among American Christians, Baird showed surprising charity to non-Calvinists. The two chief classes of Christianity were the evangelical and nonevangelical denominations. In the former classification Baird lumped Episcopalians, Congregationalists, Baptists, Presbyterians, and Methodists, "the five most numerous," followed by such "smaller orthodox" denominations as the Lutherans, German and Dutch Reformed, Associate and Reformed Presbyterians, Quakers, and Protestant Methodists. Even though these churches represented significantly different teachings on sin and grace, church government and authority, and the meaning and practice of baptism and the Lord's supper, Baird contended that what united these various Protestants were fundamental doctrines (such as the Trinity and the Atonement), a similar conception of the morality required of believers, and a demand that church members demonstrate evidence of having been "born again."[7]

Nonevangelical denominations, accordingly, did not meet Baird's three criteria. In this category he put Roman Catholics, Unitarians, Christians (Disciples of Christ), Universalists, Swedenborgians, Jews, Shakers, Mormons, and for good measure atheists, deists, socialists, and Fourierists.[8] Whatever blinders Baird may have unknowingly worn while compiling his catalog of American religion, as R. Laurence Moore concedes, *Religion in America* was "pioneering" as the first "broadly based account" of religious attitudes in the new nation.[9]

The soundness of Baird's classification was apparent some fifty years after the appearance of *Religion in America* when H. K. Carroll wrote the opening volume in Philip Schaff's American Church History series, entitled *The Religious Forces of the United States* (1893). Even after a civil war, the first fruits of industrialization and urbanization and a larger influx of non-English-speaking immigrants than the United States had previously witnessed, Carroll decided that the country was still divided between Baird's evangelical and nonevangelical camps. Unlike Baird, Carroll had a harder time determining what comprised evangelical beliefs, though he defined these churches as ones holding to the "inspiration, authority and sufficiency" of the Bible, the Trinity, the deity of Christ, justification "by faith alone," and the work of the Holy Spirit "in the conversion and sanctification of the sinner." This meant that Universalists and Adventists, for instance, were excluded from most evangelical groups because of their views on future punishment, even though on the cardinal doctrines these communions were "generally evangelical." Still, as fuzzy as the dividing line may have been, Baird's two parties in American religion were yet in force, with Methodists, Baptists, Congregationalists, Presbyterians, and Episcopalians heading up the list of evangelicals, and Catholics, Mormons, Jews, and "Communistic Societies" filling out nonevangelical ranks.[10]

When it came to discerning which group had the larger influence, Carroll had little trouble. "Evangelical Christianity," he asserted, "is the dominant religious force . . . it shapes the religious character of the American people." And the reason for evangelicalism's decided influence was its overt relevance. Instead of being polemical, evangelicalism was "intensely practical." According to Carroll,

> It emphasizes more than it used to the importance of Christian character and of Christian work. It is less theological in its preaching, making more, indeed, of biblical exposition, but less of doctrinal forms and definitions. And yet it would be wrong to say that it makes little or no account of belief. All that it says, all that it does, is based upon profound and unshakable belief. It is the gospel it declares and is trying to work out in a practical way.[11]

Again, after the 1920s, and especially after the 1940s when evangelicalism became synonymous not just with conservative Protestantism but also with the sort of Christianity promoted by the likes of Billy Graham, the lines drawn by Baird and Carroll between evangelical Christians and the rest of Americans became confusing. Over the course of the twentieth century, evangelicalism took on a narrower meaning and now has become the conservative alternative to the Protestant mainstream.[12] But as anachronistic as these nineteenth-century portrayals of American Christianity may seem, these historians grasped the characteristics that made Anglo-American Protestantism the dominant faith in the United States and that established the criteria for evaluating religion in American culture. American Protestantism of an evangelical persuasion held sway, according to Baird and Carroll, because of superior motives and techniques for transforming individuals and society. This outlook in turn encouraged the phenomenon of giving high marks to religious groups and traditions that demonstrate practical benefits.

The particular genius of the nineteenth-century American Protestant mainstream was revivalism. This, at least, was the implicit argument of Baird's *Religion in America*. In a section of the book dedicated to the official capacities of churches (e.g., preaching and church membership), Baird inserted a lengthy apology for revivals. It would not be a stretch to say that this is the heart of *Religion in America*. Baird argued that revivals emerged simply out of the zealous piety of America's Puritan forefathers who were devoted to preaching and prayer, the two necessary ingredients for all "extraordinary seasons of religious interest." American revivalism's first fruits, in Baird's narrative, were harvested during the Calvinistic preaching of Jonathan Edwards during the 1730s. But except for the diversion of interest to "war and civil commotion" between 1750 and 1800, revivals continued to flower, so much so that by the time of Baird's writing he could claim that they were "a constituent part of the religious system of the country."[13] Baird did concede that some Protestants had abused revivalism. Still, these excesses could not detract from the "great and lasting reformations with which [revivals] have actually blessed the American churches."[14] And the reason for revivalism's success was its appeal to "certain original principles" that lay at the foundation of human psychology and motivation. Baird's list of nine principles had less to do with Christian doctrine or the Bible than it did with the hidden reaches of the self. Yet, that was precisely revivalism's attraction. By changing the hearts of sinners, revivals promised the dramatic transformation of society.

Baird made the social and public aspects of revivals explicit at the conclusion of his effort to answer revivalism's critics. One of the most uncomfortable expressions of this form of Protestantism was the camp meeting. But even here Baird stressed their orderliness and civic mindedness. He observed that it was increasingly common for the sites of camp meetings to be used for Sunday schools, temperance societies, and gatherings on the Fourth of July where those assembled would hear "addresses far more religious than political" and unite in prayer for God to bless the nation.[15]

Mainstream American Protestantism, because of its significant debt to revivalism, not only facilitated the production of holy persons through the spiritual make over rendered by conversion. It also encouraged a variety of reforms that promised a holy society. Carroll made this same point fifty years after Baird. To prove that evangelical churches were "the mightiest, most pervasive, most persistent, and most beneficent force" in American civilization, Carroll listed a series of endeavors in the following order: the churches were a "large" property holder, a corporation, a "public institution," a capitalist structure (i.e., "gathers and distributes large wealth"), an employer, a relief organization, a university, a reformatory influence, a philanthropic association, an organized beneficence, and a facilitator of commerce. Carroll then added a few rhetorical questions that left no doubt about the good the churches were accomplishing: "Who that considers these moral and material aspects of the church can deny that it is beneficent in its aims, unselfish in its plans, and impartial in the distribution of its blessings? . . . What is there among men to compare with the church in its power to educate, elevate, and civilize mankind?"[16] Of course, the nonevangelicals in the United States might answer these questions differently from Carroll. But the noteworthy element in his assessment of American Protestantism was not its myopia but the effort to demonstrate religion's worth by its practical results. Even if America's Protestant churches were not accomplishing all that Carroll said they were, almost no one in mainstream Protestant circles would have questioned whether the churches should be doing those things or be evaluated by their performance of such functions.[17]

Since Carroll wrote at the end of the nineteenth century, a time when academic theology was moving to the left, the temptation to historians has been to chalk up Protestant activism to the liberalizing tendencies commonly associated with the Social Gospel.[18] To be sure, Carroll showed less concern for theological precision than Baird. And the Social Gospel was a factor in the responses of the largest Protestant denominations to the problems posed by a rapidly industrializing economy. Nevertheless, the choice that Baird and Carroll both made in calling the mainstream Protestant denominations evangelical was apt because the energy and activities for which both authors praised the churches was not a tangential byproduct of born-again Christianity but an inherent feature of revivalist-inspired Protestantism.[19] As historians have recently begun to notice, in contrast to an older body of literature that featured revivalism's stress on the subjective experience of converts, evangelical Protestantism was a much larger phenomenon that affected a person's whole way of life, both secular and religious, public and private.[20] In fact, the logic of evangelical Protestantism was such that conversion, being as total and radical as the Spirit who caused it, would produce an obviously unique form of religious devotion that could not be sequestered in the observance of certain devotional ceremonies or practices. As a variety of pietism, revivalism stressed the relevance of the faith for all areas of human endeavor. In other words, as much as revivalists like Billy Sunday may have preached about the world to come, the piety they sought from converts was essentially this-worldly. It is no wonder, then, that Baird identified evangelical Protestantism as the most influential church in nineteenth-century America. The engine driving the mainstream denominations could not help but produce such impressive and visible results.

Revivalist-Styled Christianity

Revivalism is not a word generally associated with the large-scale, corporate institutions into which America's mainstream denominations were turning during the last third of the nineteenth century. The word itself conjures up uneducated preachers in rural settings, not bureaucratic managers in center city office buildings. Although the camp meeting may be the image that comes to mind when many Americans think of revivals, this form of American Protestantism has a broader meaning that applies as much to the ministry of mainline pastors as it does to itinerant evangelists. In fact, in its wider dimensions, revivalism blossomed as the most successful means for Christianizing the United States.

In their controversial book, *The Churching of America*, Roger Finke and Rodney Stark offer a relatively straightforward reason for dubbing the nineteenth century, as church historian, Winthrop Hudson, did, "the Methodist Age" of American history.[21] In 1800, when the Methodists were a small group, they comprised roughly 2.5 percent of the religious adherents in the United States. But by 1850 they had become the largest Protestant denomination, accounting for 34 percent of church membership in the country. Methodists would continue to be the largest Protestant group in the United States until 1906 when they were overtaken by the Baptists, whose own record of success after 1850 would be reason enough for limiting the Methodist Age to the first half of the nineteenth century. Even so, the lesson that Methodist and Baptist examples teach is the centrality of revivalism to the expansion of American Protestantism. Finke and Stark argue that the reason why upstart groups like the Methodists and Baptists succeeded while more established denominations like Presbyterians, Episcopalians, and Congregationalists declined owed to the use of "enthusiastic preaching, revival campaigns, and camp meetings," all of which "were potent methods for mobilizing religious participation."[22]

What Finke and Starke also note about Methodist and Baptist success is an important point that demystifies revivalism and shows its broader meaning. As opposed to believers who might interpret revivals as the direct outpouring of the Holy Spirit, or the secular habit of regarding revivals as bizarre expressions of religious enthusiasm, these sociologists conclude that revivals "aren't simply spontaneous, happenstance events, but require careful planning and the application of appropriate methods."[23] As Charles G. Finney, the most popular revivalist during the first half of the nineteenth century, argued, revivalism was actually a "science" that promised certain religious procedures would produce definite spiritual results.[24] From a wider perspective, then, revivalism is not merely a certain style of preaching, in a specific location that involves definite kinds of experiences among converts. It does include these activities and circumstances. But broadly construed revivalism also involves a new and unique way of being a Christian.

Finke and Starke also rightly observe that nineteenth-century Methodists and Baptists were not the first to harness the power of revivalism for recruiting the faithful. The way of revivals gained prominence a century earlier during the First Great Awakening, the time when evangelical Protestantism emerged. Here the phenomenal success of George Whitefield (1714–1770) is crucial for understanding the specific dynamics that would alter the practices of American Protestants. A Church of England priest who traveled to the New World initially to raise support for an orphanage in Georgia, Whitefield eventually emerged as the leader of a transAtlantic revival that swept through the American colonies between 1739 and 1741. Prior to Whitefield's arrival, American Protestants had witnessed revivals on a smaller scale, first in the late 1720s among the Dutch Reformed and Presbyterians in New Jersey thanks to the pointed preaching of Theodore Freylinghuis (1691–1747) and then a well-publicized reinvigoration of church life in Northampton, Massachusetts, under the ministry of Jonathan Edwards (1703–1756). But although similarities existed between these local forerunners of the Great Awakening, Whitefield's preaching and techniques forged a unique style of Protestantism that would come to dominate the practice of Christianity in the United States.

What Whitefield shared in common with his fellow small-time revivalists was an ability to prick the wounded consciences of listeners through an affective and colloquial style of preaching. But his probing of the conscience would go much deeper than his peers. Aside from his oratorical powers, which were considerable (it was said that women would faint when they heard him pronounce the word *Mesopotamia*), Whitefield hammered away on the theme of personal conversion. In contrast to older pulpit habits in which sermons on the new birth would be more doctrinal and objective, Whitefield turned the subject into a chance to explore the feelings and experiences of his audience. According to one of his biographers, the Anglican revivalist addressed "neither the understanding nor the theologically informed" but "spoke simply and overwhelmingly of the passions of the heart."[25] In other words, Whitefield encouraged the idea that faith was principally felt, not known, and so initiated the idea that conversion could be detected mainly by the degree to which a believer emoted. And he played on his audience's emotions by painting vivid pictures of heaven and hell, inviting potential converts to imagine the pain of eternal damnation and the pleasures of heavenly bliss. What is more, Whitefield showed a remarkable knack for communicating Christianity in a way that was easily accessible to the circumstances of his listeners. As Franklin Lambert has well shown, the English revivalist cast his message in terms of the mercantile revolution that was transforming Anglo-American society, thus making him a "pedlar in divinity." He employed ideas such as "shopping, spending, insuring, banking, selling" because these notions were "most likely to be understood and remembered by the common people."[26]

Whitefield's appeal to his listeners' emotions gained reinforcement from the antics he performed as he spoke. Aside from his dramatic way of delivering his message, Whitefield, contrary to the preaching fashions of the day, would raise his arms, sometimes act out the biblical narratives, and even weep. As one listener recalled about Whitefield's manner, "I could hardly bear such unreserved use of tears, and the scope he gave to his feelings, for sometimes he exceedingly wept, stamped loudly and passionately, and was so overcome, that for a few seconds, you would suspect he never could recover."[27] Not without some plausibility, Whitefield's critics accused him of manipulating his audiences. But they were also undoubtedly jealous because Whitefield's style proved remarkably successful, not only because his ways were novel but also because he brought religion out of the formalities of study and ceremony and made it accessible to the very real experiences of the average man and woman.

In addition to what he did while speaking, Whitefield's activities outside the pulpit were just as crucial for his success. He not only spoke in the language of the marketplace, but he used the techniques of the market to his own advantage. The English evangelist along with his associates followed a strategy of self-promotion and publicity that was unheard of in religious circles. Part of this stemmed from Whitefield's efforts on behalf of the orphanage in Georgia. But some of his religious marketing was done clearly to boost his own stature. For instance, Whitefield drew large crowds at open-air meetings but would sometimes inflate the numbers to generate greater attention in the press. What is more, Whitefield and his handlers would sometimes stage events again to draw crowds and publicity in newspapers. These reports created a sense of immediacy and drama about the revivalist's affairs that dovetailed with the excitement converts experienced in their own encounter with the divine. Whitefield also allowed his own journals to be published; these offered a firsthand account of God's work through the revivalist. All of this publicity not only redounded to the success of the revivals but also pleased colonial publishers who were searching for novelties that would boost sales of newspapers, pamphlets and books. Whitefield's friendship with Benjamin Franklin, a man not necessarily known for religious enthusiasm, testifies to the intentional links between the new form of Christianity and the emerging market.[28]

The long-term significance of Whitefield's remarkable achievement was to make Christianity accessible to common people, rather than confining it to elites or formal ecclesiastical structures. Whitefield proved that if packaged in new wrapping and reduced to its most personal and intimate aspects, the Christian religion could attract broad support. For this reason, Whitefield deserves credit for discovering and implementing the tools that would become staples of the evangelist's trade after American independence. Charles G. Finney may have popularized the so-called new measures, and Dwight L. Moody and Billy Sunday may have adapted revivalism for big-city America, but these evangelists were only building on the foundation of Whitefield, who first figured out a way of making Christianity voluntary (e.g., conversionism) and then orchestrated a system of attracting volunteers for the Christian faith.[29]

Even though the fires of religious zeal would burn less intensely as British colonists in North America fought a war for independence and established a new nation, the revolution and its political settlement would prove how brilliant Whitefield's achievement had been. When the United States ratified the Constitution, the First Amendment prohibited Congress from making any law that established or restricted religion. This left the United States free from the taint of the Old World's ecclesiastical establishment. Ironically, this measure, which was a hard-fought victory for Enlightenment political philosophy, also played directly into the hands of the sort of religion that Whitefield had made successful. The First Amendment made religion a private matter. And even though many states would continue to use taxes to support established churches, the model of the federal government would eventually become the norm for all religious bodies in the United States. American political philosophy taught that government had no right to interfere with private matters of conscience. People were free not only from the tyranny of the king but also of the bishop or pope. As such they were free to choose their own religion.[30]

The result of religious disestablishment was a free-market approach to questions of faith and the consequences were far-reaching. Churches that had previously been assigned parishioners in a particular locale were now forced to compete for adherents. In other words, the separation of church and state put an end to the welfare state for religious bodies and in turn made churches dependent on the people for support. Not surprisingly, the primary means that churches used in their search for members was something akin to revivalism. It is no wonder that in this setting the churches that grew the fastest—namely, Methodists and Baptists—were the ones least encumbered by tradition and formalism and most willing to use revivalist techniques. According to Roger Finke, religious markets inherently cater to individuals and make faith "an individual decision." Although Christianity was still a group phenomenon and relied on "the support, control, and rewards" of a local congregation, the American system of disestablishment inevitably stressed "personal conversion and faith." Conversion, Finke writes, "is an individual decision set in the context of a religious market with a wide array of diversity. The religion of the unregulated market is of the people, by the people and for the people."[31]

If revivalism provided a successful means of popular appeal, it also yielded a form of piety that made faith an important factor in everyday life. As Marilyn J. Westerkamp has argued, revivalists gave the laity greater control over conversion when they taught that genuine faith was evident in holy affections or feelings, as opposed to correct beliefs regulated by clergy. Each person who listened to an evangelist could readily relate to the descriptions of the passions that accompanied conversion since all people had some firsthand acquaintance with the emotions of joy, love, fear, and desire. A harder sell, however, was a theological understanding of Christianity that required some familiarity with biblical narratives along with the historic creeds of the church. The emotional appeal of revivals, according to Westerkamp, gave laity power by circumventing the doctrinal process by which clergy had in effect controlled participation in the church and identification with the Christian religion.[32]

But if the average Christian experienced some measure of liberty from clerical oversight through revivalism's reformulation of conversion, they were not so free when it came to the rigors of the new faith. Instead of limiting Christian devotion to formal church activities on Sunday or other holy days, being a believer now became a full-time duty, with faith making demands in all areas of life. The practical character of revivalist Protestantism is sometimes overlooked because of the common assumption that conversion is a way to escape the fires of hell by way of heaven's pearly gates. But the faith that Whitefield established in America, in fact, was far more oriented to moral reform in this world than to the comforts of the world to come. Daniel Walker Howe captures this dimension of revivalist Protestantism well when he writes that "the essence of evangelical commitment to Christ is that it is undertaken voluntarily, consciously, and responsibly, by the individual for himself or herself." Howe makes this point in the context of discussing the degree to which evangelical Protestantism encouraged a form of social control in the moral reforms its adherents promoted. That context in and of itself demonstrates the practical or this-worldly nature of revivalist-inspired Christianity. But when Howe adds that evangelical

Protestants were "people who have consciously decided to take charge of their own lives and identities," he highlights the kind of self-discipline that revivalism required.[33]

Signs of the demands that conversion placed on believers were evident from the beginning of Whitefield's ministry. For instance, he argued with listeners that the internal change wrought in conversion should make an outward difference in their lives, even in the way they dressed. Here Whitefield denounced interest in worldly possessions and insisted that those really converted would manifest a form of self-denial that associated luxury with godlessness. As *Gentlemen's Magazine* observed of Whitefield's converts, "several of fine ladies, who us'd to wear French Silks, French Hoops of four yards wide, . . . Bob Wigs and white Satin smock Petticoats," once they became Methodists began to wear "plain Stuff-Gowns, no Hoops, common Night Mobs, and plain Bays."[34] The moralistic tone of Whitefield's sermons and writings may help to explain his friendship with Ben Franklin. Although Franklin was by no means abstemious, he admired Whitefield's call for Christians to abandon lives of hypocrisy and perform "works of kindness, charity, mercy and public spirit." What is more, Franklin recognized in Whitefield's revivals a form of Christianity not far removed from his own enlightened version where the forms and doctrines of the faith were secondary to real faith and obedience, and where denominational differences were simply petty quarrels among defensive clerics.[35]

The self-discipline and moral striving required by revivalism would continue to flower wherever the new version of Christianity took root. Rhys Isaac, for instance, shows how the awakening of revivalist sentiments among colonial Virginians incited a religious conflict between evangelical Protestants and the Anglican establishment that was truly revolutionary, not so much for the politics of the colony, though its political implications were momentous, but also for the order and routines of everyday life. Contemporary accounts of the 1760s upsurge of revivalist Protestantism could not help but notice the contrast between "traditional Virginia formal exchange" and evangelicalism's "solemn fellowship." The new converts' "solemnity, austerity, and stern sobriety" were a direct assault upon the forms of propriety and modes of association necessary for maintaining social cohesion in colonial Virginia. As Isaac puts it, "conversion could ultimately be validated among church members only by a radical reform of conduct." The revivalist churches took aim at the "hurly-burly" culture of traditional Anglican elites and disciplined adherents for drunkenness, quarreling, slander, and property disputes. In other words, conversion involved much more than adhering to certain religious beliefs or following specific devotional practices. Instead, it extended to changes in behavior and appearance. Just as Whitefield had railed against the finery of the well-to-do, so Virginia's evangelicals renounced the manners and clothing of gentlemen. In the revivalists' religious system, conversion was simply the beginning of a whole new way of life.[36]

The radical demands of revivalist Protestantism would be no less revolutionary after the founding of the United States. In fact, as Christine Leigh Heyrman demonstrates, the strenuous and sober life that ensued from conversion showed no signs of letting up in the early decades of the nineteenth century. To be sure, antebellum revivalism continued to make conversion and the rewards of eternal life central, the basis for the rest of evangelicalism's many demands. But once having sorted out one's eternal destiny, an all encompassing way of life followed that was designed to set revivalist Protestants clearly apart from either nonbelievers or complacent Christians. Worldly pleasures, such as "the thrill of the hunt, the sociability of the tavern, the lure of the fiddle," were obvious signs of infidelity. And churches that tolerated such lapses, such as the Episcopalians, were guilty of leading souls astray. Evangelical Protestants, in turn, established an alternative culture that undermined the existing lines of deference and structures of community. "Evangelicals drew people away," Heyrman writes, "from the familiar settings of sociability in rural counties—horse races and taverns, barbecues and balls." They regarded "drinking and joking, gambling and dancing, fiddling and cockfighting not as innocent amusements that made strangers into neighbors but as sinful frivolities that set men and women on the path to hell." And so the radical change of desire and emotion that conversion accomplished in the human heart inevitably trickled down to visible and outward displays of piety that set evangelicals apart from the rest of the world. Much like Whitefield before them, the converts Heyrman studied altered their physical appearance by shedding "all ruffles, bows, rings, and feathers"; women "hitched up bodices to conceal their cleavages"; and men "cut their long hair."[37]

For most of Heyrman's Protestants, the work of being a Christian resulted mainly in small-scale transformations of individuals and families whose faith puts them at odds with the ways of the dominant southern society. But she also observes how revivalist Protestantism had the potential to be a force that could inaugurate a dominant social order of its own making.[38] And this is precisely what happened in the North, where the self-discipline of evangelical piety was more congenial with an emergent industrialism and where revivalist Protestants held greater power. Here, in fact, the Second Great Awakening spawned a host of voluntary associations that helped to offset the cultural instability that could conceivably have developed in a new nation that did not have the restraints provided by crown or established church. According to Donald G. Mathews, it is useful to think of this revival "in its social aspects as an organizing process that helped to give meaning and direction to people suffering in various degrees from the social strains of a nation on the move."[39]

The social order supplied by revivalist Protestantism to the new nation, in the estimate of Daniel Walker Howe, was "the functional equivalent of an established church." The agencies of this religious establishment were not so much the churches but the so-called benevolent empire, an affiliated set of voluntary organizations, both local and national, whose purpose was to have the moral seriousness of the individual convert writ large in the soul of the nation. Lay Protestants and clergy alike formed associations to eliminate slavery; protect the Sabbath from the desecration of postal service; restrain the consumption of alcohol; thwart the aims of the papacy; assist widows and orphans; reform prisons, print and distribute Bibles; teach reading, writing, and arithmetic to poor children—the list goes on. Howe also notes that this network of voluntary societies was the "religious counterpart" to the American System of Henry Clay and the Whig Party. The goal of both the Benevolent Empire and the Whig political program was "to impose system and direction upon the amorphousness of American society."[40] So congenial was American society to revivalist Protestantism that Jon Butler concludes the new nation by 1850 "was overrun with reform societies."[41] And so ingrained was the logic that began with the premise of a dramatic and immediate conversion and finished with a completely transformed person that few Anglo-American Protestants questioned the revivalist way of being a Christian and hence the aptness of referring to it as a religious establishment.

But revivalist Protestantism was not technically an ecclesiastical establishment, in part because of the barrier posed by the First Amendment and, more important, because the institutional church played such a relatively small role in Anglo-American Protestant success. This does not mean that the denominations looked on from the sidelines during the First or Second Great Awakenings. To the contrary, not only did the Methodist and Baptist denominations grow through revivalist methods and beliefs, but other Anglo-American denominations also adopted revivalist ways and supported the institutions of the Benevolent Empire. The methods of revivalism and the earnest piety by which revivals transformed individuals and society were in many respects an extension of the churches.

That being conceded, revivalist Protestantism did not rely on or even make use of the formal structures and practices of Protestant church life. What is more, the kind of Christianity that Whitefield fanned into flame outside the churches and that had by the nineteenth century become the norm, was hostile to the very efforts that had historically characterized Protestant Christianity. This is a point that Nathan O. Hatch makes so convincingly in his book, *The Democratization of American Christianity*.[42] In this work he writes about populist forms of Christianity during the antebellum era, among them revivalist Protestantism, and how they led a religious revolution that established a new religious system that took faith and practice out of the hands of elites and put them squarely within the reach of the common man and woman. According to Hatch, revivalist Protestants inverted "the traditional modes of religious authority." They scorned the "tradition, learning, solemnity, and decorum" of Protestant clergy and followed instead "a diverse array of populist preachers who exalted youth, free expression, and religious ecstasy." Furthermore, in a phrase that could just have easily been written by Rhys Isaac or Christine Leigh Heyrman, Hatch asserts that for revivalist Protestants "divine insight was reserved for the poor and humble rather than the proud and learned."[43] The implications of this revolution, as Hatch rightly notes, were momentous. Christianity in the United States has thrived at the popular level but has failed to penetrate the elite sectors of society. But what Hatch does not fully develop is what this form of Protestantism meant for the Protestant clergy, the one group of elites most closely identified with the faith and whose work defined the Christian life corporately conceived. Making this point is easier to do by highlighting the three main features of populist Christianity—namely, anticreedalism, anticlericalism, and antiritualism—and how these affected the institutional church.[44]

When revivalist Protestants repudiated theological formulations, whether the Calvinistically inspired *Westminster Confession of Faith* or briefer statements such as the Apostles' Creed, they were obviously displaying their anticreedal credentials. But the reason for this hostility to dogma had important repercussions for pastors and clergy. Creeds, according to revivalist logic, were man-made documents and so of no binding authority. Even worse, creeds had become little more than a device to keep the theologically illiterate under the thumb of clerical tyrants. In God's kingdom, especially as it was emerging in the democratic confines of the United States, no believer was superior to another, nor were the words of some Christians better than those of other adherents. Many democratically oriented revivalists took aim at Calvinism, which was at the time the chief theological tradition in the United States. And the particular objections by Baptists and Methodists to Calvinist theology was the way Reformed orthodoxy made people passive in salvation. As one Kentucky pastor who joined the Disciples of Christ put it, "we are not personally acquainted with the writings of John Calvin, nor are we certain how nearly we agree with his views of divine truth; neither do we care."[45] Even so, the egalitarianism that informed revivalist anticreedalism showed profound contempt for all traces of systematic thought, whether Arminian, Lutheran, or Socian. Christianity admitted no expertise, nor did it privilege learning since all people, the laity and clergy alike, held the same status before God.

Of course, the people generally responsible for writing creeds were clergy and church officials. Therefore, anticreedalism inevitably led to one form or another of anticlericalism. Some of the contempt for clergy may be attributed to the circumstances of early nineteenth-century America where established churches still existed in several states, and anticlericalism took the form of protests against the preferences that some clergy received from government at the expense of others. Still, as understandable as some of this resentment may have been, revivalist Protestantism's profoundly anti-elitist presumption remains, and that animus was aimed squarely at clergy who represented a barrier to egalitarian Christianity. In fact, in its more radical forms, revivalist Protestantism leveled all sorts of hierarchies, but especially those that presumed to come between God and the faithful. According to Daniel Parker, a Kentucky Baptist, "[T]he preaching manufactories of the east appear to be engaged in sending hirelings to the west, and should any of those *man-made, devil sent,* place-hunting gentry come into our country, and read in our places, we shall likely raise against *them* seven shepards [*sic*], and eight principle [*sic*] men."[46] Chances are that seminary graduates in the northeast who were learning about polite manners in the home and proper decorum in the pulpit had little interest in going into Parker's country.[47]

Even so, what lay behind revivalist Protestant forms of anticreedalism and anticlericalism was a strong antipathy to any person, institution, or activity that presumed to come between God and the people. This explains the tendency among Anglo-American Protestants to turn ceremonies performed by clergy that communicate divine grace, such as baptism and the Lord's Supper, into symbolic gestures that express the faith of converts. Although Hatch does not develop the antiritualism of democratic Christianity, a strain of it runs through the poems and songs from revivalist Protestants that he includes in the appendices to his book.[48]

But arguably the most explicit rejection of Christianity's historic forms of formal devotion were the events led by Charles Grandison Finney, whose "New Measures" substituted the science of revivals for historic liturgical forms. These novel ways of generating and sustaining the faithful were by no means new to Finney since he likely picked them up from Methodists and Baptists. Still, the notoriety of his revivals ensured that such novel practices as devoting days to religious services (as opposed to a one-time service), using lay male and female exhorters, and designating a pew at the front of the church the "anxious bench," for those under conviction to sit and receive prayer, would be identified with Finney. These activities so weakened the historic churchly practices of preaching, the sacraments, and prayer that conducting church life apart from revivals and its characteristic form of piety became almost unthinkable. Meanwhile, the arrival of large numbers of Roman Catholics in the 1830s and 1840s, which encouraged Protestant fears of the Pope and the Catholic Church, guaranteed the victory of revivalist over churchly Protestantism because the people's religion of mainstream Protestantism could be clearly differentiated from the perceived priestcraft of Rome.[49]

The glue keeping these antiformal sentiments together was the conviction that the Bible was the only legitimate authority. Of course, the Protestant Scriptures were not free from the taint of human hands, having been composed by Jewish prophets and Christian apostles. But the way around this problem was the convenient circumvention of divine inspiration. The words contained in a holy writ were different from every other word written by men because they came with divine sanction. Thus, the Protestant doctrine of *sola scriptura* became in revivalist Protestant hands the notion of Bible-onlyism. In contrast to the teaching of fallible men whose guidance was optional, only the Bible could command the assent of men and women because it was divine. What is more, the Bible gave direct access to God, making the interpretations of clergy and theologians unnecessary. The immediacy, perfection, and authority of biblical truth became clinching arguments for doing away with forms of religious devotion or churchly hierarchy, such as creeds, clergy, or ceremonies, that came between God and believers. The cumulative effect of revivalist-styled Christianity, then, was to take the faith away from the institutional church and give it to the people. Christianity was a religion to be practiced in the marketplace, the home, and statehouse, not something to be confined to the church, under the control of clergy.[50]

The Legacy of Pietism

By 1860, two "great" awakenings combined with religious disestablishment and the prevalence of revivalist methods to leave mainstream Protestantism with an indelible stamp. Perhaps the best word to describe it is pietism. Of course, generalizing about mainstream Protestantism prior to 1900 runs the risk of committing the same errors of which Baird and Carroll were guilty when they used the category of evangelical Protestantism while glossing significant differences between, for instance, German Reformed, Methodists, and any branch of American Lutheranism. Nevertheless, the relative ease with which nineteenth-century Protestant historians could group together churches and traditions that disagreed fairly vigorously over creed, liturgy, and church government invites some explanation. And the most sensible one is to recognize pietism as the vital center of American Protestantism's dominant expressions, thus making Baird and Carroll's use of "evangelical" Protestantism particularly apt.

Definitions of pietism vary, in part because of the different historical circumstances in which it emerged. Some scholars feature seventeenth-century developments among Lutherans in Germany, others the devotional zeal of seventeenth-century Puritans, while still others look to strains of spiritual intensity in Dutch Calvinism.[51] One of the most common traits of these different strains of pietism is the effort to define the Christian religion apart from its particularities and locate its essence in "the heart."[52] The evangelical theologian, Donald Bloesch, writes that the hallmarks of pietism are the conversion experience or new birth, the supremacy of the Bible (often studied in private, small-group settings), moral earnestness, and a social conscience. This form of faith could even find expression among Roman Catholics since one of the figures whom Bloesch cites in support of his definition is the Jansenist theologian Saint-Cyran, who said, "The essence of piety is in the right ordering of the heart . . . in a heart living in this dependence and peace. It is not in the sacraments, not even in that of the body of Christ."[53] Comments such as this have prompted a less sanguine estimate of pietism such as that from James Tunstead Burtchaell. He agrees with Bloesch in the main by defining pietism as "the primacy of spirit over letter, commitment over institution, affect over intellect, laity over clergy, invisible church over visible," all in an effort to return to the simplicities of the first Christians. But this form of piety, Burtchaell adds, "repressed any strong sense of the visible church." Consequently, pietism begot religious zeal "unsustained by morality, church without theology, preaching without sacrament, community without order."[54]

An important note sounded in both of these assessments is the small role the institutional church plays in the religious life of the pietist. This is exactly what revivalist Protestantism had taught American believers to expect. Clergy, creeds, rituals, and church order did not matter since they did not affect the heart noticeably. Instead, what mattered were preachers who could convict sinners of their wrongful ways and lead them to conversion, converts who studied the Bible for daily guidance, and Christians who led personal lives that were obviously different from those who had not experienced conversion. Going to church and participating in public worship, to be sure, were fine activities and should not be neglected. But these acts of devotion had no real bearing on one's personal salvation. Like a vitamin, the institutional church was merely supplemental.

Ironically, pietism was not an obvious threat to the largest denominations. The dominant forms of piety in American Protestantism did not prevent churches from gaining more members or from growing into large-scale corporations. Indeed, after the Civil War the leading denominations developed agencies, structures and financial systems of support that made the likes of H. K. Carroll gush.[55] At the same time, the fortunes of revivalism thrived. Dwight L. Moody was the leading practitioner of techniques Whitefield had honed 150 years earlier, though Moody's business instincts made his crusades more urban-friendly than the Anglican priest's had been. Still, the Christianity forged by revivalist Protestantism did not create a zero sum game, as if Moody's success came at the expense of the churches or vice versa. Membership in a Congregationalist, Presbyterian, or Methodist congregation came without strings. Protestant church members could flock to a revival in good conscience or join a religious voluntary organization because they had already learned that revivalist devotion was no different from the way Anglo-American Protestants conceived of churchliness. And this explains why it was so easy for the northern Presbyterian Church to bless revivalism when it ordained Billy Sunday, a man without seminary training who would have likely had trouble explaining why baptism or the Lord's supper were part of the Christian religion.

Still, the fluidity between the Protestant churches and revivalism may not have been as important a part of pietism's legacy as the interdenominational cooperation that came to the fore in postbellum American Protestantism. Beginning with the establishment of the Evangelical Alliance's American chapter in 1873 and culminating in the formation of the Federal Council of Churches (FCC) in 1908, Protestant denominations put aside creedal, liturgical, and governmental differences and began to live out the form of pietist ecumenism upon which revivalists from Whitefield to Sunday depended. Just as Whitefield had hoped his activities would break down barriers among the denominations and unite those who had experienced a sudden and dramatic conversion in deeds of mercy and love, so the largest Protestant denominations in the late nineteenth century pursued with greater vigor common endeavors that slighted historic differences among Protestants. According to Leonard Wolsey Bacon, who wrote the final volume in the series that Carroll's began, "the greatest addition to the forces of the church in the period since the war has come from deploying into the field hitherto unused resources of personal service." These forces included the Young Men's Christian Association (YMCA), Young Women's Christian Association (YWCA), women's societies, Sunday school, and Christian Endeavor.[56]

Of course, the FCC would later emerge as the institutional embodiment of liberal Protestantism. Consequently, tracing its roots to revivalistic Protestantism surely sounds a strange historiographical note since much of the history of American Protestantism has been written from the perspective of the divide between liberals and evangelicals. But as odd as it may seem, treating the FCC as the culmination of pietism makes perfect sense. The practices and beliefs that had made Methodists different from Baptists, Congregationalists, or Presbyterians had been melting away thanks to over 150 years of revivalism. The sort of ecumenism that the FCC advocated was the logical outcome of a form of Christianity that looked for the reality of faith in everyday life as opposed to church ordinances.

The earliest histories of Protestant ecumenism and the FCC bear out this relationship between revivalism and the attenuation of American Protestantism's confessional and liturgical identity. The one that draws the strongest tie between early twentieth-century ecumenism and revivalism came from the pen of John A. Hutchison, then an instructor in philosophy at the College of Wooster who would eventually chair the religion department at Columbia University, thanks no doubt to his time of study at Union Theological Seminary which he acknowledged in the preface. Among the important forerunners of ecumenism, in Hutchison's narrative, is the First Great Awakening where "strict denominational lines were blurred and a common religious pattern . . . was begun." The revivals also spurred interest in "moral and social problems," thus proving that the federal council's efforts were not a "new thing." In fact, the FCC was the natural outgrowth of "the American religious situation," which Hutchison described as common endeavor for "practical service in a variety of humanitarian causes." These were the deep waters of American Protestant piety that stirred beneath the "placid surface" of denominationalism.[57] From all appearances, Hutchison, a Presbyterian minister and philosopher was firmly a part of the Protestant establishment and so far removed from the spiritual enthusiasm and religious zeal usually associated with revivalist Protestantism. But underneath the ecstasy of the conversion experience and the rigors of revivalism's stern moral code, as Hutchison's book shows, was a reappropriation of Christianity that essentially linked the apparently conservative and liberal wings of American Protestantism. Revivalism secured the victory of pietism, which in turn directed mainstream American Protestantism, whether of a Social Gospel variety or an evangelistic stripe, away from the formal and corporate beliefs and practices of the church toward the informal settings and personal affairs of believers.

According to Nathan Hatch, the triumph of pietist Protestantism promoted by revivalists from Whitefield to Sunday has had enormous consequences for the place of religion in American culture. The "driving force behind American Christianity," he writes, "is not the quality of its organization, the status of its clergy, or the power of its intellectual life." Instead, it is "its democratic and populist orientation" that has caused religion to flourish at the level of popular culture but wither "in the realms of high culture."[58] The point made here is related but somewhat different. It is hard to disagree either with Hatch's account of antebellum religion or his assessment of its long-term consequences. Still, an equally important consideration is not simply what the legacy of pietist Christianity has meant for American society but also for the Christian religion itself—the way it is practiced, passed on, and cultivated. And on this score the consequences of pietism (in its revivalist Protestant expression) are enormous. For at the same time that the American Protestant mainstream was winning boasting rights as the religious establishment, it was losing its ties to previous generations of adherents who had been Christians in markedly different ways. Whether or not this transformation also resulted in the American Protestant mainstream losing its soul is a question historians naturally avoid and that obviously (though unevenly) divides Protestant adherents. But the reorientation of American Protestantism did establish the personal and the practical as benchmarks for identifying genuine faith and determining religion's importance. It is no wonder that religion in America is so popular since it is so accessible. It is a wonder, though, that revivalist Protestantism ever passed as conservative.

Notes

1. This account comes largely from William G. McLoughlin Jr., *Modern Revivalism: Charles Grandison Finney to Billy Graham* (New York: Ronald, 1959), 400–10. For other treatments of Sunday, see Lyle W. Dorsett, *Billy Sunday and the Redemption of Urban America* (Grand Rapids, Mich.: Eerdmans, 1991); and Roger Bruns, *Preacher: Billy Sunday and Big-Time American Evangelism* (New York: Norton, 1992).

2. McLoughlin, *Modern Revivalism*, 407.

3. H. L. Mencken, "Doctor Seraphicus et Ecstaticus," *Baltimore Evening Sun*, March 14, 1916.

4. Mencken, "Doctor Seraphicus et Ecstaticus."

5. See the introduction, note 11, for a discussion of the use of the word *mainstream*. The revivalist dynamic that Sunday urged on his listeners in trying to make

faith relevant for everyday affairs, as this chapter argues, was crucial to the formation of a Protestant mainstream and its attendant placing of groups uncomfortable with such formulations in the position of outside the mainstream.

6. For a good overview of the different meanings of evangelicalism, see George Marsden, "Introduction: The Evangelical Denomination," in *Evangelicalism and Modern America*, ed. George Marsden (Grand Rapids, Mich.: Eerdmans, 1984), vii–xix.

7. Robert Baird, *Religion in America; Or, An Account of the Origin, Progress, Relation to the State, and Present Condition of the Evangelical Churches in the United States* (New York: Harper, 1844), 184, 219.

8. Baird, *Religion in America*, 269–91.

9. R. Laurence Moore, *Religious Outsiders and the Making of Americans* (New York: Oxford University Press, 1986), 5.

10. H. K. Carroll, *The Religious Forces of the United States*, vol. 1, American Church History Series (New York: Christian Literature, 1893), xlv, lvi.

11. Carroll, *The Religious Forces*, lix.

12. See chap. 3.

13. Baird, *Religion in America*, 196, 202.

14. Baird, *Religion in America*, 207.

15. Baird, *Religion in America*, 218.

16. Carroll, *Religious Forces*, lx–lxi.

17. One of the companion volumes in the American Church History series of which Carroll's was a part, Leonard Woolsey Bacon, *A History of American Christianity*, vol. 13 (New York: Christian Literature, 1897), 361–73, makes a point similar to Carroll when he observes the series of Protestant initiatives, from the Young Men's Christian Association to the Salvation Army, all of which confirm "the tendency of the Christian life toward a vigorous and even absorbing external activity" (369).

18. Standard accounts of the Social Gospel include Charles Howard Hopkins, *The Rise of the Social Gospel in American Protestantism, 1865–1915* (New Haven, Conn.: Yale University Press, 1940); and Henry F. May, *Protestant Churches and Industrial America* (New York: Harper, 1949).

19. See Timothy L. Smith, *Revivalism and Social Reform: American Protestantism on the Eve of the Civil War* (1957; reprint, Baltimore: Johns Hopkins University Press, 1980).

20. See Daniel Walker Howe, "Religion and Politics in the Antebellum North," in *Religion and American Politics: From the Colonial Period to the 1980s*, ed. Mark A. Noll (New York: Oxford University Press, 1990), 125–30.

21. See Winthrop Hudson, "The Methodist Age in America," *Methodist History* 12 (1974): 3–15.

22. Roger Finke and Rodney Starke, *The Churching of America, 1776–1990: Winners and Losers in Our Religious Economy* (New Brunswick, N.J.: Rutgers University Press, 1992), 72–83, 96.

23. Finke and Starke, *The Churching of America*, 104.

24. See Charles G. Finney, *Lectures on Revivals of Religion*, ed. William G. McLoughlin (1835; reprint, Cambridge, Mass.: Harvard University Press, 1960).

25. Harry S. Stout, *The Divine Dramatist: George Whitefield and the Rise of Modern Evangelicalism* (Grand Rapids, Mich.: Eerdmans, 1991), 39. Much of my analysis of Whitefield follows Stout's perceptive rendering of the evangelist.

26. Frank Lambert, *"Pedlar in Divinity": George Whitefield and the Transatlantic Revivals* (Princeton, N.J.: Princeton University Press, 1994), 47, 48.

27. Quoted in Stout, *Divine Dramatist*, 41.

28. On Whitefield's commercial strategies, see Lambert, *Pedlar in Divinity*, chap. 2, especially 60–68. On the evangelist's relationship with Franklin, see Stout, *Divine Dramatist*, chap. 12.

29. On the voluntaristic nature of American religion, see Sidney E. Mead, *The Lively Experiment: The Shaping of Christianity in America* (New York: Harper, 1963), chap. 7; and Winthrop S. Hudson, *The Great Tradition of the American Churches* (New York: Harper, 1953).

30. On the significance of America's decision to disestablish religion, see R. Laurence Moore, *Selling God: American Religion in the Marketplace of Culture* (New York: Oxford University Press, 1994), chap. 3.

31. Roger Finke, "Religious Deregulation: Origins and Consequences," *Journal of Church and State* 32 (Summer 1990): 625, quoted in Mark A. Noll, *The Scandal of the Evangelical Mind* (Grand Rapids, Mich.: Eerdmans, 1994), 66.

32. Marilyn J. Westerkamp, *The Triumph of the Laity: Scots-Irish Piety and the Great Awakening, 1625–1760* (New York: Oxford University Press, 1988), 209–12.

33. Howe, "Religion and Politics," 128.

34. Quoted in Lambert, *Pedlar in Divinity*, 49.

35. Quoted in Stout, *Divine Dramatist*, 229.

36. Rhys Isaac, *The Transformation of Virginia, 1740–1790* (Chapel Hill: University of North Carolina Press, 1982), chaps. 7–8, quotations from 164, 168, 169.

37. Christine Leigh Heyrman, *Southern Cross: The Beginnings of the Bible Belt* (New York: Knopf, 1997), 8, 18, 19.

38. Heyrman, *Southern Cross*, 26.

39. Donald G. Mathews, "The Second Great Awakening as an Organizing Process, 1780–1830," *American Quarterly* 21 (1969): 23–43, reprinted in *Religion in American History: Interpretive Essays*, ed. John M. Mulder and John F. Wilson (Englewood Cliffs, N.J.: Prentice Hall, 1978), 199–217, quotation from 203.

40. Howe, "Religion and Politics," 130, 131.

41. Jon Butler, *Awash in a Sea of Faith: Christianizing the American People* (Cambridge, Mass.: Harvard University Press, 1990), 278.

42. Nathan O. Hatch, *The Democratization of American Christianity* (New Haven, Conn.: Yale University Press, 1989).

43. Hatch, *The Democratization of American Christianity*, 35.

44. The following paragraphs are based on a section of D. G. Hart, "Overcoming the Schizophrenic Character of Theological Education in the Evangelical Tradition," in *A Confessing Theology for Postmodern Times*, ed. Michael S. Horton (Wheaton, Ill.: Crossway, 2000), 111–30.

45. Robert Marshall and J. Thompson, quoted in *A Confessing Theology for Postmodern Times*, 174.

46. Quoted in *A Confessing Theology for Postmodern Times*, 178.

47. For an example of some of that advice from theological faculty to seminarians, see Samuel Miller, *Letters on Clerical Manners and Habits: Addressed to a Student in the Theological Seminary at Princeton* (New York: Carvill, 1827).

48. See, for instance, *The World Turned Upside Down* (1815) and *Priest-Craft Float Away* (1811), reprinted in Hatch, *Democratization of American Christianity*, 230–31.

49. On nineteenth-century American Protestant anti-Catholicism, see John Wolffe, "Anti-Catholicism and Evangelical Identity in Britain and the United States, 1830–1860," in *Evangelicalism: Comparative Studies of Popular Protestantism in North America, the British Isles, and Beyond, 1700–1990*, ed. Mark A. Noll, David W. Bebbington, and George A. Rawlyk (New York: Oxford University Press, 1994), 179–97.

50. On Bible-onlyism, see Noll, *Evangelicalism: Comparative Studies*, 179–83; and George M. Marsden, "Everyone One's Own Interpreter? The Bible, Science, and Authority in Mid-Nineteenth-Century America," in *The Bible in America: Essays in Cultural History*, ed. Nathan O. Hatch and Mark A. Noll (New York: Oxford University Press, 1982), 79–100.

51. See F. Ernest Stoeffler, *German Pietism during the Eighteenth Century* (Leiden: Brill, 1973); and James Tanis, *Dutch Calvinistic Pietism in the Middle Colonies: A Study in the Life and Theology of Theodorus Jacobus Frelinghuysen* (The Hague: Martinus Nijhoff, 1967).

52. To say that pietism is basically a religion of personal experience is obviously an abstraction that divorces it from its own historical and cultural origins. But since pietists themselves believed that "heart" religion transcended the constraints of history and culture, such a definition is appropriate and serves to unite the proponents of pietism wherever or whenever they sense the internal movement of the Spirit.

53. Quoted in Donald G. Bloesch, *The Evangelical Renaissance* (Grand Rapids, Mich.: Eerdmans, 1973), 105.

54. James Tunstead Burtchaell, *The Dying of the Light: The Disengagement of Colleges and Universities from their Christian Churches* (Grand Rapids, Mich.: Eerdmans, 1998), 839, 841.

55. For Presbyterian developments, see, for example, Louis B. Weeks, "The Incorporation of the Presbyterians," in *The Organizational Revolution: Presbyterians and American Denominationalism*, ed. Milton J. Coalter, John M. Mulder, and Louis B. Weeks (Louisville, Ky.: Westminster/John Knox, 1992), 37–54; and James H. Moorhead, "Presbyterians and the Mystique of Organizational Efficiency, 1870–1936," in *Reimagining Denominationalism: Interpretive Essays*, ed. Robert Bruce Mullin and Russell E. Richey (New York: Oxford University Press, 1994), 264–87.

56. Leonard Wolsey Bacon, *A History of American Christianity*, vol. 13, American Church History Series (New York: Christian Literature, 1897), 361–71, quotation from 361–62.

57. John A. Hutchison, *We Are Not Divided: A Critical and Historical Study of the Federal Council of the Churches of Christ in America* (New York: Round Table Press, 1941), 5, 297. See also Charles S. Macfarland, *Christian Unity in the Making: The First Twenty-five Years of the Federal Council of the Churches of Christ in America* (New York: Federal Council, 1948), 15–34; and Elias B. Sanford, *Origin and History of the Federal Council of the Churches of Christ in America* (Hartford, Conn.: Scranton, 1916), 87–95.

58. Hatch, *Democratization of American Christianity*, 211, 213.

Confessional Protestantism

John Williamson Nevin (1803–1886) is one of those figures in American Protestant history who is well known more for his eccentricity than the popularity or influence of his views. Like his contemporaries, Horace Bushnell or Orestes Brownson, Nevin was caught between a recognition that the Protestant past could not be recovered completely and an understanding that the present religious tendencies were moving in unfavorable directions. Consequently, he can be read as a breath of fresh air compared to the utopian reformers and even mainstream progressives of his day. Yet, Nevin was not able to chart a path that would endure. And so he remains a historical curiosity. But his oddness is important for understanding the triumph of pietism in mainstream American Protestantism and what that victory meant for alternative forms of Protestant faith.

Nevin was reared in a devout Scotch-Irish Presbyterian family in Carlisle, Pennsylvania. He attended Union College in Schenectady, New York, before enrolling in 1823 at Princeton Seminary to train for the ministry. During the first part of his career, he worked in the Presbyterian circles in which he had been reared, first teaching at Princeton Seminary to fill in for Charles Hodge, who was studying in Germany, and then in 1829 joining the faculty at Western Seminary, a relatively new Presbyterian school on the frontier in Pittsburgh. But changes and disputes in the Presbyterian Church along with his own reflections on what was happening to Protestantism in the United States prompted Nevin in 1840 to accept a call to Mercersburg Theological Seminary, an institution that was geographically close to his boyhood home but, as an agency of the German Reformed Church, was religiously and ethnically distant from his Scotch-Irish Presbyterian roots. Still, Nevin's foreignness to the language, customs, and creeds of the German Reformed were no barrier.

In addition to teaching at the seminary, he presided over Marshall College, another German Reformed institution, until it merged in 1853 with Franklin College in Lancaster to become Franklin and Marshall College. In 1866 he would serve again as college president over the united institution. His other notable contributions to the German Reformed Church were to found and edit, from 1849 to 1852, the *Mercersburg Review* and to rewrite the church's liturgy in the 1860s. But Nevin's greatest achievement was his devastating critique of American revivalism in his 1843 pamphlet, *The Anxious Bench*. This work not only offers a perspective on nineteenth-century Protestant developments that defies the categories of liberal and evangelical but also accounts in part for Nevin's move from the Scotch-Irish Presbyterian to the German Reformed branch of the Calvinistic tradition.[1]

In 1870 Nevin began to write an autobiographical series for the *Reformed Church Messenger*. The articles consisted mainly of developments in his life until 1840, the year he transferred from the Presbyterian to German Reformed Church. Nevin recalled that "being of what is called Scotch-Irish extraction," he was reared in the Presbyterian faith, especially since both his parents were "conscientious and exemplary professors of religion." The senior Nevin's Presbyterianism, however, was far removed from that of such Presbyterian revivalists as Charles Grandison Finney or Billy Sunday. Nevin described "the old Presbyterian faith" in the following terms. It was:

> based throughout on the idea of the covenant family religion, church membership by God's holy act in baptism, and following this a regular catechetical training of the young, with direct reference to their coming to the Lord's table. In one word, all proceeded on the theory of sacramental, educational religion, as it had belonged properly to all the national branches of the *Reformed* Church in Europe from the beginning.[2]

Nevin's claim to have been reared according to the historic Reformed tradition was clearly important in his own conception of Christianity and its organic development. But it also enabled him to stand apart from the contemporary religious scene. In this regard, his appeal to Calvin was telling. As opposed to the American habit of getting religion by means of revival in its broadest sense, Nevin argued that historic Presbyterianism was essentially a churchly faith in the sense that "the Church in her visible character" was "the medium of salvation for her baptized children." For Nevin, no image better captured this churchly devotion than Calvin's idea of the church as mother. By this Nevin meant, quoting Calvin, "there is no other entrance into life, save as she may conceive us in her womb, give us birth, nourish us from her breasts, and embrace us in her loving care to the end."[3]

Ironically, the turning point for Nevin as a young man occurred not when he grew up to become a communicant member of the Presbyterian Church but instead when he went off to college and experienced another way of becoming a Christian. In Nevin's own words, the New England Puritan faith that informed Union College under president Eliphalet Nott was a serious challenge to "the educational and churchly scheme of religion" in which he had been reared.

> I had come to college, a boy of strongly pious dispositions and exemplary religious habits, never doubting but that I was in some way a Christian, though it had not come with me yet (unfortunately) to what is called a public profession of religion. But now one of the first lessons inculcated on me indirectly by this unchurchly system, was that all this must pass for nothing, and that I must learn to look upon myself as an outcast from the family and kingdom of God.[4]

Nevin remembered having no power to "withstand the shock." And when a "'revival of religion,' as it was called," took place at Union, he submitted to the "anxious meetings, and underwent the torture of their mechanical counsel and talk," finally converting at the age of seventeen.[5]

However, much of Nevin's memory may have played tricks on him, his reflections as an older man on the differences between revivalist Protestantism and the churchly forms inherited from his Scotch-Irish forebears were sufficiently weighty to explain his transfer to the German Reformed Church. For Nevin, revivalism pitted "an intense subjectivity" against "the grand and glorious *objectivities* of the Christian life." When he returned home, he noticed that the new ways of revivalism were also replacing older Presbyterian habits in Pennsylvania. "The notion of a new sort of religious life," Nevin explained, "was silently at work in the minds of many; caused it to be felt, more or less, that the modes of thought and worship, handed down from the fathers, had become a good deal prosy and formal, and needed at least to have infused into them a more modern spirit."[6] He would persevere for almost two decades more in the Presbyterian fold. But after seeing revivalism eat away the vitals of churchly Presbyterianism, Nevin welcomed the opportunity to move into the German Reformed communion where revivalism was being kept at bay. Nevin himself was not entirely aware of his move's significance, nor had he arrived at a point where he could articulate a churchly understanding of Protestantism like he did later in life. But early on in his tenure at Mercersburg he began to marshal arguments against pietistic Protestantism, first by taking aim at Finney's methods, and then by debating Charles Hodge over the real presence of Christ in the Lord's Supper, which over time pushed Nevin to the periphery of the mainstream churches while also making him one of the nineteenth century's most perceptive critics of American Protestantism.[7]

By twenty-first-century standards, the churchly Protestantism that Nevin defended sounds more Roman Catholic than Protestant. To be sure, the Lutheran and Anglican traditions also represent churchly and liturgical expressions of Protestantism, but in the United States, thanks to the influence of pietism, they have always appeared to be Romish. Nevin himself was aware of these attitudes when he recalled that at Union College the idea of repeating the Apostles' Creed was perceived as being "one of the questionable relics of Popery."[8]

However much Nevin might be thought to be a traitor to Protestantism because of his churchly ways, he is very instructive for pointing out the eccentricities of mainstream Protestantism. Nevin not only criticized the assumptions that guided revivalist Protestantism but also attempted to recover and perpetuate an older form of Protestant devotion that is best termed confessionalism. Like Nevin, confessional Protestantism has not been a major influence on American religious life. Yet, this variety of Protestantism maintained and perpetuated older forms of Christian belief and practice that showed just how innovative and novel mainstream American Protestantism was and continues to be.

Old World Presbyterians

The Scotch-Irish Presbyterians from whom Nevin descended have not received sustained attention from religious historians, especially the ones who practiced a form of Christianity that was more formal and churchly than that promoted by revivals. Prior to the nineteenth century, the better-known Presbyterians were those such as Gilbert Tennent, Samuel Davies, or Jonathan Dickinson who ministered in the regions of Philadelphia, New Jersey, and New York City and who in 1746 led the way in founding the College of New Jersey (later Princeton University), a revival-friendly liberal arts institution dedicated to training pastors who could preach fiery sermons that seared cold hearts. Prorevival Presbyterians in 1741 became known as the "New Side," a label that distinguished them from their opponents, appropriately named, the "Old Side," whom Leonard J. Trinterud damned with faint praise when he observed that they "were the bearers of the old tradition." Trinterud also noted that the region in which Nevin was reared, south-central Pennsylvania, was along with the Shenandoah Valley, an Old Side stronghold. Not only were Old Side Presbyterians isolated from the provincial towns of New York and Philadelphia, but they were largely an immigrant church, newly settled after relocating from Northern Ireland. According to Trinterud, Scotch-Irish immigrants who settled in the Appalachian Mountains came without pastors and so became the Old Side's "greatest missionary field."[9]

The image of Presbyterian itinerants, traveling by horseback on bad trails to conduct services for farmers, hunters, and trappers is as sympathetic a view as one can find in much of the literature on Old Side Presbyterianism. Trinterud, whose path-breaking study has not been equaled in comprehensiveness, also established the early line on Old Side historiographical fortunes. The Old Side was a failure. They could not attract a following among the laity, they failed to establish a school to train ministers, and the Old Side left no mark on colonial Presbyterianism. "Despite their arrogant pretensions to superiority" over the prorevival party, Trinterud concluded, "the clergy of the Old Side left behind them little or no lasting contribution to the Church." And to add insult to injury, he asserted that even their opposition to the revivals of the First Great Awakening "was a cover for immoralities of the grossest kinds in their own lives."[10]

With friends like this, it has been little wonder that the guild of American religious historians have not been inclined to give the Old Side much of a hearing. For instance, in standard survey texts Old Side Presbyterians are either ignored or extinct. Winthrop S. Hudson referred to them as "the antirevivalist group," noting their decline in numerical strength while failing to mention any of the Old Side's objections to the Awakening.[11] Sydney E. Ahlstrom gave little more notice in a survey known for its inclusiveness. He dismissed the Old Side's concerns as "superficial" and portrayed them as theological thugs who were intent on bullying their rivals even though the New Side conducted its "affairs with diligence and decorum."[12] To be sure, some of the neglect owes to the small number of sources that survived the Pennsylvania and Virginia frontiers, thus preventing revisionist historians from offering their spin. Francis Alison, who taught philosophy at the College of Philadelphia (later University of Pennsylvania), is the best-known, most studied, and perhaps least representative figure of the Old Side Presbyterians.[13] Still, in some of the recent re-evaluations of the First Great Awakening, the Old Side emerges as at best "polemical,"[14] "contentious,"[15] "mean,"[16] and "extreme."[17] Unlike the prorevival Presbyterians, the Old Side's views were so difficult to comprehend that only negative adjectives would suffice. Even the most sympathetic account from Elizabeth Nybakken quickly passes over the heart of Old Side objections to revivalism on the way to establishing an interesting point, but hardly a rehabilitating perspective, about the Irish character of this form of Presbyterianism and its subsequent defeat by Scottish Presbyterianism.[18]

The Old Side's reputation for nastiness is ironic if only because of the way the 1741 division between the Old and New Sides transpired. On the eve of the Great Awakening, Presbyterianism in the American colonies was just beginning to achieve some semblance of self-identity. The first act of collective Presbyterian endeavor was the founding in 1706 of the Presbytery of Philadelphia. This brought together ministers from different Protestant backgrounds, primarily Scotch-Irish Presbyterian and New England Puritan. These traditions were both Calvinistic but differed on worship and church polity.[19] What is more, these early Presbyterian ministers had not been commissioned by a church as part of a mission work and were operating more or less independently. The same could be said of Presbyterian church members. Unlike some other Protestant groups that migrated to the New World as congregations, complete with their own pastor, most of the Presbyterian laity came for economic, not religious, reasons. Presbyterianism, then, was something of a chosen identity for both clergy and laity, though, of course, both groups had some familiarity with the tenets and practices of the Reformed branch of Protestantism back in the Old World.

From 1706 until 1741, then, Presbyterians in the Middle Colonies were trying to figure out what it meant to be part of a Presbyterian Church. Aside from including new congregations and establishing structures of church governance, a major task was to determine the requirements for the ordination of clergy. This is where Presbyterian fraternity broke down and the diversity of backgrounds in the new church became evident. During the 1720s, Presbyterians arrived at the theological standard that ministers would be expected to know and teach. In 1729, in its Adopting Act, the Presbyterian Church agreed that the *Westminster Confession of Faith*, along with the Westminster Assembly's *Larger* and *Shorter Catechisms*, would be the doctrinal basis for admittance into the ministry. But even here, debates lingered into the 1730s about what subscription to these creedal standards required—for instance, whether candidates could take exception to parts of the confession and catechisms, or whether the Adopting Act required assent to the Westminster Standards in their entirety and specificity. At the same time that Presbyterians debated the meaning of creedal subscription, antagonisms surfaced over educational requirements for clergy. In 1735 William Tennent Sr. founded the Log College in Bucks County, slightly north of Philadelphia, as a place to train pastors. Other Presbyterian ministers, however, were dubious about Tennent's school and preferred to see candidates for the ministry train at universities in Scotland or Northern Ireland.[20]

Adding heat to disputes over ordination requirements were the flames of revival. Here the family name of Tennent is significant, since one of William Sr.'s sons, Gilbert, gained a reputation during the late 1720s and 1730s for stirring up zeal and earnest commitment among the Presbyterian laity. Not only did the younger Tennent preach the terrors of the law as a way of dramatizing the ultimacy of the Christian message, but he also drew upon a pietistic understanding of conversion that called upon would-be believers to undergo an immediate and powerful experience of grace. The affect of revivalism had direct consequences for Presbyterian debates surrounding ordination. Those ministers who advocated revivals argued that subscription to the Westminster Standards and a university degree did not a minister make. What candidates for the ministry also needed was to demonstrate signs of conversion or the ability to recount an experience of divine grace.

On March 8, 1740, Gilbert Tennent made his case for the necessity of conversion among clergy in a sermon delivered in Nottingham, Pennsylvania, and entitled, "The Danger of an Unconverted Ministry." The context for what would arguably become the most important Presbyterian sermon of the eighteenth century was not simply the debates surrounding ordination. Tennent had in view more immediately the arrival of George Whitefield in 1739 and the emergence of revivals on a grand scale. The content of the Anglican priest's sermons along with his habit of preaching in places where he had not been invited occasioned criticisms from some Presbyterian clergy, many of whom would form the Old Side party. Tennent, however, was certain that the response to Whitefield was a divine work and the Presbyterian revivalist would not tolerate any opposition to the evangelist or his meetings. His sermon on the dangers of unconverted ministers was not simply a hypothetical argument about a remote possibility. Tennent was convinced that the opponents of revivals were dangerous because their opposition to Whitefield (and, it should be added, to him, his father, and the Log College) proved these critics to be unconverted.[21]

Tennent's sermon text was a verse from the Gospel of Mark (6:34) that mentions Christ's compassion for people lacking sound religious leaders. In the first part of the sermon, Tennent had little trouble identifying the Pharisees as the teachers with whom Christ was at odds or in comparing them to the revivals' opponents. The next section enumerated the sufferings of laity who were forced to sit under the preaching of such incapable leaders. In his concluding remarks of application, Tennent specified what the people needed to do. One thing was to stock the church with faithful ministers and the way to accomplish this was by encouraging places like the Log College, since the academies were "much corrupted and abused" and private schools such as his father's were "under the Care of skillful and experienced Christians" and only admitted those who could give "plain Evidences of experimental Religion." The other remedy was for the laity to seek out good preachers and listen to them wherever and whenever they could, even if it meant not attending a congregation in which they were members. "To bind Men to a particular Minister, against their Judgment and Inclinations, when they are more edified elsewhere," Tennent exclaimed, was "a cruel Oppression of tender Consciences . . . a Yoke worse than that of *Rome* itself." This logic had a measure of appeal to parishioners, but it was precisely the issue that had prompted opposition to the revivals since itinerant evangelists were disrupting the work of settled clergy in local congregations. But Tennent believed he could see through such objections to the "Rottenness and

Hypocrise" that resided in the antirevivalists' hearts. In his mind, the revival and ministers associated with it were so good and true that those who lived "under the Ministry of dead Men, whether they have got the Form of Religion or not" should repair "to the Living" where they could be edified.[22]

It is hard to imagine what a charitable reaction to this sermon from those who disagreed with Tennent would look like. In fact, the sermon forced some ministers who may have appreciated aspects of the revivals to side with the antirevivalists since Tennent not only questioned the character of fellow ministers in a public forum but also encouraged the laity to look for another church if their minister did not live up to expectations. Even though the formal breach between the New and Old Sides did not occur until May 1741 at the meeting of the synod of Philadelphia, Tennent's sermon threatened whatever stability and order the young Presbyterian Church had obtained after thirty-five years. Tennent not only had said that it was permissible for the laity to sever the bonds with their own minister but also had undermined the trust and respect between fellow ministers.

Nevertheless, Tennent's sermon possessed a certain persuasiveness if only because of a general presumption that favored revivalism. After all, what minister would reasonably oppose a development that brought new converts into the church, generated greater interest in Bible reading and prayer, and raised the moral standards for lay members and clergy? In other words, those who opposed genuine religion had to be hypocritical, selfish, and proud; there was no other reasonable explanation for the Old Side's opposition.

The important issue, of course, is what constitutes genuine religion. For those in the pietist tradition, in this case, the New Side, the forms of religion are not as important as what happens to believers in their hearts or souls. But for Old Side Presbyterians, whose position was an early embodiment of confessional Protestantism, forms do matter to authentic faith. What particularly mattered at the decision of the synod of Philadelphia in 1741 to exclude the prorevival members was church order and the procedures of Presbyterianism, not simply in the training and ordination of ministers but also in abiding by and submitting to the decisions of ecclesiastical assemblies. For the Old Side, then, the trouble with revivalism was that its promoters did not submit to the legitimate authority of the church. In effect, the Old Side alleged that the prorevival party, according to its own conception of Christian piety, was changing the rules by which the church operated.[23]

This was the argument of John Thomson (ca. 1690–1753), one of the Old Side ministers who opposed revivalism because it challenged church authority. Born in Northern Ireland and having studied for the ministry at the University of Glasgow, in 1715 Thomson migrated to the New World and assumed a pastorate in Lewes, Delaware. He quickly gained the esteem of fellow presbyters, being chosen moderator of synod twice and of presbytery on three occasions. Thomson also proposed and persuaded his colleagues in 1729 to adopt the Westminster Standards as the basis for ministerial fellowship in the Presbyterian Church. In 1730 he moved to southeastern Pennsylvania (Octorara) and pastored congregations there until 1744 when he moved to North Carolina to establish a congregation among recent Scotch-Irish immigrants. The places where and conditions under which Thomson ministered did not facilitate the preservation of his papers, thus, making much of his life and thought a mystery. But in 1741 at the peak of the controversy among Presbyterians over the revivals, Thomson wrote a pamphlet, *The Government of the Church of Christ . . .* , which states Old Side objections to the new forms of religion and offers a confessional Protestant alternative to what was emerging as the dominant strain of Protestant piety in the New World.

For Thomson, a direct corollary to personal devotion was the order and discipline of the church. Just as the life of the believer should be characterized by decorum and propriety, so the affairs of believers gathered into a unified whole should also demonstrate restraint and dignity. This was one of the reasons for Thomson's objection to the revivalists' understanding of conversion and the certainty by which it could be detected, both by the convert and by clergy. Revivalists interpreted Old Side criticism here as an admission that the state of persons could not be known. But as Thomson explained, the question was not whether faith could be detected but rather what constituted fitting evidence of belief. For Tennent and the prorevival party, the evidence of conversion was immediate and obvious, comparable to the way one might feel the blowing of the wind or a knife wound. In Thomson's view, however, the marks of grace were much more subtle and ordinary. In the case of a prospective minister, he denied that the examination should include questions about a man's personal experience. Instead, all that was needed was to ask whether a candidate for the ministry adhered to the doctrines and beliefs of the Presbyterian Church. "These personal and secret things" were appropriate for "free intimate private voluntary

Conversation between or among intimate Bosom-Friends," but no church judicatory on earth had a "just right" to inquire into the "Secrets of [the] heart."[24]

By raising the issue of intimacy and privacy, Thomson was questioning the very propriety of revivalism's piety. He argued that what was fitting in private settings was not appropriate for public ones—for example, the language and emotion of prayer at home would not be suitable for corporate worship. In other words, revivalist piety bordered on vulgarity because it made experiences and emotions of a more intimate nature the norm for settings that were formal and public. Thomson was not even sure whether some of the revivalists or their converts' antics were fitting at any time. He doubted, for instance, whether the Spirit of God was genuinely at work in the use of "such hellish Words and Expressions, as they often use in their Sermons, which they borrow from the most profane, black guard Ruffians, Cursers and Swearers." Thomson also objected to the cries and convulsions that accompanied such preaching. Rather than regarding these displays of piety as marks of genuine religion, Thomson asserted that his Presbyterian forefathers _____ ____ __ ___ form of devotion, one in which both ministers and the people _____ _____ _____ _____ Affairs in a regular manner, according th_____ _____ _____ _____ment, every Pastor having his ow_____

As dis_____ _____ _____ _____ _____ tion could be, the rights of pastors t_____ _____ _____ _____ omson's larger concern. The Old Side_____ _____ _____ _____ the ministry of pastors—was a means_____ _____ _____ _____ edification of members. A sacred bo_____ _____ _____ _____ nd their clergy, which revivalists threate_____ _____ _____ _____ ters of unbelief and by invading other_____ _____ _____ _____ 'the Relation between a Minister of the_____ _____ _____ _____ y Person belonging to it, [is] a sacred_____ _____ _____ _____ he called revivalism a "new-fangle Meth_____ _____ _____ _____ away People's minds from their own mini_____ _____ _____ _____ ticularly egregious and "profane Vi-olati_____ _____ _____ _____ ncouraged the laity to abandon their min_____ _____ _____ _____ ns given and proven before a lawful Ch_____ _____ _____ _____ ssued an Old Side maxim that has re-ma_____ _____ _____ _____ aluations of American religion since 17_____ _____ _____ _____ yourselves of it that you are not most edified or profited when you are most pleased. False Doctrine and mere Amusements do too often please an unskillful Auditory, to their Hurt."[26]

In this pamphlet Thomson also defended the Presbyterian form of government, extending the bond between clergy and laity to include the ties among clergy in the various courts of the Presbyterian system of church order.[27] Although this part of his argument was the most relevant to the specific circumstances that forced the breach between the New and Old Side branches of the Presbyterian Church, the damage was already done once Thomson had defended the formal procedures of the church as the appointed way of being Presbyterian. When he called revivalism a novel form of Christianity, Thomson introduced the notion that pietistic Protestantism—the form that would fill the mainstream of American religion—was at odds not with a rationalist, protoliberal Protestantism but with an older, churchly Protestant faith.[28] In fact, if Thomson's Presbyterianism can be construed as a form of confessional Protestantism, the Old Side–New Side split was the first stage of a perennial rivalry in American religious history not between conservative and liberal Protestantism but between conversionist or pietistic Protestantism and its churchly or confessional competitor.

Subsequent developments among colonial Presbyterianism, however, would obscure this hostility, partly because the Old Side would fare so poorly and partly because the Old and New Sides would reunite. In 1758 the Old and New Sides agreed to resume their previous relationship as fellow Presbyterians in one denomination. The terms were so favorable to the New Side that one historian has called the Presbyterian reunion a "victory" for the prorevival party.[29] Although candidates for the ministry would have to demonstrate adequate learning and be able to subscribe to the Westminster Standards, anyone seeking ordination would also have to show evidence of conversion. Presbyterians were trying valiantly to recognize the legitimacy of both sides. But subsequent events in the united church would show the fundamental tension between the Old and New Side's methods of religion.

The source of controversy continued to be the examination of candidates for the ministry. The Old Side continued to insist that only formal questions were legitimate, with the New Side wanting some demonstration of a conversion experience. Despite the expressions of good will and concessions offered during the 1750s, the 1760s proved how difficult it was for the two parties to coexist. Consequently, in 1762 a second presbytery in Philadelphia was formed precisely to give Old Side ministers freedom to conduct examinations as they saw fit. A similar pattern emerged in rural southeastern Pennsylvania, an area of continuing Scotch-Irish strength. Tensions between the Old and New Sides became so intense that at first the denomination reorganized the presbyteries of Donegal and New Castle to weaken the strength of the Old Side.

But this action only made the Old Side clergy more belligerent. Finally, the denomination relented and allowed the formation of a separate body, "the true Presbytery of Donegal," to accommodate Old Side concerns. Yet, despite these small victories, the New Side constituted the majority in the denomination as a whole and represented a New World form of Presbyterianism, where revivalism and Reformed practices would coexist.[30] Some candidates for the Presbyterian ministry, especially those studying with Old Side educators, sensed the atmosphere and switched to the formalities of the Anglican church. New Side ministers used these Anglican "converts" as evidence of the Old Side's disloyalty.[31] But these Presbyterians-turned-Episcopalians could just as likely demonstrate the rejection of revivalism by younger Presbyterians whose churchly piety made the Church of England a more suitable place of worship and ministerial endeavor.

From one perspective, then, the 1758 reunion was a classic compromise with each party apparently finding a place in the church. But this view is premised on the idea that revivalism and traditional Presbyterian forms of ministry could coexist. The split of 1741 had proved precisely the opposite of such a position. The Old Side had argued in opposition to the New Side that the church had no legitimate authority to search the subjective experience of members for evidence of conversion or even sufficient criteria for evaluating alleged evidence. In contrast, the New Side contended that revivalism was the surest way to promote the faith and guaranteed the integrity of ministers. These two views could not be easily reconciled. But in the aftermath of the two sides' separate existence that saw the New Side church grow and the Old Side decline, the latter party did not have leverage to insist on its views in the reunited church or to persist outside the other Presbyterian body. The Old Side–New Side reunion, then, may not have been a complete victory for revivalism, but it did forge a view popular in American Protestantism since 1758 that revivalism and conservative Protestantism are mutually reinforcing. In the case of Presbyterianism, this notion has encouraged a mix of Presbyterian traditionalism and revivalistic pragmatism. This amalgam has proved to be a winning combination as long as Presbyterian particularities have not impeded personal piety or evangelistic outreach. From 1758 on, the New Side's effort to combine doctrine and experience would be the guiding premise of future developments in mainstream Presbyterian churches. The Old Side–New Side controversy, then, foreshadowed the lesson of nineteenth-century American Protestantism: for churches and their members to grow they had to use the reliable methods of revival. Confessional Protestantism's old measures were not as effective in the environment of the New World as revivalism's novelties.

Old World Lutherans

To argue that the tensions at work in colonial Presbyterianism were the same as those that emerged among nineteenth-century American Lutherans is to indulge in a form of oversimplification. Unlike Presbyterians who spoke a common language, Lutherans, thanks to their different places of origin, could not speak to each other and be understood, let alone worship together with a common liturgy. Also, because they migrated from different parts of Germany or Scandinavia, Lutherans confronted not only the discrepancies between Old World customs and New World practices but also the cultural barriers that would separate Lutherans from each other. One further difference between colonial Presbyterians and nineteenth-century Lutherans was the potential rivalry between Lutherans who had lived in North America since the seventeenth century and recent Lutheran immigrants. Whereas colonial Presbyterians were all new to America and shared a similar status, the nineteenth-century Lutheran experience had the potential of elevating the older families and persons who had successfully assimilated to the customs of the new nation above the unwashed ethnics who persisted in living by the old ways.

Indeed, what stands out in nineteenth-century American Lutheran history is the reality of immigration. Although Lutherans had established churches in the New World in the seventeenth century that by the time of the American Revolution would be recognized as a legitimate partner in the denominational system, nineteenth-century immigration upset the stability that colonial Lutherans had achieved. Between 1830 and 1880, approximately three million Germans migrated to the United States, 190,000 Norwegians, and 85,000 Swedes, the three largest groups going into the Lutheran church.[32] Of course, not all of these immigrants were practicing Lutherans. Even so, with 90 percent of the Scandinavian and 50 percent of the German immigrants making a nominal profession of Lutheran faith, these new faces easily swamped the capacities of the existing churches. And when the churches began to catch up with the new Lutherans in America, the Lutheran presence became even more chaotic. Between 1840 and 1875, Lutherans formed fifty-eight different church bodies to accommodate this large influx of immigrants, from the Evangelical Lutheran Synod of the West, founded in 1840, to the Wartburg Synod, commencing in 1875.[33] Although the stakes were lower, uniting Lutherans looked to be a more arduous proposition than preserving the union of the United States.

Another important difference between nineteenth-century Lutherans and colonial Presbyterians is the relation of each group to pietism. In contrast to Presbyterians who may have encountered it for the first time when they settled in the New World, by 1850 Lutherans had lived with pietism for two hundred years. Lutheran pietism, narrowly considered, was a reaction against scholastic orthodoxy and sought a revitalization of believers and the church more through deeds and devotion than through correct beliefs. Its leader was Phillipp Jacob Spener (1635–1705), who desired a renewal of Lutheran churches through small groups of believers gathering for prayer and Bible study. The pietist movement also spawned a number of charitable and educational institutions, along with missionary societies. Although the formal aspects of church life were less important to pietist devotion than the gatherings of laity for edification, only the most radical pietists left the institutional church completely. Still, wherever it emerged, pietism tapped sentiments of discontent with the formalities of correct theology and liturgy that defined Lutheran orthodoxy.[34]

The revivals that Lutherans in the British colonies witnessed were technically different from seventeenth-century pietism, but revivalists and pietists were on the same side of the question about what counted for genuine religion. Among the different denominations of British Protestants, only the Methodists advocated small-group meetings in ways comparable to pietism. The revivals of the First Great Awakening, consequently, flourished more from the work of itinerant preaching and the lay people who turned out than from any sort of systematic plan to generate lay-directed small groups. Even so, Old World pietism pre-disposed colonial Lutherans to welcome revivalists such as George Whitefield and Gilbert Tennent. Henry Melchior Muhlenberg (1711–1787), the patriarch of American Lutheranism, invited Whitefield in 1760 to preach at a confirmation service and maintained cordial relations with Tennent. Indeed, according to L. DeAne Lagerquist, Tennent's sentiments in "The Danger of an Unconverted Ministry" would have sounded to Muhlenberg, who trained at Halle, the academic center of pietism, like those of Spener.[35] The experience of the eighteenth-century revivals showed that German pietism and its Anglo-American equivalent were united by a concern for religion of the heart as opposed to the head or of internal sincerity as opposed to external observance. At the beginning of the nineteenth century, then, Lutheranism in America was fairly assimilated. To be sure, Lutherans had not abandoned their liturgy, hymns, or confessions and catechisms. But few saw any tension between the dominant forms of piety among Anglo-American Protestants and those of German-American Lutherans.

The dominant figure of nineteenth-century Lutheranism, Samuel Simon Schmucker (1799–1873), accelerated Lutheran assimilation of American ways. A graduate of the University of Pennsylvania and Princeton Theological Seminary, Schmucker was able to dispense with any charge of Lutheran provincialism. What is more, the aim of much of his work as a church leader and professor at Gettysburg Seminary was to move the Lutheran church into the mainstream of American Protestantism. To that end, in his 1855 book, *The Definite Synodical Platform*, Schmucker hoped to give American Lutheranism a theological foundation that would allow the church to adapt better to its cultural setting. He specifically called for revision of five areas of the *Augsburg Confession*, the theological standard for ministry and membership in the church. Schmucker's *Platform* stripped Lutheran teaching on baptismal regeneration and the real presence of Christ in the Lord's Supper of their foreignness and moved it in the low church direction of the American Protestant mainstream. At the same time, he proposed that Lutherans act more like native Anglo-Americans by observing the Sabbath in a fashion comparable to Puritan practice. Finally, to show that Lutherans were different from another group of foreigners recently to arrive and stir up a good deal of protest, Schmucker believed his church should condemn such Roman Catholic practices as the mass and private confession. This was not simply a strategy for mainstreaming

Lutheranism. Schmucker was also active in ecumenical circles, having attended the first meeting of the Evangelical Alliance in London (1846), and he hoped to unite all the evangelical churches in the United States in some measure of cooperation. In fact, a list of essential doctrines that he prepared in 1851 shows striking resemblance to the theological platform adopted in 1873 by the American branch of the Evangelical Alliance.[36] The *Platform* was one way of facilitating such cooperation by rounding off some of Lutheranism's angularities. It also fit with the pietist and revivalist habit of setting aside formal theological and liturgical differences as unimportant compared to the more significant bonds of love that unite all believers, no matter what denomination or tradition, in the weighty tasks of missions and evangelism.[37]

The only problem for Schmucker was that by the time the *Platform* was published, the composition of American Lutheranism had changed considerably thanks to immigration. Some of these Lutherans arrived in the United States with a strong dose of theological self-consciousness that was clearly at odds with Schmucker's hopes for a more tolerant form of Lutheranism. Consequently, instead of shepherding the Lutheran faithful into more generically Protestant pastures, Schmucker sparked a controversy about Lutheran identity that ironically highlighted differences between historic Lutheranism and the American Protestant mainstream he had hoped to cover.

The year before Schmucker's *Platform* appeared, Philip Schaff, professor of theology at the German Reformed seminary in Mercersburg, Pennsylvania, and a recent immigrant to the United States, returned to his homeland and described three parties among Lutherans in the New World. He characterized Schmucker's contingent as the "Neo-Lutheran" party, "an amalgamation of Lutheranism with American Puritanism and Methodistic elements." This group was most emphatic in calling itself the American Lutheran Church, and in Schaff's view it was "the most active, the most practical and progressive, and is best acquainted with the English spirit." Neo-Lutherans were, in fact, so familiar with English ways that he could call them "English, un-German, not only in language, but also in [their] sympathies and antipathies." At odds with the Neo-Lutherans were the "Old Lutherans," whom Schaff described as recent immigrants from Germany, "still totally German" and foreign to "the English and American spirit." These Lutherans were so intolerant that they would not even consider admitting pious non-Lutherans to the observance of the Lord's Supper. Schaff's third group was the Moderates. They stood midway between the "two extremes," but he could not help distinguishing them more from the Old than the Neo-Lutherans, because they partook of the breadth of pietism and were "too Americanized already" to sympathize with the Old Lutherans' "exclusive spirit."[38]

Schaff's reading of mid-nineteenth-century Lutheranism may have revealed more about his own ecumenical preferences than the actual situation. To be sure, he rightly detected what immigration had done to American Lutheranism—namely, exposing important differences between the dominant forms of Anglo-American piety and their German Lutheran counterparts. But country of birth could not entirely explain the crisis over denominational identity that American Lutheran churches experienced in the 1850s. Indeed, one of the reasons for questioning Schaff's categorization, as perceptive as it was, is that one of the Lutheran pastors he placed in the Moderate camp was William Julius Mann (1819–1893), an emigrant to the United States in 1845 (at Schaff's urging), minister to St. Michael's and Zion's Congregation in Philadelphia (the congregation that Muhlenburg had pastored) and, most important, Schmucker's most vigorous opponent. In response to Schmucker's *Platform*, Mann wrote *A Plea for the Augsburg Confession* (1856), a book suggesting that even though the Moderates were not as "rigid" as the Old Lutherans, the Neo-Lutherans were trying to fit the square peg of historic Lutheran faith and practice into the round hole of mainstream American revivalist Protestantism.[39]

Because of his *Plea* and another polemical work, *Lutheranism in America* (1857), Mann emerged as one of the leaders of Lutheran confessionalism.[40] As with Lutheran pietism, the origins of Lutheran confessionalism also go back to European developments. In the early nineteenth century in Germany and Scandinavia, a variety of circumstances, some religious and some political, prompted a greater Lutheran self-consciousness and reacquaintance with the confessional standards of the tradition. Many Lutheran immigrants brought to the United States a greater attachment and concern to maintain the beliefs and practices of historic Lutheranism. As the term *confessionalism* suggests, Lutheran traditionalists placed a high priority on the teachings of the Lutheran confessions, especially the *Augsburg Confession* (1530). In contrast to Protestants in the evangelical mainstream and Lutherans such as Schmucker who insisted on the right of private judgment and made experience (e.g., conversion) the norm for determining religious truth, confessionalists held that the Lutheran doctrinal standards taught what the Bible revealed and so were objectively true. What is more, adhering to the teaching of *Augsburg* was essential to Lutheran identity. This high estimate of church teaching also affected the confessionalists' method of passing on the faith. As opposed to the revivalist practice of forcing individuals to choose their religious identity, confessionalist Lutherans advocated catechetical training since the process of learning Lutheran doctrine would have the effect of nurturing a Lutheran outlook. Theological instruction was not the only form of fitting nurture for confessionalists. They also defended a traditional Lutheran understanding of the sacraments, baptism, and the Lord's Supper, as the essence of the church. Through corporate worship, confessionalists argued, the liturgy strengthened church members' faith.[41] In sum, confessionalist piety was essentially churchly; participation in the forms and rites of the church, as opposed to the convert's solitary quest to lead an earnest moral life, was the way to be a Christian.

Mann exhibited each of these strands of Lutheran confessionalism in his *Plea for the Augsburg Confession*. He took up each of Schmucker's five areas of confessional revision and defended historic Lutheran teaching. As Schaff had noted, Mann's views were thoroughly plausible. But they were also definitely at odds with the American Protestant mainstream into which Schmucker hoped to lead American Lutherans. For instance, to Schmucker's charge that Lutheranism perpetuated Roman Catholic beliefs about the Mass, Mann resolutely refuted what he deemed the abuses of Catholicism and defended the reforms introduced by Martin Luther and Philip Melanchthon. But this did not mean Lutherans were left with a simple choice between Schmucker's Americanist faith and Rome. The Lutheran position, according to Mann, was one that avoided the abuses of Rome while still affirming that the Lord's Supper conferred grace. Here he quoted *Augsburg*: this sacrament is "a means to awaken our faith and to comfort the hearts and consciences of men, by reminding them . . . that Christ has promised them grace and forgiveness of sins" (Art. 24).[42] Many have interpreted the difference between Schmucker and Mann as simply the classic difference between Ulrich Zwingli and Martin Luther on the Lord's Supper, and Mann left evidence to support this contention. But he also stated that his difference with Schmucker went deeper to the very purpose of the sacraments in the life of the believer. For mainstream Protestants, according to Mann, the sacraments were tangential compared to the individual Christian's personal life of piety. But for confessional Lutherans, the sacraments had "intrinsic value" because they were divinely appointed means of conveying grace.

The corporate character of confessional Lutheran piety also came through in Mann's response to Schmucker's accusation that *Augsburg* continued the Roman Catholic practice of private confession and absolution. Again, Mann quoted Lutheran formulas to good effect, showing how the Lutheran practice of absolution differed from that of Rome not just in form but also in substance. Still, this did not mean that Schmucker was correct, as if the only options were absolution as administered by Catholic priests or the revivalist Protestant habit of offering none at all. Consequently, Mann again argued for a middle way, one where the Lutheran pastor actually declares pardon to those who confess their sin, but does so in the context of public worship and in response to a corporate confession of sin, not in a confessional with one church member at a time.[43] What is more, Mann contended that absolution was "nothing but what the Bible authorizes, and ha[d] been the practice of the Lutheran Church from the beginning."[44]

Mann's defense of confessional Lutheranism was more than an expression of one party in a specific denominational struggle. For him and other confessionalists, the very identity of Lutheranism in the United States hung in the balance. If Schmucker had wanted to "ponder with a prayerful and searching spirit" points of received Lutheran teaching, Mann asserted, he should be able to do so. But to "proclaim publicly [his] apostasy from Luther and the Augsburg Confession" was "unbecoming and unwise." What is more, Schmucker's criticism of his church's views was un-Lutheran, showed "a spirit foreign to our Church," and demonstrated that the views of other Protestants had "gained ground in our own mind" against those of Luther. Mann did not intend these observations to be prejudicial because he thought the history of Lutherans in the United States made the situation inevitable. A variety of circumstances had contributed to ignorance of Lutheranism's "peculiar" teachings"—the influence of German rationalism and the lack of a Lutheran seminary (which meant prospective pastors had to train at other denominational schools). It was understandable, then, that "our Lutheran home became rather uncomfortable for many of its own children . . . and invited strangers into the family circle." But these unfavorable circumstances could not hide the fact that many Lutheran churches had "done away with the peculiar doctrines, with the old forms of worship, and with the Old Lutheran Church's usages."[45]

Mann concluded with comments on the Lutheran church's relation to other American Protestants. Here he stressed a choice that was confronting

American Lutherans. They could have a larger presence by giving up their "peculiar doctrines" and following the ways of other denominations. But this choice would result in a church that was no longer Lutheran in character. Or they could make known how "excellent" Lutheranism was, "what a treasure of deep, solid, comforting Bible truth."[46] Either way, the Lutheran Church could not be both generically Protestant and particularly Lutheran. By posing the Lutheran dilemma in this way, Mann was speaking not just for Lutherans but for all confessional Protestants who sensed a loss of churchly identity in the face of American Protestantism's evangelical mainstream. In other words, the low church piety of revivalism did not mix with the churchly teachings and practices of historic Protestantism's confessional traditions.

But, as Mann's *Plea* also demonstrated, the churchly ways of confessionalists were becoming harder and harder to distinguish from Catholicism in the eyes of many Americans, thanks to the influence of revivalism. To maintain that Protestant ministers declared forgiveness of sins, or that baptism and the Lord's Supper conferred grace, or that being a church member required affirming the doctrines of a particular denomination was by the 1850s to do the same things that Roman Catholics did. Undoubtedly, the recent arrival of Catholic immigrants in the 1830s and 1840s on a large scale, and the subsequent stoking of anti-Catholic prejudices, accounted for some of the misunderstanding confessional Protestants endured. But just as significant was the dominance of revivalism among American Protestants. Protestant revivalism, with its pietist disregard of forms, teachings, and rites in favor of a religion that consisted of devout feelings and good intentions, had become so deeply ingrained in the American soul that Protestant confessionalism looked and sounded as foreign as Catholicism. To those whose piety revolved around the ceremonies and creeds of Lutherans, Presbyterians, and Episcopalians, however, revivalism was the foreign element in American Protestantism.[47]

A Different Way of Getting Religion

The experience of colonial Presbyterians and nineteenth-century Lutherans demonstrates that a form of Protestantism at odds with the mainstream's pietist faith was alive even if not well during the defining years of American Protestantism. Confessional Lutheranism and Presbyterianism represented a different way of appropriating and passing on the Christian faith from the dominant modes of broadly defined revivalism. In contrast to the moment of crisis that resulted in a conversion experience, confessional Lutherans and Presbyterians stressed the acquisition of theological knowledge and participation in the life of the congregation. To become steeped in the way that other Presbyterians or Lutherans understood and practiced the faith was the path to becoming a mature Christian, not the solitary encounter of the individual with the supernatural and mysterious workings of the Spirit. The corporate nature of confessional Protestant devotion also involved church members in a high degree of dependence on the clergy. Rather than being left to their own devices in private Bible reading or small-group meetings outside church, confessional Protestantism expected Christians to be under the direct supervision of ministers either through the acts of public worship or periodic pastoral visits in homes.[48]

In the case of colonial Presbyterians, who believed a sacred bond existed between a pastor and his flock, revivalists and itinerants showed disrespect for that bond, not only by invading alien parishes but also by casting despite on ministers who raised questions about the methods and preaching of evangelists. What is more, challenges to established clergy, rather than being made public through the printed or spoken word, had to be scrutinized by appropriate church authorities, such as the presbytery or synod. For confessional Lutherans the walk of church members was tied to the minister's acts of declaring corporate forgiveness and in administering the sacraments. Lutheran creeds defined the significance of these rites, and participation in them was at the core of Lutheran identity. Consequently, the institutional church set confessional piety apart from revivalism's rugged spiritual individualism and low regard for clergy, liturgical rites, and creeds. And as the examples of colonial Presbyterians and nineteenth-century Lutherans show, revivalism was no less hostile to confessional Protestantism than to the errors of Rome. In fact, on a spectrum of Christianity that placed creeds, clergy, and rites at one end, and religious experience and personal morality at the opposite end, Protestant confessionalists would be located closer to Roman Catholics than to revivalist Protestantism.

John Williamson Nevin made precisely this point in the little pamphlet he wrote in 1843 against the techniques that made Charles Grandison Finney famous. Over the course of this essay, Nevin criticized specifically many of the so-called new measures that Finney and others were using to gain converts and revitalize churches. But in the conclusion, Nevin turned from specifics to more general observations about what was happening to Protestantism in the United States. "Two different theories of religion," according to Nevin, were "at war."[49] The anxious bench stood for a shallow system of Christianity in which faith was presumed to "authenticate itself." "With very little instruction, and almost no examination, all who can persuade themselves that they are converted, are at once hailed as brethren and sisters . . . and with as little delay as possible gathered into the full communion of the Church."[50] This was almost opposite of the bench's rival system of religion, signified in Nevin's mind by the catechism. By this he did not mean simply the memorization of catechism answers as was the practice among the German Reformed and Scotch-Irish Presbyterians. Instead, the catechism stood for a more comprehensive and churchly system of Christian practice that revolved around sermons, teaching in the church, pastoral visitations, and, of course, catechesis. In sum, the catechism symbolized "patient perseverance in the details of ministerial work"—that is, in the "agencies, by which alone the kingdom of God may be expected to go steadily forward." The differences between these two ways of religion were so great that Nevin could conclude, "The Bench is against the Catechism, and the Catechism against the Bench."[51]

Almost sixty years after Nevin wrote these words, the German Reformed Church was still trying to maintain a churchly system of religion in the face of the individualistic and experiential faith that dominated United States' Protestantism. At the end of its twentieth-century edition of the *Heidelberg Catechism*, a pocket-sized, hardcover book, the German Reformed Church appended instructions to catechumens about the meaning of confirmation and how this method of conversion differed from the model dominant in the Protestant churches. It read:

> Some persons, not understanding our church life and customs, foolishly think that we confirm our young people no matter what their state of mind and heart is, and that we do not believe in conversion. This is a great mistake. We require a high degree of fitness for confirmation, namely, an intelligent, sincere, and unreserved taking of three most searching and far-reaching vows in the name of the holy Trinity.[52]

The process of confirmation, the appendix explained, was sort of like conversion, but it was not "sudden," did not necessarily consist of "wonderful religious experiences, such as you hear about in others," nor was it the sort of thing you could date precisely. Instead, confirmation took time—"the growth of years"—and happened in "a very quiet way." This advice to cat-echumens concluded with the reassurance that confirmation was "the Re-formed doctrine of 'getting religion.' We get religion, not in bulk but little by little. Just as we get natural life and strength, so spiritual life and strength, day by day."[53]

The German Reformed Church's understanding of confirmation, as this advice to catechumens demonstrated, was in the authors' minds at odds with ways of acquiring and practicing the Christian religion that revivalist-inspired Protestantism had fashioned into the mainstream American faith. Consequently, the experience of the German Reformed at the beginning of the twentieth century was a variation on the theme that has been played out in the history of various confessional Protestant groups in the United States—namely, that the old ways of the Protestant religion were no longer effective in the new American society. In fact, historic Protestant practices and beliefs had been refashioned in such a way that the clergy and public acts of worship were no longer essential to zealous and sincere Christian faith. Over the course of the twentieth century, this tension would still ex-ist as controversies within the mainstream denominations would redefine the meaning of conservative Protestantism. Although these developments would obscure further the habits and beliefs of confessional Protestants, their churchly faith still stands in marked contrast to the seemingly conser-vative zeal of fundamentalists and evangelicals.

Notes

1. On Nevin, see Theodore Appel, *The Life and Work of John Williamson Nevin* (1889; reprint, New York: Arno, 1969); Same Hamstra Jr. and Arie J. Griffioen, eds., *Reformed Confessionalism in Nineteenth-Century America: Essays on the Thought of John Williamson Nevin* (Metuchen, N.J.: Scarecrow, 1995).

2. John W. Nevin, *My Own Life: The Earlier Years* (Lancaster, Pa.: Historical So-ciety of the Evangelical and Reformed Church, 1964), 2.

3. Nevin, *My Own Life*, 3; quotation from Calvin, *Institutes of the Christian Reli-gion*, IV.3.i.

4. Nevin, *My Own Life*, 9.

5. Nevin, *My Own Life*, 9–10.

6. Nevin, *My Own Life*, 11, 14.

7. For Nevin's response to Finney's revivals, see Nevin, *The Anxious Bench* (Chambersburg, Pa.: Weekly Messenger, 1843); for his differences with Hodge, see Nevin, *The Mystical Presence: A Vindication of the Reformed of Calvinistic Doctrine of the Holy Eucharist* (Philadelphia: Lippincott, 1846).

8. Nevin, *My Own Life*, 11.

9. Leonard J. Trinterud, *The Forming of an American Tradition: A Re-examination or Colonial Presbyterianism* (Philadelphia: Westminster, 1949), 137.

10. Trinterud, *The Forming of an American Tradition*, 135–36, 143.

11. Winthrop S. Hudson, *Religion in America*, 3d ed. (New York: Scribner's, 1981), 70.

12. Sydney E. Ahlstrom, *A Religious History of the American People* (New Haven, Conn.: Yale University Press, 1972), 271, 272.

13. See, for instance, Elizabeth Ingersoll, *Francis Alison: American Philosophe* (Ann Arbor, Mich.: UMI, 1974); and J. L. McAllister, "Francis Alison, and John Witherspoon: Political Philosophers and Revolutionaries," *Journal of Presbyterian History* 54 (1976): 33–60.

14. Marilyn J. Westerkamp, *The Triumph of the Laity: Scots-Irish Piety and the Great Awakening, 1625–1760* (New York: Oxford University Press, 1988), 197.

15. Milton J. Coalter Jr., *Gilbert Tennent, Son of Thunder: A Case Study of Continental Pietism's Impact on the First Great Awakening in the Middle Colonies* (Westport, Conn.: Greenwood, 1986), 82.

16. Janet F. Fishburn, "Gilbert Tennent, Established 'Dissenter,'" *Church History* 63 (1994): 44.

17. Ned C. Landsman, *Scotland and Its First American Colony, 1683–1765* (Princeton, N.J.: Princeton University Press, 1985), 250.

18. Elizabeth I. Nybakken, "New Light on the Old Side: Irish Influences on Colonial Presbyterianism," *Journal of American History* 66 (1981–1982): 813–32.

19. On these differences, see Horton Davies, *The Worship of the English Puritans* (London: Dacre, 1948).

20. On these developments among colonial Presbyterians, see Leonard J. Trinterud, *The Forming of an American Tradition: A Re-Examination of Colonial Presbyterianism* (Philadelphia: Westminster, 1949); Milton J. Coalter Jr., *Gilbert Tennent, Son of Thunder: A Case Study of Continental Pietism's Impact on the First Great Awakening in the Middle Colonies* (Westport, Conn.: Greenwood, 1986); and Westerkamp, *The Triumph of the Laity* (New York: Oxford University Press).

21. See Coalter, *Gilbert Tennent*, chap. 3.

22. Gilbert Tennent, "The Danger of an Unconverted Ministry," in *The Great Awakening: Documents Illustrating the Crisis and Its Consequences*, ed. Alan Heimert and Perry Miller (Indianapolis: Bobbs-Merrill, 1967), 85, 89, 95, 97.

23. See *A Protestatation Presented to the Synod of Philadelphia, June 1, 1741* (Philadelphia: B. Franklin, 1741).

24. John Thomson, *The Government of the Church of Christ, and the Authority of Church Judicatories established on a Scripture Foundation* . . . (Philadelphia: A. Bradford, 1741), 22–25, quotation from 25.

25. Thomson, *The Government of the Church of Christ*, 127.

26. Thomson, *The Government of the Church of Christ*, 126, 127.

27. Thomson, *The Government of the Church of Christ*, 27, 32.

28. This is a notion generally missed in the history of colonial Presbyterianism in which the anti-revivalists are generally regarded as protoliberals. See, for instance, Trinterud, *Forming of an American Tradition*, chap. 8.

29. Coalter, *Gilbert Tennent*, 156.

30. Trinterud, *Forming*, paints the Old Side–New Side controversy in Old World–New World colors: "Behind this long and bitter struggle over the ministry, and the nature of the reunited Church, was the rising sense of a new world and the dwindling power of the old world and its norms. For the Old Side, the source and fountain of all true Presbyterianism lay 'at home,' across the sea. . . . The New Side, on the other hand, in their determination to build the Church according to what they conceived to be its own genius, born of the mingled bloods of its members and of the Great Awakening, may often have been unduly harsh in their generalizing of the bad character of a section of the Scotch-Irish clergy" (164).

31. Trinterud, *Forming*, 159.

32. E. Clifford Nelson, *The Lutherans in North America*, rev. ed. (Philadelphia: Fortress, 1980), 159–63; Theodore G. Tappert, ed., *Lutheran Confessional Theology in America, 1840–1880* (New York: Oxford University Press, 1972), 25.

33. Nelson, *Lutherans*, 125, 175.

34. On Lutheran pietism, see Nelson, *Lutherans*, 62–67; L. DeAne Lagerquist, *The Lutherans*, Denominations in America, no. 9 (Westport, Conn.: Greenwood, 1999), 15–16; and Paul P. Kuenning, *The Rise and Fall of American Lutheran Pietism* (Macon, Ga.: Mercer University Press, 1988), chap. 1.

35. Lagerquist, *Lutherans*, 53.

36. S. S. Schmucker, "Vocation of the American Lutheran Church," in S. S. Schmucker, *The American Lutheran Church, Historically, Doctrinally, and Practically Delineated* . . . (1851; reprint, New York: Arno, 1969), 248.

37. On Schmucker, see Lagerquist, *Lutherans*, 51–55, 221–22; and Kuenning, *Rise and Fall*, 60–68. For accounts of Protestant cooperation that adopt Schmucker as a forerunner of church union, see Charles S. Macfarland, *Christian Unity in the Making: The First Twenty-five Years of the Federal Council of Churches of Christ in America, 1905–1930* (New York: FCCCA, 1948), 19, 20, 26; and John A. Hutchison, *We*

Are Not Divided: A Critical and Historical Study of the Federal Council of the Churches of Christ in America (New York: Roundtable, 1941), 10–11.

38. Schaff quote in Nelson, *Lutherans*, 211–212.

39. William Julius Mann uses similar categories in *Lutheranism in America: An Essay on the Present Condition of the Lutheran Church in the United States* (Philadelphia: Lindsay & Blakiston, 1857).

40. See David A. Gustafson, *Lutherans in Crisis: The Question of Identity in the American Republic* (Minneapolis: Fortress, 1993), 130–38.

41. On Lutheran confessionalism, see Gustafson, *Lutherans in Crisis*, 18–19; Nelson, *Lutherans*, 217–27; Walter H. Conser Jr., *Church and Confession: Conservative Theologians in Germany, England, and America, 1815–1866* (Macon, Ga.: Mercer University Press, 1984), chap. 3; and Tappert, *Lutheran Confessional Theology* (New York: Oxford University Press).

42. W. J. Mann, *A Plea for the Augsburg Confession, in Answer to the Objections of* The Definite Platform . . . (Philadelphia: Lindsay & Blakiston, 1856), 15.

43. Mann, *A Plea for the Augsburg Confession*, 20–22.

44. Mann, *A Plea for the Augsburg Confession*, 23.

45. Mann, *A Plea for the Augsburg Confession*, 43–45.

46. Mann, *A Plea for the Augsburg Confession*, 46.

47. For a good discussion of these tensions among American Episcopalians, see Allen C. Guelzo, *For the Union of Evangelical Christendom: The Irony of the Reformed Episcopalians* (University Park: Pennsylvania State University Press, 1994), chap. 1.

48. What I am calling confessionalism, Robert Bruce Mullins, *Episcopal Vision/American Reality: High Church Theology and Social Thought in Evangelical America* (New Haven, Conn.: Yale University Press, 1986), designates as "high church" for the Episcopalians he studies. They are related in the sense that both stand over against pietism's (i.e., evangelicalism's) low regard for the ministry of the church and high regard for individual piety. Mullins writes, "High church writers would not deny the evangelical claim of *sola gratia* nor would low churchmen dispute the value of the bishops and ordinances. Rather, they differed as to whether the role of the Episcopal Church in antebellum America was to emphasize its points of commonality with the rest of the religious milieu or instead to emphasize the points that distinguished it from the wider religious environment. On this key attitudinal difference all of the persons considered under the rubric *high church* would have concurred—the Episcopal Church was an alternative to evangelical theology and culture and not part of it" (xv). Although Lutheran, Presbyterian, and Reformed confessionalists would have differed with Episcopalians on church government, creeds, and liturgy, they would have viewed their identity in similar ways, as an alternative to pietist Protestantism.

49. Nevin, *Anxious Bench*, 57.

50. Nevin, *Anxious Bench*, 39–40.

51. Nevin, *Anxious Bench*, 55–56.

52. Reformed Church in the United States, *The Heidelberg Catechism of the Reformed Church in the United States, Twentieth-Century Edition* (Philadelphia: RCUS Publication and Sunday School Board, 1902), 183–84.

53. Reformed Church in the United States, *The Heidelberg Catechism*, 184.

Defining Conservatism Down 3

In his 1970 book, *Righteous Empire*, Martin E. Marty, the dean of American religious historians, argued that 1912 marked a watershed for the American Protestant mainstream. This was the year when Billy Sunday, still laboring in small venues in the Northeast and Upper Midwest, stopped at Columbus, Ohio, to lead a revival. One of the town's ministers, the Congregationalist Washington Gladden, was not very impressed with the results of Sunday's antics, even though the revival had attracted the support of most Protestant ministers and favorable coverage in the local press thanks to over eighteen thousand converts (ten percent of the population), greater opposition to liquor traffic, and more support for the city's blue laws. Gladden, a minister of the Social Gospel, faulted Sunday for impure motives—the revivalist's take-home pay was $21,000 in free-will offerings. He also questioned Sunday's theology, comparing it to the backward ideas of medieval Europe, and wondered how genuine the conversions really were. According to Marty, the antagonism revealed in this brief episode culminated almost sixty years of developments in American Protestantism that saw the emergence of two distinct parties. On the left, Gladden stood for a wing of the churches that put the salvation of society ahead of saving individual souls. His rival, Sunday, represented the older approach of revivalist Protestantism that believed society could only be reformed by the conversion of individuals. This division into two parties, one individualistic and the other social, was "one of the fateful events of American Protestant history."[1]

Marty acknowledged in his notes to this book that his understanding of the two-party division among Protestants in the early twentieth century was indebted to the work of a graduate student, Jean Miller, who traced the fundamentalist controversy of the 1920s to the antagonism between individualistic and social forms of Christianity. The thesis of her 1969 dissertation was straightforward and simple: American Protestantism was split in two camps and was still divided by the time she was writing; the basic disagreement between evangelicals and liberals was "the church's role in the world." According to Miller, "essentially the division is between those who see the church's task as the transformation of society, and those who see its mission as individual salvation."[2] By the time of her dissertation's publication in 1991, a lot had changed, from Miller taking on the name of her husband, to the avalanche of literature to be published on American religious history. Yet, despite these changes, Schmidt (nee Miller) indicated that her mind was unchanged. The division between individual and social Christianity, or between private and public Protestantism was still key to understanding twentieth-century American Protestantism. Schmidt even extended her argument by claiming that this division not only cut across denominational lines, but was more important than "denominational divisions."[3]

In the same year that Schmidt's research appeared as a book, another volume was published that seemed to prove Schmidt right for not changing her mind. James Davison Hunter's *Culture Wars* extended Schmidt's two-party-analysis from American Protestantism to the culture at large. According to Hunter, the United States is divided between two antagonistic parties, one orthodox, the other progressive. Interestingly enough, his use of religious imagery to describe a cultural conflict is intentional since these parties each start with differing moral assumptions that dovetail with the older conflict between liberal and fundamentalist Protestants. The orthodox party, Hunter argued, is committed *"to an external, definable, and transcendent authority,"* while the progressives *"resymbolize the prevailing assumptions of contemporary life."*[4] The parallels between this culture war and Protestant battles during the 1920s are even more striking for Hunter since the orthodox are concerned to protect institutions, such as families, schools, and churches, that sustain the lives of individuals, as opposed to the aim of progressives to bring all institutions into conformity with national norms.[5] Yet, as the subtitle of Hunter's book indicates, both sides are engaged in a conflict to "define America." Con-

sequently, just as Schmidt ended her study of the two parties in American Protestantism with reflections on the way each side had radically different ideas about how to change the world, so Hunter demonstrates that
each party in America's culture war has radically different ideas about
how to transform the American nation.

As much as the two-party-interpretation of twentieth-century Protestantism appears to explain the differences between mainliners and evangelicals, it fails to grapple with an ideal that both sides share. To be sure, evangelicalism, the conservative side of American Protestantism's two parties,
has always looked to the salvation of individuals as the primary task of
evangelists, pastors, and lay people. But evangelicalism is hardly a private
faith. Sunday's crusades prove this point. A prominent feature of his revivals was to encourage support for a variety of social reforms that dovetailed with Anglo-American Protestant cultural norms, such as temperance
and Sabbath observance. What is more, the orthodox party identified by
Hunter demonstrates how socially minded the individualist Protestant
party is. After all, the question Hunter asks in his subtitle is not how to define the family or the church but how to define the United States of America. Where evangelicals and liberals differ, then, is not on whether faith or
religion should have an affect on public life, or extend beyond the transformation of individuals to all levels of society. Instead, the difference is
that each side has a different program for defining America, the evangelical
one relying more on the efforts of individuals, families, and churches (i.e.,
mediating structures), the mainline version stressing legislation and government programs. But neither side wants to limit religion to the private
worlds of family devotions or worship services.

Perhaps the public and political side of pietist Protestantism, especially
evangelicalism, would be more obvious if scholars and observers of American religion were more familiar with confessional Protestantism's churchly
and liturgical sensibility. Indeed, of all the varieties of Protestantism in the
United States, confessionalism is arguably the most consistently otherworldly
or privatistic. This otherworldliness, however, is not the kind associated with
the hellfire sermons of itinerant evangelists or a faith that encourages active
withdrawal from the so-called worldly affairs of politics and culture. Instead,
confessionalism's otherworldliness resides in its sense that this life is not the
highest reality, and that ultimately the sort of social transformation achieved
either by politicians or believers is trivial compared to the work of the church

in establishing a holy society of believers and preparing them for the world to come. Confessionalism, in contrast to the pietism of both evangelicalism and liberalism, regards the purpose of the church as fundamentally different from, though not inherently antagonistic to, the aim of polities such as the United States. Ironically, because confessionalism is formally liturgical and not revivalistic, its otherworldliness has been ignored, so deeply ingrained is the two-party understanding of American Protestantism. Yet, the conservatism of confessionalism is a long way from the conservative Protestant faith that many associate with evangelicalism.

The irony of twentieth-century religious history is that Billy Sunday, as good an example of revivalistic Protestantism as exists, came to stand for *the* conservative expression of Protestantism in the United States. Again, in the light of Old Side Presbyterians, Lutheran confessionalists, and the German Reformed, Sunday's version of Protestantism was novel. It neglected the ministry of the church that included not merely the general work carried out by clergy but specifically the preaching of the word in public worship, the administration of the sacraments, and the public assemblies of the church for supervising and conducting ecclesiastical endeavors. What is more, confessional Protestantism's concern for creed, liturgy, and polity respected the differences among Protestant denominations, even if it did not facilitate greater interdenominational cooperation. In contrast, Sunday's pietistic Protestantism nurtured an individualistic conception of Christian devotion that began with conversion (a conscious decision) and was sustained by private and small-group religious exercises as well as public displays of good works, which included personal evangelism, observance of a strict moral code, and support for social reforms that would create and sustain a righteous nation. Sunday's faith may have retained better than the Social Gospel did the chief features of nineteenth-century American Protestantism. But it was no less practical or removed from the everyday concerns of America's white Protestants. Sunday's preservation and application of a revivalist faith was, however, very different from the churchly forms of Protestantism that surfaced at the time of the Reformation.

The Emergence of Conservative Protestantism

Reporters following the religious controversies of the 1920s were at a loss for words to describe the divisions between Protestants that were then becoming obvious. For instance, in 1924, a writer for *Time* magazine described William T. Manning, bishop of New York, as displaying a model of "Churchmanship." The occasion for the story was a sermon Manning had delivered in the Cathedral of St. John the Divine, which at the time still needed $15 million for completion. The forcefulness of Manning's remarks may not have been the most useful for fund-raising, however. He said that it would be better that the Cathedral "should never be built than that a Bishop of this Church should fail to bear his witness for the full truth of Jesus Christ." Manning went on to clarify what such a witness involved for Episcopalians:

> this Church calls upon her clergy and people to believe the fact that Our Lord went into the place of departed spirits, the fact that He is now at the right hand of God, the fact that He will one day come again in judgment, and she certainly calls upon us to believe and expects us to believe and teach, the fact that He, who for our sakes, came down from Heaven, was born of the Virgin Mary, the fact of His bodily resurrection from the tomb, and the fact of His return to the place which He had, before the worlds were, at the right hand of the Father.

Manning's affirmation of fundamental Christian doctrines would have warmed the heart of most fundamentalist listeners, even if the Protestant Episcopal Church's *Book of Common Prayer* did not. Nevertheless, the editors at *Time* chose to feature Manning as a conservative churchman, rather than a fundamentalist.[6]

A year earlier *Time*'s coverage of Episcopalians had differed starkly. Under the headline "War," the reporter listed the four denominations in which a religious dispute was breaking out: Baptists, Episcopalians, Methodists, and Presbyterians. The bulk of the story concerned Harry Emerson Fosdick's controversial preaching at First Presbyterian Church, New York City, and the subsequent efforts of his opponents to oust the flamboyant and charismatic sermonizer. *Time* called this the "first skirmish" in a religious war between "old-timers" who called themselves fundamentalists and "new-timers" whom the fundamentalists called modernists. Among Episcopalians the controversy was even more intense. After sixty-five bishops in the Protestant Episcopal Church assembled at Dallas, Texas, to instruct all Episcopal clergy to teach the literal meaning of the Apostles' Creed, priests and rectors from every state "denounced [the Bishops] for their insistence on literal interpretation of the creeds and for their arrogation of the right to dictate the theology of their church." One of the most vociferous spokesmen for modernists was Manhattan's Leighton Parks, who publicly defied Bishop Manning, one of the leaders of the Dallas gathering. According to *Time*, Parks defended the denial of Manning's "full truth" and challenged his bishop to bring him to trial.[7]

Time was not alone in its confusion about how to designate the opponents of liberal Protestantism in the mainline denominations. In a four-part series for *World's Work*, Rollin Lynde Hartt began his analysis with a list designed to highlight the diversity of conservatives:

> Hence a phenomenon. Billy Sunday and Bishop Manning, Dr. Arcturus Zodiac Conrad and Mr. Bryan, Dr. Clarence Edward Macartney and Dr. Reuben Torrey, Professor Machen and Dr. W. B. Riley, Doctor Goodchild and Dr. Laws, Princeton Seminary and the Moody Bible Institute (entrance requirement, "a common school education or its equivalent") are all up in arms together, valiantly combating modernism.[8]

Part of the reason why Hartt had some difficulty in grouping together such a disparate list of bedfellows, from an Episcopal bishop to a Southern Baptist pastor, or from an itinerant revivalist who lacked a formal theological education to well-respected seminary professors, came from the second and third installments in this series. The first of these subsequent articles focused on evolution and the efforts by some to eliminate it from public school curricula, while the second featured the doctrine of biblical inerrancy. Neither of these matters of theological controversy were shared by everyone on Hartt's original list. For that matter, Manning's sermon in 1924 on the fundamental doctrines of the Apostles' Creed made no mention of scriptural infallibility or creation and evolution. Hence, Hartt may not have been entirely comfortable identifying Manning and Sunday as participants in a joint endeavor.[9]

Yet, what convinced many, Hartt included, that Protestants as diverse as confessional Presbyterians and Bible school leaders shared a common agenda was the fact of the stridency of their opposition to modernism. In fact, in Hartt's final article in this series, it was their perceived dogmatism as much as any particular doctrine or belief that characterized fundamentalism. This dogmatism—that is, the idea that certain theological assertions could not be denied if one wanted to claim to be a believer—was the weak point in fundamentalist public relations. Hartt quoted the Princeton theologian Benjamin B. Warfield, who declared that Christianity rested upon an "external authority" and that without it, to rely on "religious experience," "the inner light," or "the immanent Divine," was to "discard Christianity and revert to natural religion." Unfortunately for conservatives, this point sounded much like the Roman Catholic line that modernism had "at last revealed to the light of day what was always at the bottom of the Protestant doctrine of private judgment applied to the religion of Christ." Indeed, modernists took up the tack of charging fundamentalists with denying the "the right of individual interpretation and authority," and so reduced the controversy to the historic dispute between the Catholic and Protestant ideals.[10] In such a contest, conservatives were sure to be perceived as religious bigots. This was clearly how several hundred undergraduates at Cornell University perceived the matter when they printed and distributed a statement defending Harry Emerson Fosdick as "the leading American interpreter of the Christian religion for men of scientific training."[11] Such was an ominous affirmation since it would be the scientifically trained for the most part who would emerge as the leading interpreters of the conflict.

H. L. Mencken, who had uncanny instincts about American religion, thought the analogy with Roman Catholicism worked equally well in explaining modernism, but his depiction of fundamentalism did as much as any reporter's during the 1920s to fix the image of conservative Protestantism. In a 1926 essay for the *American Mercury*, the Baltimore journalist observed two distinct forms of the Protestantism, the one "moving, with slowly accelerating speed, in the direction of the Harlot of the Seven Hills," the other "sliding down into voodism." Interestingly enough, Mencken avoided the ideological labels of liberal and conservative, preferring instead the liturgical ones of high and low church Protestantism. In the upper reaches, Protestants were doing their best to imitate the ways of Rome, as "the more solvent Methodists and the like are gradually transmogrified into Episcopalians, and the Episcopalians shin up the ancient bastions of Holy Church." From Mencken's perspective, then, it was the liberals, the very ones who feared Rome's repression, who were also ironically succumbing to the "lascivious advances" of Catholic worship and the church calendar.[12]

Although Mencken departed from the standard takes on modernism, his rendering of fundamentalism confirmed most educated Americans' worst fears. In the netherworld of Protestantism, "in all those parts of the Republic where Beelzebub is still real," fundamentalists were plunging headlong "into an abyss of malignant imbecility," declaring "a holy war upon every decency that civilized men cherish." The particular part of civilization on which conservatives directed the greatest measure of their ire, according to Mencken, was education. Here, Mencken's essay showed all the marks of having been written after the Scopes trial, an incident that so offended him that he not only ridiculed backwoods religion but also continued to mock William Jennings Bryan mercilessly even after his sudden death only one day after the trial's finale. With Bryan clearly in mind, Mencken wrote that "what one mainly notices about the clerics who lead [the fundamentalists] is their vast lack of sound information and sound sense." Conservatives constituted, he added, "perhaps, the most ignorant class of teachers ever set up to guide a presumably civilized people." They were even "more ignorant than the county superintendents of schools."[13] Thus, Mencken added to the image of conservative Protestants as unreasonably bound to an interpretation of the Bible that made them mentally unprepared for life in modern society and incapable of adjusting to a world of ideas that was fast leaving them behind.

By the 1930s, a scholarly consensus had emerged on conservative Protestantism (i.e., fundamentalism). One gauge to this early assessment of fundamentalism was the University of Chicago church historian William Warren Sweet, who in 1930 came out with his popular survey *The Story of Religions in America*. In the first edition, Sweet spent little time on fundamentalism as he moved hastily through contemporary events, jumping from the Ku Klux Klan to fundamentalism all under the theme of reactions to the Great War. Even so, Sweet defined conservatism as "an organized attempt to preserve the authoritarian position of historic Protestantism." The two episodes that Sweet featured were the efforts of Presbyterian conservatives to "bring Harry Emerson Fosdick to trial for heresy," and the Scopes trial. The overall impression that Sweet gave in 1930 was that fundamentalism was simply one among many facets of the "churches in the age of big business."[14] By 1939, the time of the revised edition's release, Sweet had linked fundamentalism directly to the Klan, stating that "students of society" had recognized both movements to be "identical types of reactionism." He then expanded his coverage of the controversy by conflating squabbles among Methodists, Baptists, Disciples, and Presbyterians, along with the Scopes trial as part of the 1920s pattern of "declining idealism and growing nationalism."[15]

Part of the reason for the difference between Sweet's assessments at the beginning and end of the 1930s was the publication of the first sustained treatment of fundamentalism. Stewart G. Cole, who wrote *The History of Fundamentalism*, was a professor at Crozer Theological Seminary in Chester, Pennsylvania, a school sponsored by the Northern Baptist Convention, one of the denominations affected by the debates between liberals and conservatives. As such, Cole was by no means an impartial observer. Still, his interpretation received the blessing of the Protestant establishment along with the scholarly guild in which Protestants continued to receive sympathetic treatment. According to Cole, "fundamentalism was the organized determination of conservative churchmen to continue the imperialistic culture of historic Protestantism within an inhospitable civilization dominated by secular interests and a progressive Christian idealism."[16] Why he did not appear to recognize any tension between secularism and progressive Christianity is a question that haunts Cole's argument. His modernists wanted Christian civilization instead of secular society as much as fundamentalists. What made fundamentalists different was their inability to adjust to new social and intellectual realities. Evangelical theology was the product of agricultural society in which religion gave comfort "in the face of the stubborn forces of nature." In this environment, the church was "a regulative agent of the first magnitude," playing the role of either "mediaeval martinet" or "humanitarian savior."[17]

But the forces of industrialization, the discoveries of modern science, and the demands of international politics undermined the old absolutes of church and theology. Urban Christians assimilated the outlook of modern society and "realized the church could not continue its aristocratic policy." As such, the conflict between liberals and conservatives was one of two competing Christian cultures, one southern and rural, the other northern and urban.[18] In the words of H. Richard Niebuhr, who wrote the article on fundamentalism for the *Encyclopedia of Social Science*, conservative Protestantism in its more aggressive forms was most prevalent in isolated communities where "the traditions of pioneer society had been most effectively preserved" and were "least subject to the influence of modern science and industrial civilization."[19]

As much as the early pictures of fundamentalism that journalists and scholars developed now look tattered and even doctored, these initial reactions created a larger impression of conservative Protestantism that is still influential.[20] In an essay for the Fundamentalism Project, cosponsored by the University of Chicago and the American Council of Learned Societies, Nancy T. Ammerman traces the emergence of fundamentalism to changes in society and ideas, the efforts of some Protestants to adapt to these changes, and a growing sense among conservatives "that adaptation constituted nothing less than heresy."[21] What is more, the lynchpin of conservative beliefs was the reliability of the Bible. Consequently, inerrancy of the Bible, opposition to modern study of Scripture, and maintaining the Bible as the standard for national life are at the heart of conservative Protestantism. If a communion or person holds to such a view of the Bible and opposes efforts to accommodate Christianity to modernity or secularism, he or she qualifies as a fundamentalist. Oddly enough, a definition this broad should include Roman Catholicism, a Christian communion that prior to Vatican II was not partial to scholarship that suggested the Bible was partly myth or well known for welcoming modernization.[22] In effect, the initial and ongoing understanding of fundamentalism leaves out consideration of such aspects of Christian faith as creeds, church polity and ordination, and liturgy, except in the case of Catholics, whose polity and liturgy were hard to ignore. Instead, all Protestants who tried to hold onto the traditional teachings and practices of their denomination or communion end up being fundamentalists. Bishop Manning and Billy Sunday become part of the same faction.

Some Protestants, even in the 1920s, had trouble recognizing themselves in the emerging understanding of conservatism. Confessional Protestantism especially did not fit the generic depiction of believers intent on preserving the social order of rural life. For instance, J. Gresham Machen, a Princeton Seminary professor of New Testament and the leader of confessional Presbyterians, but usually taken for a fundamentalist, declined the offer of Bryan Memorial University' trustees to preside over the institution dedicated to the Great Commoner precisely because Machen saw a difference between his concerns for the Presbyterian Church and those of other conservatives, like Bryan, who believed the nation was veering from its Christian orientation. As Machen explained, "I never call myself a "Fundamentalist." Of course, if the only options were the labels, fundamentalist or modernist, then he was "willing to call [himself] a Fundamentalist of the most pronounced type." But Machen preferred to refer to himself as a Calvinist—"that is, an adherent of the Reformed Faith," thus standing "in the great central current of the Church's life" that ran down from the Bible, to Augustine, Calvin, and the Presbyterian churches.[23]

Other confessional Protestant communions, such as the Lutheran Church Missouri Synod and the Christian Reformed Church, also had trouble fitting the pigeonholes of fundamentalist and liberal. The former denomination, for example, held a similarly high view of the Bible, opposed evolution, and recognized liberalism as a serious breach of the Christian faith. Yet, these Lutherans did not join fundamentalist organizations for both theological and political reasons. Fundamentalists, Lutherans thought, were generally noncreedal and upset the proper boundaries between the kingdom of God (the church) and the kingdom of man (the state).[24] Likewise, the Christian Reformed Church had affinities with fundamentalism but did not join the fray, partly because the denomination had no liberals and partly because it had its own internal struggle over the implications of Calvinism's doctrine of election.[25]

Part of the problem in making sense of the 1920s controversy was the frequent use of the phrase "historic Protestantism" to describe fundamentalism. In a sense, these conservatives were truly the heirs of the Protestantism that became the mainstream faith in the United States. But, as argued in chapter 2, this Protestant faith was hardly the historic expression that emerged in the sixteenth century and dominated most European churches throughout the seventeenth and eighteenth centuries. Fundamentalism perpetuated most of the features that have been described as revivalist or pietist Protestantism. It stressed the necessity of conversion, moral earnestness, and zealous devotion through private study of Scripture and witness to nonbelievers. Fundamentalism did not, however, regard highly the aspects of church life that mattered greatly to confessional Protestants, such as creeds, clergy and polity, and corporate worship. In fact, when compared to confessionalists' commitment to the particulars of a specific Protestant tradition, fundamentalism appears to be another example of the tendency, also exhibited by liberalism, to reduce Christianity to its essence and to regard the circumstances of creed, ordination, and liturgy as peripheral to genuine faith. To be sure, the fundamentalist essentials, such as the deity of Christ, virgin birth, and vicarious atonement, were a long way from the liberal shibboleths of the fatherhood of God and the brotherhood of man. And for that reason, confessionalists had little trouble deeming fundamentalism a better brand of Christianity than liberalism. But in the end, confessional Protestants were reluctant to identify with fundamentalism because it was a truncated and novel form of Christianity.

Confessional Protestants were also leery of the way fundamentalists politicized religion or—perhaps a better way of putting it—sacralized politics. Here, it is worth noting the irony of fundamentalism's reputation for being an otherworldly and privatistic faith. Of course, as heirs of revivalist Protestantism, fundamentalists stressed the need for regeneration and taught that eternal life in heaven was the reward for true believers. But their piety hardly consisted of sitting around in Bible studies waiting for the second coming of Christ. Conversion changed lives, and so the gospel made a difference in individual persons and in society at large as converts sought to eradicate all forms of evil. The activism inherent in revivalist Protestantism, then, makes sense of widespread fundamentalist support for Prohibition and legislation to prohibit the teaching of evolution in public schools. Confessionalists, however, were less inclined to support these reforms, partly because their cultural and religious heritage did not condemn alcohol and partly because they put their educational energies into parochial or Christian day schools. Some of the confessional Protestant ambivalence toward fundamentalist politics, then, owed to the immigrant experience. But it also stemmed from a different understanding of Christianity in which churches and families were more important in perpetuating the faith than nations such as the United States or their office holders.

These differences between fundamentalists and confessionalists, however, were lost on most observers of American religion in the two decades after World War I. Consequently, fundamentalism became synonymous with conservative Protestantism. Nuances among different forms of conservatism became obscure thanks in large measure to the way revivalist Protestantism came to dominate American understandings of religion. The pietist criteria of conversion, personal holiness, and reverence for the Bible apparently left Americans with a choice between fundamentalists who defended Protestant verities and liberals who equivocated.

The Neoevangelical Wrinkle

With the image of conservative Protestantism as backward, stupid, and mean firmly fixed by the denominational and educational controversies of the 1920s and 1930s, it was not surprising that some conservatives in the 1940s began to look for and offer an alternative. Signs of that search were noticeable throughout the decade as what some have dubbed "progressive fundamentalists" established a series of institutions that were designed to accent the positive and avoid the mudslinging. First came the National Association of Evangelicals (NAE) in 1942, and from it flowed a flurry of activity: the National Religious Broadcasters (1944); the Evangelical Foreign Missionary Association (1945), World Relief Commission (1945), the National Sunday School Association (1946), and the National Association of Christian Schools (1947). These institutions also were closely linked to a resurgence of conservative interest in the life of the mind. The first president of the NAE, Harold John Ockenga, was also the first president of Fuller Theological Seminary, founded in 1947, and Ockenga, along with one of Fuller's original faculty members, Carl F. H. Henry, in 1956 teamed up with Billy Graham to start *Christianity Today* as a theologically informed magazine for these more open-minded and kinder conservatives.[26]

The appearance of the word *evangelical* in the name of many of these organizations was as important as it was successful. The term certainly sounded better than *fundamentalist,* and, importantly, it ended up sticking, at least in the sense that the term *evangelical* became over the course of the last half of the twentieth century the exclusive coinage of conservative Protestants. Prior to the 1940s, all Protestants, with the exception of Unitarians, claimed to be evangelical—even avowed liberals such as Harry Emerson Fosdick and Shailer Mathews did so. But with so many institutions promoting an evangelical identity, the mainstream churches conceded the term to the conservative Protestants who may not have been fundamentalists but clearly were not part of the Protestant establishment.

A certain irony attends the identification of evangelicalism with conservative Protestants who may be in—but are not really of—the mainline Protestant denominations and their related organizations. This irony concerns the chief difference that is supposed to distinguish progressive fundamentalists from paleofundamentalists—namely, separatism. For instance, at the beginning of the 1940s, several conservatives were looking for ways to pool resources and present a united front that would rival such mainline agencies as the Federal Council of Churches. Carl McIntire, who would later distinguish himself for anticommunism as well as longevity, led one such effort with the American Council of Christian Churches (ACCC), an organization in which he hoped all fundamentalists would unite and op- pose together the errors of liberalism, both religious and political. But the men who led in founding the NAE, such as J. Elwin Wright, an earnest real estate developer and leader of the New England Fellowship, Harold John Ockenga, pastor of Boston's historic Park Street Church, and Will Houghton, president of Moody Bible Institute, wanted to go beyond fun- damentalist cussedness in order to unite conservatives in the larger and more important project of reaching a lost nation. The old agenda of op- posing theological liberalism was too narrow. If conservatives were going to restore Christianity in America, they would have to find a more positive and attractive rationale than McIntire's. As Stephen W. Paine, president of Houghton College, said at the NAE's first conference, "many sincere Chris- tians are impelled to united action by negative motives." But such move- ments always lacked "*cohesive* qualities" and for that reason "constructively- minded Christians" hesitated joining them.[27]

As much as these evangelicals were endeavoring to be positive and con- structive, they still wound up drawing lines that would make them separate (even if not separatists) from other Protestants. Unlike McIntire's ACCC, for instance, the NAE did not require a joining church to renounce its membership in the mainstream Federal Council of Churches. This made many fundamentalists, McIntire included, conclude that the NAE was soft on modernism. But even though the evangelicals did not make hostility to modernism essential to their identity, they did end up creating a set of ri- val institutions to those of mainstream Protestantism that made them dif- ferent from and clearly had little to do with the liberal denominations. What is more, the founders of the NAE declined McIntire's overtures, thus creating a sense of rivalry between evangelicals and fundamentalists. As much as evangelicals wanted to be cooperative and positive, the very act of founding separate institutions from those of liberals and fundamentalists embodied a form of separatism; evangelicals may have been willing to wel- come some from the mainstream churches and some fundamentalists into their ranks, but such transfers had to play by evangelical rules, as upbeat and affirming as they may have been.[28]

Modernism aside, evangelicals also displayed a number of traits that showed a much greater affinity with fundamentalists than they may have noticed. Fundamentalists and evangelicals are both heirs of revivalist Protestantism; the examples of Billy Sunday and Billy Graham help back up this assertion. What this means is that both sets of Protestants, if such differentiation is truly possible, promote born-again forms of Protestant piety, as opposed to confessionalism's churchly form of devotion, that are supposed to make a difference in individual converts as well as the life of the nation. The revivalist Protestant impulse was firmly behind several of the evangelical initiatives of the 1940s. The institutionalization of evangelicalism was necessary, in fact, because such religious work as foreign missions, chaplaincy, and radio evangelism required national offices that could take on the labor of coordinating the various evangelical denominations, parachurch organizations, or individuals with the appropriate federal agency for the sake of obtaining the proper governmental certification.

What is more, the evangelical initiatives of the 1940s also exhibited the older revivalist Protestant concern to come to the aid of the American nation in a time of religious and political crisis. Ironically, imagery well supplied by World War II suffused the words of those advocating this positive form of evangelicalism. Harold John Ockenga identified three religious threats to the United States: the vast growth of Roman Catholicism, the "terrible octopus of liberalism," and secularism. "Let us learn something," Ockenga added, "from the Soviets and the Nazis," that if the "children of this world are wiser than the children of light, then it is time for the children of light to open their eyes and learn how to carry on God's work." It was no longer time for "defensive tactics," like those Western democracies trying to avoid the war. Instead, it "was the day for the offensive."[29] William Ward Ayer, pastor of Calvary Baptist Church in New York City, attempted to generate support for the new initiative by reminding delegates to the NAE's first annual convention that "evangelical Christianity has the America of our fathers to save." Thus, just as the United States Army and Navy were fighting the "enemy without," so evangelicals had an "enemy at home to battle" who was "more dangerous than the enemy abroad."[30] For this reason, evangelicals like Ockenga and Ayer advocated throwing aside the fundamentalist tactics of polemic and turned instead to cooperation. "A terrible indictment may be laid against fundamentalism," Ockenga asserted, "because of its failures, divisions, and controversies."[31] The first plan of action, then, was to seek unity.

The second plan involved a series of committees in which revival would prove to be once again the tried and true method of righting America's wrongs. The NAE established an evangelism committee to coordinate the work of local congregations and denominations in outreach. Another was the Special Committee on Religious Broadcasting. And this explains the need for an evangelical agency to interface with the federal government; a number of fundamentalists and evangelicals, such as Charles Fuller, Donald Grey Barnhouse, and Will Houghton had turned to the radio as a medium to conduct evangelistic crusades on a grand scale. Consequently, it made no sense to allow the Federal Council of Churches to obtain all the good air time when evangelicals could implement a lobby every bit as forceful to work with the Federal Communications Commission. As the committee on religious broadcasting put it, "no one factor" in recent developments that led to the formation of the NAE "has contributed more than the dissatisfaction engendered over the present system of time allotment" on network radio.[32]

Yet, for all of their similarities with fundamentalists, evangelicals were clearly trying to go beyond the old Protestant guard and accomplish something significant for the cause of Christianity and in the life of the nation. An important book that summarized the new evangelical enterprise was Carl F. H. Henry's *The Uneasy Conscience of Modern Fundamentalism* (1947). This book, which historian Joel Carpenter has described as the new evangelicalism's manifesto, was a direct and confrontational plea for conservatives to move beyond their narrow concerns and respond to the needs of the postwar world. Henry argued that the collapse of Western civilization, as evidenced by war-torn Europe, provided the church with a tremendous opportunity. But fundamentalists had failed to respond to the crisis. Here, he agreed with Protestant liberals when they claimed that fundamentalists had "no social program calling for practical attack on acknowledged world evils." Fundamentalists were betraying Christianity since a "globe-changing passion certainly characterized the early church."[33] The problem with fundamentalists' foes, the liberals, then, was not that they had worked for world peace, the brotherhood of mankind, or resolution between management and labor. Instead, their trouble was in trying to accomplish these things "without any reference to the vicarious atonement and redemptive work of Christ."[34] What Henry advocated was an orthodox Social Gospel where "the evangelical task" of "preaching the Gospel, in the interest of individual regeneration" also functioned as "the best solution of our problems, individual and social." For Christianity produced not merely saved souls but "a divine society that transcends national and international lines."[35]

Henry's argument was less nationalistic than that of other American evangelical leaders, though he did believe that in "Anglo-American democracy" lingered traces of "Hebrew-Christian ideology."[36] But his effort to apply the message of Christian to social evils, as much as it was intended to set evangelicals apart from liberals and call fundamentalists to a better way, ended up misreading history and obscuring the differences that were supposed to separate Protestantism's two parties. For instance, William Bell Riley, a prominent fundamentalist in northern Baptist battles during the 1920s and the man who single-handedly ran the World Christian Fundamentals Association, established a reputation for civic reform in the first two decades of the twentieth century, organizing political opposition to gambling and liquor while also preaching against the greed of the nation's corporations. As Riley's biographer, William Vance Trollinger Jr., admits, the alliance between evangelism and reform "jarringly clashes with the common scholarly perception that the social gospel clergy and the evangelistic clergy were in mutually exclusive camps." In fact, during the fundamentalist controversy "a host of conservative evangelicals were involved in urban uplift programs."[37] Part of the reason for Henry's ignoring this feature of fundamentalism may have stemmed from different political preferences (unlikely) or from the widespread perception that after the Scopes trial fundamentalists retreated from politics. Just as likely is that Henry's interest in a national evangelical presence tended to discount the politics of progressive urban reform in which fundamentalists had often participated. But even here, the examples of William Jennings Bryan leading a well-publicized fight against the most important form of secularism that he could detect (i.e., evolution) and Billy Sunday conducting campaigns in support of World War I and Prohibition reveal that Henry and the new evangelical movement of the 1940s were at least disfiguring history to set themselves apart from the common run of conservative Protestants. And from this longer perspective of revivalist support for social reform, the fruit of new evangelicalism did not fall far from the tree of revivalist Protestantism.[38]

What Henry along with his evangelical peers also failed to see was how the concern to Christianize the social order moved their brand of conservative Protestantism closer to that of the mainstream churches, while distancing it from confessional Protestantism's traditionalism. To be sure, evangelicals, like their civic-minded fundamentalist forerunners, faulted the liberal Protestant Social Gospel for putting the social order ahead of the individual soul. Fundamentalists and evangelicals alike thought it impossible to have a Christian society apart from first converting the members of that society. In fact, evangelicals, fundamentalists, and liberals all were convinced that a Christian society was not simply a possibility but a necessity. According to Henry, the gospel possessed a "social imperative."[39] But the social and political side of Christianity was not so obvious to other Protestants, especially confessionalists, for whom the temporal realities of American society and international politics were secondary compared to the task of the church in caring for souls and conducting worship. Indeed, for confessionalists, the "Divine society" of which Henry wrote was the visible church, not any particular nation or system of international peace. Thus, the evangelical move to apply Christianity to society not only perpetuated the older fundamentalist pattern but showed that the legacy of pietism was alive and well in both the "liberal" and "conservative" branches of the revivalist Protestant mainstream. Whether there were two parties (fundamentalist and liberal) or three (fundamentalist, liberal, and evangelical), all were committed to the pietist vision of making faith relevant to everyday life. Moreover, these varieties of pietism were distinct from confessionalism's overarching assumption about the permanence of the eternal realities communicated through the ministry of the church compared to the passing affairs of life in this world.

Therefore, whatever the affinities between evangelicalism and liberal Protestantism in the arena of applying Christianity to social life, one thing was clear from the new and improved version of fundamentalism to emerge in the 1940s: it was markedly different from confessional Protestantism. Confessional Protestantism, in fact, came up short in meeting the requirements established by the new conservative Protestantism. Its creedalism, concern for church polity, and the prominence it assigned to public worship could not unite Protestants in a set of evangelistic and educational endeavors that would revive the United States and give fresh blood to overseas missions. What evangelicals needed was a minimalist creed, a well-oiled machine, some funding, and lots of zeal. They also needed a form of Protestantism that measured its effectiveness by the impact it made on individuals and society. Consequently, as much as the new evangelicalism helped rejuvenate the image of conservative Protestantism, it further obscured the creedal, churchly, and liturgical aspects of historic Protestantism.

A Conservative Social Gospel?

By the end of the twentieth century, Henry's call for a more politically involved form of evangelicalism appears to have paid unwanted dividends.
Since the presidential election of 1976, evangelical Protestants have been
among the more prominent, although by no means the most welcome, participants in American politics through such organizations as the Moral Majority and the Christian Coalition. Studies of the new evangelicalism of the
1940s have not connected Henry's uneasy fundamentalist conscience to the
emergence of the religious right. But David Moberg, the author of a widely
read book on evangelicalism and social reform, *The Great Reversal* (1972),
did. "The first widely heard spokesman calling for a revival of interest in
social issues," he argued, "was Carl F. H. Henry, who . . . called for a 'new
reformation' which would make clear the implications of personal regeneration for social as well as individual problems."[40] In Moberg's estimation,
Henry had helped reverse an earlier reversal that saw fundamentalism abandon evangelicalism's historic social involvement as part of its opposition to
liberal Protestantism's Social Gospel.

With the religious right, however, Henry and Moberg may have received
more than they bargained for since it has further solidified the identification between conservative Protestantism and conservative politics. This
would certainly be the conclusion of Richard V. Pierard, whose book *The
Unequal Yoke* (1970) on evangelicals and politics appeared in the same series
for which Moberg wrote. According to Pierard, whose disdain for the Republican platform of small government was more explicit than Moberg's,
"the ties linking evangelical Christianity to political conservatism are so numerous and pervasive that it is possible to say the two are 'yoked together.'"
Just as obvious to Pierard was the danger of evangelical Protestants, in the
words of the Bible, being unequally yoked "to the way of the world." "The
evangelical church," he concluded, "has tied itself to the *status quo* of contemporary middle-class America and traded its prophetic ministry for a
pottage of public acclaim and economic well-being."[41]

Keeping in mind that these statements came well before the election of
Ronald Reagan in 1980 or the prominence of such popular religious right
figures as James Dobson, Jerry Falwell, Pat Robertson, and Ralph Reed, it
takes little ingenuity to suspect that evangelicals such as Pierard and
Moberg who called for greater social involvement from evangelicals were
not entirely pleased with the results of that solicitation. Their call was not

really to reverse evangelicals' abandonment of politics but instead to be-come socially engaged in the right (actually, center-left) way. As Pierard pointed out, it was not as if evangelicals weren't voting during the 1960s; instead, it was that too many voted for Barry Goldwater.[42]

Yet, Pierard and Moberg repeated at the beginning of the 1970s the same historical mistake that Henry made in the 1940s. They figured that evangelicals who did not see it their way were not involved politically, when in fact they missed the worldly orientation of the evangelical tradition, both in the good times (from their view) when it was progressive (such as the nineteenth-century campaigns against slavery) and in the bad when it was conservative and generated support for probusiness Republicans. Indeed, one of the ironies of much of the literature on evangelicalism is that this form of Christianity ever gained the reputation of being otherworldly. To be sure, its individualistic conception of faith has nurtured suspicions about various governmental programs to correct social wrongs. But this op-position was not a form of escapism. Instead, it was an affirmation that so-cial change of a lasting nature comes only through the conversion of indi-viduals. Nevertheless, evangelicals never had any trouble insisting that faith should and, indeed, would make a difference in everything from the do-mestic relations of families to the international politics of nations.

Most scholars date the origins of the religious right in the late 1960s and early 1970s.[43] The chief catalysts for evangelical politics were a series of developments that threatened the family, such as the sexual revolution, feminism, and abortion. Closely related were national debates that changed the character of public schools, at least in the religious right's mind, such as bussing to achieve racial integration and banning prayer and Bible read-ing. Finally, disputes over the United State's involvement in Vietnam nur-tured a sour estimate of the country that did not sit well with many Protes-tants who regarded America as at the very least a generically Protestant nation that had been mightily blessed by divine favor.[44] Historians, politi-cal scientists and sociologists may differ on how profound these changes were for American society, but the estimate of Sydney E. Ahlstrom, long-time historian of American religion and civilization at Yale, seems particu-larly apt for understanding the rise of the religious right:

> [T]he exploration and settlement of those parts of the New World in which the United States took its rise were profoundly shaped by the Ref-

ormation and Puritan impulse, and . . . this impulse, through its successive transmutations, remained the dominant element in the ideology of most Protestant Americans. To that tradition, moreover, all other elements among the American people—Catholic, Orthodox, Lutheran, Jewish, infidel, red, yellow, and black—had in some way, negatively or positively, to relate themselves. Or at least they did so *until the 1960s*, when the age of the WASP, the age of the melting pot, drew to a close.[45]

This is another way of saying that the reversal of Protestant fortunes during the 1960s was responsible for the reemergence of pietist Protestant politics in the form of the religious right. In other words, the connections between Jerry Falwell and Carl F. H. Henry are not as remote as they sometimes seem.

The emergence in the 1970s of an evangelically inspired and aggressive form of conservative politics in the United States usually obscures the pattern of evangelical politics prior to the 1960s when evangelicals and mainline Protestants were indistinguishable in American party politics. In fact, mainline and evangelical Protestants are both heirs of an earlier revivalist Protestant understanding of political reflection about the government and the destiny of the United States. From the middle of the nineteenth century until today, most Protestants of Anglo-Saxon stock have identified politically with the Whig-Republican tradition that drew heavily upon pietist Protestantism. This ideology in turn leaned heavily on the conversionist impulse that made individual commitment to Christ and a concerted effort to live a disciplined life the chief elements of Christian piety. As Daniel Walker Howe has argued, the revivalist emphasis on individual responsibility and self-denial was a crucial ingredient in a Whig outlook that promoted "rational order over irrational spontaneity" and "self-control over self-expression."[46] What is more, it fed naturally the demands of an expanding market economy which the Whigs and Republicans favored, and hatched any number of social reforms that were designed to Christianize America (a revivalist desire) and enforce Anglo-conformity (a Whig goal).[47] Revivalist Protestants gave the Whig and Republican Parties a particular religious stamp after the arrival in the 1840s of large numbers of Catholic immigrants who identified with the Democratic Party. To be sure, some of these differences were explicitly political. But they also stemmed from divergent convictions about Christian faith and practice. Unlike Democrats who believed in a limited, populist government that did not legislate social behavior but rather gave room for the expression of self-interest and local autonomy, Republicans trusted government to enact laws based on eternal truths which would nurture virtuous citizens and a righteous society.[48]

By the late nineteenth century, the Democrats had also begun to incorporate reformist and moralistic perspectives as evidenced by the evangelical politician, William Jennings Bryan, and his less evangelical colleague, Woodrow Wilson, both of whom were Presbyterian and who represented regional constituencies of Anglo-American Protestants that would not countenance voting for the party of Lincoln. As such, even though evangelicals could be found in both parties, their politics were virtually indistinguishable from their Protestant cousins who would emerge as the religiously liberal party. Mark A. Noll offers as good a summary as any of the basic evangelical political outlook:

> Protestants in the progressive era relied instinctively on the Bible to provide their ideals of justice. They believed in the power of Christ to expand the Kingdom of God through the efforts of faithful believers. They were reformists at home and missionaries abroad who felt that cooperation among Protestants signaled the advance of civilization. They were thoroughly and uncritically patriotic. On more specific issues, they continued to suspect Catholics as being anti-American, they promoted the public schools as agents of a broad form of Christianization, and they were overwhelmingly united behind prohibition as the key step toward a renewed society.[49]

To be sure, during the period from 1925 to 1965, a distinct form of millennialism colored evangelical political thought, especially in the way they viewed international politics. But domestically this theology only reinforced a prior suspicion of big government and centralization.[50] What is more, life in the United States for white Protestants, whether evangelical or liberal, was usually comfortable. In fact, whatever plausibility Moberg's thesis about a "great reversal" has, conservative Protestants during the middle decades of the twentieth century benefited from the Christian culture that the Protestant establishment patched together. The schools included prayer and Bible reading, abortion was illegal, federal officials were not proposing to bus children far from home for schooling, and domesticity was still an ideal for most American women. Consequently, even if mid-twentieth-century evangelicals were not politically active, they did not need to be.[51]

The two-party analysis of American Protestantism, which pits the gospel of individuals against the Social Gospel, has caused many to miss the history and legacy of revivalist Protestantism that both evangelicals and mainliners share. Throughout the twentieth century, evangelicals and liberals have differed over the way to prioritize evangelism, but they have agreed that faith will make an obvious and uplifting difference in individual and social life. This is because fundamentalists, evangelicals, and liberals all trace their roots to revivalist Protestantism's understanding of Christianity as inherently activist and reform minded; it creates virtuous individuals who pursue an equally virtuous society. In sum, evangelical and mainline Protestants both believe that Christianity inevitably produces a Social Gospel that will produce a Christian social order. This is why Ralph Reed, Pat Robertson's point man for the Christian Coalition, could write with some plausibility, even after discounting for his public relations aims, that the religious right begins with "a principle from the Social Gospel" outlined by Reinhold Niebuhr that "the purpose of politics is to establish justice in a fallen world."[52]

The revivalist heritage of both evangelicalism and mainstream Protestantism not only calls into question many of the accepted definitions of conservative Protestantism, but the differences between pietism and confessionalism make such categories even more slippery. If evangelicals and fundamentalists make up the sector of American Protestantism that favors small-government, individual responsibility and traditional roles for men and women, then they are conservative, as that term is commonly used in American politics. But this definition, ironically, relies on political categories to designate one of the factions in America's two-party Protestant system that is supposed to avoid politics for evangelism. Furthermore, if evangelicals and fundamentalists make soul winning a greater priority than liberals, then again they are conservative in the prevailing understanding of American Protestantism. But this categorization ignores the heritage of confessional Protestantism and the churchly and liturgical features of historic Protestantism that revivalist Protestants abandoned. What discussions of American Protestantism need is the addition of another category, much like one that has entered assessments of American politics. Instead of distinguishing simply between political liberals and conservatives, some now speak of two wings within the latter's ranks—namely, neoconservatives and paleoconservatives. In the same way, for the purpose of distinguishing between evangelicals and confessional Protestants, it might be best to speak of the former as neo-Protestants and the latter as paleo-Protestants. If such a linguistic turn were ever to succeed, these new designations for conservative Protestants might remind their users that just as political neoconservatives are, as the adage has it, liberals who got mugged by the 1960s, so neo-Protestants were the pietists of the nineteenth century who got mugged in the 1920s by the excesses of trying to make an otherworldly faith relevant.

Notes

1. Martin E. Marty, *Righteous Empire: The Protestant Experience in America* (New York: Dial, 1970), 178; for more details on Sunday's revival, see Jean Miller Schmidt, *Souls or the Social Order: The Two-Party System in American Protestantism* (Brooklyn, N.Y.: Carlson, 1991), 136–39; and Roger A. Bruins, *Preacher: Billy Sunday and Big-Time American Evangelism* (New York: Norton, 1992), 129–30, 152.

2. Schmidt, *Souls or the Social Order,* xxxv.

3. Schmidt, *Souls or the Social Order,* xxxii.

4. James Davison Hunter, *Culture Wars: The Struggle to Define America* (New York: Basic Books, 1991), 44, his emphasis.

5. Hunter, *Culture Wars,* especially 7–9.

6. "Churchmanship," *Time* 80 (February 11, 1924): 18, quotations from Manning in the news story.

7. "War," *Time* 80 (December 24, 1923): 20.

8. Rollin Lynde Hartt, "The War in the Churches," *World's Work* 46 (1923): 470.

9. The other two articles were "'Down with Evolution!'" *World's Work* 46 (1923): 605–12; and "Fighting for Infallibility," *World's Work* 47 (1923–24): 48–56.

10. Quotations from Rollin Lynde Hartt, "Modernism and the Coming Reformation," *World's Work* 47 (1923–24): 536, 537.

11. Quoted in Rollin Lynde Hartt, "Is the Church Dividing?," *World's Work* 47 (1923–24): 167.

12. H. L. Mencken, "Protestantism in the Republic," *American Mercury* (1925): 268–69, reprinted in *A Mencken Chrestomathy,* ed. H. L. Mencken (New York: Knopf, 1949), 76, 77.

13. Mencken, "Protestantism in the Republic," 79.

14. William Warren Sweet, *The Story of Religions in America* (New York: Harper, 1930), 512, 513; the phrase "churches in the age of big business" comes from Sweet's chapter title for the 1920s.

15. Sweet, *The Story of Religion in America*, 567, 568.

16. Stewart G. Cole, *The History of Fundamentalism* (New York: Smith, 1931), 53.

17. Cole, *The History of Fundamentalism*, 13, 14.

18. Cole, *The History of Fundamentalism*, 28.

19. H. Richard Niebuhr, "Fundamentalism," in *Encyclopedia of Social Sciences* (New York: Macmillan, 1937), VI:526–27.

20. For this author's assessment of the historiography of fundamentalism, see D. G. Hart, "Presbyterians and Fundamentalism" (a review article of Bradley J. Longfield, *The Presbyterian Controversy*), *Westminster Theological Journal* 55 (1993): 331–42.

21. Nancy T. Ammerman, "North American Protestant Fundamentalism," in *Fundamentalisms Observed: The Fundamentalist Project*, ed. Martin E. Marty and R. Scott Appleby (Chicago: University of Chicago Press, 1991), I:14.

22. On the Catholic version of the controversy over modernism, see Jay P. Dolan, *The American Catholic Experience: A History from Colonial Times to the Present* (Garden City, N.Y.: Doubleday, 1985), 304–20.

23. J. Gresham Machen to F. E. Robinson, June 25, 1927, quoted in Ned B. Stonehouse, *J. Gresham Machen: A Biographical Memoir* (Grand Rapids, Mich.: Eerdmans, 1954), 428.

24. See Milton L. Rudnick, *Fundamentalism and the Missouri Synod: A Historical Study of Their Interaction and Mutual Influence* (St. Louis: Concordia, 1966).

25. See James D. Bratt, *Dutch Calvinism in Modern America: A History of a Conservative Subculture* (Grand Rapids, Mich.: Eerdmans, 1984), chaps. 7 and 8.

26. Joel A. Carpenter, *Revive Us Again: The Reawakening of American Fundamentalism* (New York: Oxford University Press, 1997), is the authoritative interpretation of progressive fundamentalism and its many organizations.

27. Stephen W. Paine, "The Possibility of United Action," in Executive Committee of the NAE, *Evangelical Action! A Report of the Organization of the National Association of Evangelicals for United Action* (Boston: United Action Press, 1942), 54, 56.

28. For the standard interpretation of the differences between evangelicals and fundamentalists, see Carpenter, *Revive Us Again*, chap. 2; and George M. Marsden, *Reforming Fundamentalism: Fuller Seminary and the New Evangelicalism* (Grand Rapids, Mich.: Eerdmans, 1987), 6–7, 37–38.

29. Harold John Ockenga, "The Unvoiced Multitudes," in Executive Committee, *Evangelical Action*, 24, 25, 28.

30. William Ward Ayer, "Evangelical Christianity Endangered by Its Fragmented Condition," in Executive Committee, *Evangelical Action*, 46.

31. Ockenga, "Unvoiced Multitudes," 32.

32. "Report of the Special Committee on Religious Broadcasting," in Executive Committee, *Evangelical Action*, 116.

33. Carl F. H. Henry, *The Uneasy Conscience of Modern Fundamentalism* (Grand Rapids, Mich.: Eerdmans, 1947), 16, 28.

34. Henry, *The Uneasy Conscience*, 31.

35. Henry, *The Uneasy Conscience*, 88.

36. Henry, *The Uneasy Conscience*, 87.

37. William Vance Trollinger Jr., *God's Empire: William Bell Riley and Midwestern Fundamentalism* (Madison: University of Wisconsin Press, 1990), 63. For other examples of fundamentalists involved in urban reform, see C. Allyn Russell, *Voices of American Fundamentalism: Seven Biographical Studies* (Philadelphia: Westminster, 1976), on J. Frank Norris, and John Roach Straton; and C. Allyn Russell, "Mark Alison Matthews: Seattle Fundamentalist and Civic Reformer," *Journal of Presbyterian History* 57 (1979): 446–66.

38. Ironically, Henry cited J. Gresham Machen as one "who vigorously insisted that Christianity has a message relevant to the world crisis, however staggering the issues" (Henry, *The Uneasy Conscience*, 19), when, in fact, Machen insisted that the church had one job to do, that of preaching the good news, irrespective of the issues. This irony will be more apparent in chap. 4.

39. Henry, *Uneasy Conscience*, 32.

40. David O. Moberg, *The Great Reversal: Evangelism versus Social Concern* (Philadelphia: Lippincott, 1972), 160–61.

41. Richard V. Pierard, *The Unequal Yoke: Evangelical Christianity and Political Conservatism* (Philadelphia: Lippincott, 1970), 18, 19.

42. Pierard, *The Unequal Yoke*, 17, where Pierard shows the results of polls surveying evangelical voters in the 1964 presidential election.

43. Several of the following paragraphs are adapted from the essay by D. G. Hart, "Mainstream Protestantism, 'Conservative' Religion, and Civil Society," *Journal of Policy History* 13 (2001): 19–46.

44. On the origins and rise of the religious right, see Michael Lienesch, *Redeeming America: Piety and Politics in the New Christian Right* (Chapel Hill: University of North Carolina Press, 1993); Steve Bruce, *The Rise and Fall of the New Christian Right: Conservative Protestant Politics in America, 1978–1988* (New York: Oxford University Press, 1988); William C. Martin, *With God On Our Side: The Rise of the Religious Right in America* (New York: Broadway Books, 1996); and Clyde Wilcox, *God's Warriors? The Christian Right in Twentieth-Century America* (Baltimore: Johns Hopkins University Press, 1992).

45. Sydney E. Ahlstrom, *A Religious History of the American People* (New Haven, Conn.: Yale University Press, 1972), 1079, his emphasis.

46. Daniel Walker Howe, "Religion and Politics in the Antebellum North," in *Religion and American Politics: From the Colonial Period to the 1980s*, ed. Mark A. Noll (New York: Oxford University Press, 1990), 124.

47. On this point, see Howe, "Religion and Politics in the Antebellum North," 121–45; Robert P. Swierenga, "Ethnoreligious Political Behavior in the Mid-Nineteenth Century: Voting, Values, Culture," in *Religion and American Politics*, ed. Mark Noll, 146–71; George Marsden, "The Religious Right: A Historical Overview," in *No Longer Exiles: The Religious New Right in American Politics*, ed. Michael Cromartie (Washington, D.C.: Ethics and Public Policy Center, 1992), 1–16; and Allen C. Guelzo, *Abraham Lincoln: Redeemer President* (Grand Rapids, Mich.: Eerdmans, 1999), 26–63.

48. Swierenga, "Ethnoreligious Political Behavior," 152–53. See Lyman A. Kellstedt et al., "It's the Culture Stupid! 1992 and Our Political Future," *First Things* 42 (April 1994): 28–33, for evidence of these differences between Republicans and Democrats even after the 1930s.

49. Noll, "The Scandal of Evangelical Political Reflection," in *Being Christian Today: An American Conversation*, ed. Richard John Neuhaus and George Weigel (Washington, D.C.: Ethics and Public Policy, 1992), 73.

50. For the influence of premillennialism on evangelical politics, see Noll, "The Scandal of Evangelical Political Reflection," 74–82; and George M. Marsden, *Fundamentalism and American Culture: The Shaping of Twentieth-Century Evangelicalism, 1870–1925* (New York: Oxford University Press, 1980), chaps. 22 and 23.

51. See James Hudnut-Beumler, *Looking for God in the Suburbs: The Religion of the American Dream and Its Critics, 1945–1965*; and Paul A. Carter, *Another Part of the Fifties* (New York: Columbia University Press, 1983).

52. Ralph Reed, *Active Faith: How Christians Are Changing the Soul of American Politics* (New York: Free Press, 1996), 255–56.

The Intolerance of Presbyterian Creeds 4

If a Mormon had been elected in 2000 to the United States Senate from the state of Utah, few Americans would have batted an eye since members of the Church of Jesus Christ of Latter-Day Saints (LDS) have become, in the words of the syndicated columnist George F. Will, "quintessentially American."[1] In fact, the most nationally prominent politician from Utah, Senator Orrin Hatch, is a Mormon, a religious identity that may not have helped in his bid to become the Republican Party's nominee for the 2000 presidential race but has not impaired his emergence as a spokesman for political views shared by a wide swath of conservatives in the United States. A century ago, however, Mormons were not so highly regarded or so thoroughly assimilated. Evidence for this assertion is easy to find in the struggles that led Mormon leaders to abandon the practice and teaching of polygamy in exchange for the territory of Utah's admission as a state.[2] But even after Utah gained statehood, Mormon politicians were still regarded with suspicion. Consequently, in 1903 when the state's voters elected Reed Smoot, a Mormon apostle, to be their representative in the Senate, that house of legislators responded by appointing a committee to investigate whether this Mormon could legitimately occupy a congressional seat.

The Smoot investigation itself came at the prompting of Salt Lake City businessmen, lawyers, and Protestant clergy. Polygamy was still a live issue, and the LDS's recent reversal of its teaching did not reassure many of Utah's "Gentiles," who knew firsthand that church deliverances did not necessarily mean a change of behavior. But an even larger concern was whether a Mormon, especially an Apostle, who was "one of a self-perpetuating body of fifteen men" and who claimed "supreme authority" to "shape the belief and control the conduct" of other LDS members, could sincerely vow to uphold and defend the U.S. Constitution. In the words of the complainants, Smoot's promise to adhere to the laws of the United States "must be as threads of tow [flax]" in comparison to his Mormon vows that bound "his intellect, his will, and his affections."[3]

By contemporary standards that require the celebration of religious and cultural diversity, the objections to Smoot's being seated in the Senate look outrageous and reveal yet another side of the United States' dark and repressive ways. Nor does the fact that American citizens and public officials raised similar objections to Roman Catholic aspirants for national office, such as Al Smith and John Fitzgerald Kennedy who ran in 1928 and 1960, respectively, for the president of the United States, offer much consolation.[4] Opposition to duly elected officials of Mormon outlook appears to be a flagrant contradiction of American norms that are supposed to guarantee religious liberty, thereby granting equal access to political office by members of any particular religious tradition. No matter how objectionable a particular religious practice such as polygamy may be, the argument usually runs, religion should not be a sufficient ground for disqualifying a candidate from holding public office in a nation committed to the ideal of freedom of thought and belief.

Shocking though the actions of the Senate may be in the case of Smoot, even more remarkable was the flip side of the complaint against the Senator from Utah. For the Protestant ministers who objected to Smoot, along with much of the American public, saw no contradiction between being a member of a Protestant church or even being a lay officer in a specific denomination and holding public office. For instance, several presidents of the era were members of Protestant churches, and no investigation ensued after their elections to inquire whether the vows they had taken as church members conflicted with their promise to execute the laws of the nation.[5]

A good example on this score is Woodrow Wilson, whom some scholars believe to be one of the most religious men ever to be president and who was an elder in the southern Presbyterian Church.[6] To be a Presbyterian elder, Wilson would have had to promise loyalty to the Bible and the Westminster Confession of Faith. In effect, as a Presbyterian officer, to use the language of

Smoot's opposition, Wilson's intellect, will, and affections were every bit as bound by Scripture and a Presbyterian creed as the Mormon Senator's were by LDS polity and doctrine. Yet only the rare skeptic or atheist has ever perceived Protestantism as a religion that binds the consciences of its followers to a standard or power higher than that of the United States government or that conflicted with freedom of inquiry. Indeed, American Protestants in the nineteenth century were so adept at linking their faith to the cause of political liberty, democracy, and scientific discovery that almost no one perceived the slightest tension between membership in a Protestant church and citizenship in the United States. Accordingly, Protestants stood on the side of reason, freedom, and enlightenment, while other faiths were synonymous with bigotry, tyranny, and superstition.

Since the 1960s the link between Protestant norms and American ideals has come undone. A series of Supreme Court rulings on prayer and Bible reading in public schools helped Protestants learn what many residents of the United States already knew. Although its American adherents had managed to overlook the differences between political and spiritual liberty, Protestantism in the 1960s finally came of age as denominations wrestled with the recognition that their beliefs were in many respects arbitrary, authoritative, and exclusive, and so incapable of uniting all Americans, let alone underwriting the American experiment all by itself.[7]

The 1920s offered an earlier lecture to American Protestants about the tension between the free thinking encouraged by American culture and the intellectual constraints imposed by Christian belief. Of the several layers to the fundamentalist-modernist controversy, the conflict between science and faith was arguably the most enduring since it became a public spectacle during the Scopes trial of 1925 and has become part of the nation's oral tradition through theatrical and cinematic depictions of those sometimes comic courtroom proceedings.[8] William Jennings Bryan, in the eyes of the intelligentsia as well as the liberal clergy, stood precisely for a Protestant form of authoritarianism that was an enemy to progress, intellectual freedom, and good government. But beneath the surface of Dayton, Tennessee's hoopla, other theological conflicts simmered, many of which have been portrayed as simply another variety of fundamentalism.

In the northern Presbyterian Church, for instance, when a minority of confessionalists objected to the denomination's drift from church dogma, journalists then and historians since pigeonholed such conservatism as fundamentalism. In some respects, this was an easy mistake to make because of the mainstream churches' assumption that Protestantism was not a dogmatic faith. Nevertheless, the Presbyterian controversy of the 1920s revealed a strain of confessional thinking that would not flinch from charges of intolerance or dogmatism. These Presbyterian confessionalists, like nineteenth-century Lutherans, believed that their creed defined their church's identity. What is more, they also held that Presbyterian creedalism made the church intolerant of those who could not affirm Presbyterian beliefs. In the minds of many mainstream Protestants, such an admission was unthinkable because intolerance was incompatible with intellectual freedom and the Protestant regard for liberty of conscience. But even if Presbyterian confessionalists qualified what intolerance meant by disconnecting the private realm of religion from the public realm of intellectual freedom, they stood by the notion that creeds prohibited churches from becoming breeding grounds for free thought.

The Necessity of Intolerance

J. Gresham Machen (1881–1937) was an unlikely fundamentalist, so unlikely that his career makes more sense as that of a confessional Presbyterian. The leader of conservatives during the controversy of the 1920s within the northern Presbyterian Church (PCUSA), Machen taught New Testament at Princeton Seminary from 1906 until 1929, before helping found a series of institutions, a seminary, a missions board, and a formal protest group, which culminated in his being tried for disloyalty and suspended from the Presbyterian ministry. Although the combination of Machen's southernness and his residency north of the Mason-Dixon Line for most of his adult life encouraged a combative side, no one in his family would have expected him to devote the last sixteen years of his life to ecclesiastical politics. He came from a well-to-do professional family in Baltimore in which law, politics, and business were the most likely outlets for a career. But on the way to his undergraduate degree in Classics at Johns Hopkins University, where he graduated first in his class, Machen acquired a scholarly interest in ancient languages and literature. At Princeton Seminary, he refined that interest by pursuing New Testament studies, and he went to Germany for a year of graduate study before returning to Princeton in 1906 to teach Greek and the Bible.[9]

The book that vaulted Machen into the public eye was *Christianity and Liberalism*, which appeared in 1923, about the time that northern Presbyterians were preparing for combat. Prior to this highly polemical work, Machen had been mainly content to pursue teaching and writing, having produced a well-received study of the apostle Paul in 1921 and a New Testament Greek grammar for seminarians a year later. Because *Christianity and Liberalism* came out during the fundamentalist controversy and because he argued candidly that liberalism was an altogether different religion from Christianity, readers then and since have readily cataloged the book as a work of the right wing, no matter how much more learned and plausible it was than the ordinary fundamentalist polemic. For instance, in Richard Hofstadter's stinging critique of fundamentalist anti-intellectualism, he was forced to clarify that he was only treating these Protestants "as a mass movement," not "the more thoughtful critics of modernism" such as Machen.[10] As Hofstadter detected, something more was going on in Machen's argument, and that extra ingredient was Presbyterian confessionalism.

Although many evangelicals and liberals in the Presbyterian Church thought the book nasty, part of what made it plausible to readers who had no real interest in theology was the definitional precision that confessionalism supplied. Leaving aside all of Machen's arguments about developments in modern Protestant theology and whether those legitimately stood in line with historic Christian affirmations, his audience could easily stay with the point that many liberal Protestants were unable in good conscience to subscribe to the creeds that were supposed to be binding for the respective denominations. Here, the question, as he put it, was not one of whether creedal requirements were desirable or even worthwhile. It might be that "devotion to a creed is a sign of narrowness and intolerance" and that "devotion to the ideal of Jesus" should really be the basis for fellowship in the church. The real issue was the fact that America's Protestant denominations were "creedal churches." These creeds, in fact, stood out prominently in the denominations' public documents, namely, their articles of incorporation. "Whether we like it or not, these Churches are founded upon a creed; they are organized for the propagation of a message. If a man desires to combat that message instead of propagating it, he has no right, no matter how false the message may be, to gain a vantage ground for combating it by making a declaration of his faith which—be it plainly spoken—is not true."[11] Like confessional Protestants before him, Machen was a strict constructionist in his reading of creeds and catechisms. The meaning of Presbyterianism or Lutheranism could not evolve over time without the lawful revision of each communion's confessional standards through proper ecclesiastical channels. In other words, creeds defined religious identity; it made no sense to say you were a Presbyterian if you really believed what Mormons did.

To make the point even clearer and to turn up the heat on liberal Presbyterians, Machen underlined the questions every Presbyterian minister had to answer affirmatively in order to be ordained. One concerned believing the Bible to be "the Word of God, the only infallible rule of faith and practice." The other involved receiving and adopting the *Westminster Confession* "as containing the system of doctrine taught in the Holy Scriptures." These "constitutional" questions "clearly fixed the creedal basis of the Presbyterian Church." Yet some ministers, after taking their ordination vows, went out into congregations and criticized the Westminster Standards and the Bible "to which they have just solemnly subscribed."[12] Machen believed this was a clear instance of intellectual dishonesty.

He compared the situation to that of certain American citizens, Republicans who were opposed to the tenets of the Democratic Party, and who joined a club the purpose of which was to further the cause of the Democrats. The honest way to promote the Republican cause was to form a Republican club. "But suppose," Machen added, that these Republicans declared their "conformity to Democratic principles" for the purpose of taking over the Democratic club "and finally turning its resources into an anti-Democratic propaganda." Such a plan would undoubtedly be "ingenious." "But would it be honest?" And should not the church, he asked, which was "far more than a political club," be as beholden to the "homely principles of honesty" as political parties?[13] This was the sort of logic that led H. L. Mencken, on the occasion of Machen's death, to write that the Presbyterian conservative's falling out with "the reformers who have been trying . . . to convert the Presbyterian Church into a kind of literary and social club, devoted vaguely to good works," was an obvious "failure" but "undoubtedly right."[14]

Part of the reason why Machen could be persuasive with some of America's secular pundits was that he was willing to admit to a proposition that nonreligious Americans knew to be true—churches were intolerant. He drew on his earlier scholarship and cited the example of the apostle

Paul who condemned rival preachers in the region of Galatia because their preaching was false. It was not a case of whether the apostle had a nice or tolerant personality. The issue was "the objective truth of the gospel."[15] The dogmatism of the early church was the model for twentieth-century Christianity, in Machen's estimate. And this is why he believed liberals needed to leave the existing creedal churches and either found new denominations or join the Unitarians who provided "just the kind of church that the liberal preacher desires."[16] Liberals, he argued, had denied the truth of Christianity by cutting and trimming its doctrinal content according to the reigning intellectual fashions. This was not necessarily a bad thing. Machen admitted that one of the pressing questions facing the modern church was whether the Christian faith could be "maintained in a scientific age." Liberals said it could, and in doing so they were simply trying to defend the faith with the best of intentions. The problem, from Machen's confessional perspective, was that their apology for Christianity involved abandoning "the particularities of the Christian religion" for religious abstractions. Consequently, liberals regarded the specific affirmations of Christian creeds as "mere temporary symbols" of the faith, and such general principles as the fatherhood of God and the brotherhood of man as "the essence of Christianity."[17] By making Christianity into a religion of ideals that transcended the historical particularities of the Bible, liberalism was able to do justice to modern thought. The problem, however, was whether what was left in liberal verities resembled historic Christianity.

If churches were sites of intellectual dogmatism, places where minds were forced to conform to the teaching of a particular religious tradition, weren't they completely at odds with the sort of liberty advocated by modern science and protected by secular governments? One way that Machen responded to this apparent predicament was to distinguish between voluntary and involuntary associations—in other words, between public and private life. The reason why confessionalists like himself, he argued, were not flagrantly guilty of intolerance was because involuntary organizations "ought to be tolerant" but voluntary ones, "so far as the fundamental purpose of their existence is concerned, must be intolerant or else they cease to exist." The state was one example of an involuntary organization. "A man is forced to be a member of it whether he will or no." For government, then, to prescribe any "one type of opinion" was obviously an interference with liberty or an instance of intolerance. But beyond the state, citizens had the

freedom to "unite for some special purpose," especially in the sphere of religion, where such permission to form voluntary associations was "one of
the rights which lie at the very foundation of our civil and religious liberty."
The state was not permitted to "scrutinize the rightness or wrongness" of
the aims of religious voluntary associations because if it did "all liberty
would be gone." Instead, the state protected the right of voluntary associations. In effect, by making the church exclusive, confessionalists were doing
precisely what the American experiment was intended to produce.[18]

Machen's appeal to this distinction between public and private notions
of liberty and intolerance may help explain an early section in *Christianity
and Liberalism* where some readers may have wondered whether they had
picked up a book more about politics than theology. In an appeal to those
who may not have had any particular interest in church controversy or theological debate, Machen attempted to connect his argument to certain cultural trends, thereby showing that liberalism was part of a "lamentable decline" in the spiritual realm of American life.[19] One area of concern was a
pattern of state laws that restricted foreign language instruction in public
schools, thanks to a surge of "100 Per Cent Americanism" after World War
I. Machen believed that such legislation in states such as Oregon, Nebraska,
and New York clearly violated civil liberty. "A people which tolerates such
preposterous legislation upon the statute books is a people that has wan-
dered far away from the principles of American liberty."[20] He also thought
such laws reflected the baleful influence of a materialistic paternalism that
turned democracy into "the reduction of all mankind to the proportions
of the narrowest and least gifted of the citizens."[21] For Machen, then, religious intolerance in its proper sphere—namely, the church—was not in any
way at odds with American notions of freedom and tolerance. The trouble
was determining exactly what intolerance and liberty involved and how they
functioned in different settings.

Perhaps the best way to illustrate the way Machen thought intolerance
should function in the private and public realms is by examining his opposition to prayer and Bible reading in public schools. No fan of public education, he was not particularly keen on the way state or federal bureaucrats
in the 1920s were proposing to reform public schooling. Machen even testified before Congress in 1926 on this matter under the auspices of the
Sentinels of the Republic, a libertarian political organization founded by
Massachusetts businessmen opposed to Prohibition. Consequently, his crit-

icism of the United States' public education stemmed more from political convictions than from religious motivation, a relatively unusual feat for someone identified as a fundamentalist. For this reason, Machen's prescription for the ills besetting public schools was not to add moral or character education to the curriculum, nor was it to give God a voice through prayer and Bible reading at the start of the day. Religion, he believed, was essentially a private affair, best left to families and churches. In fact, Machen placed the brunt of educational duties upon parents, not the state or the church. In turn, he advocated Christian day schools as the appropriate vehicle for parents who wished their children to receive religious training as part of their primary and secondary education. As Machen told a rally of Christian day school teachers, "a truly Christian education is possible only when Christian education underlies not a part, but all of the curriculum of the school." Trying to add a dose of religion to normal aspects of public schooling was a "miserable makeshift."[22]

But just as Christian schools had an obligation to be profoundly Christian, so public schools had a duty to be thoroughly secular. This meant, according to Machen, the abolition not only of American patriotism and character education in public education but also of prayer and Bible reading. The function of the public school, he argued, "should be limited, rather than increased," and that limitation should be "the impartation of knowledge"—in other words, the three Rs. The moral influence in the school should derive solely from standards established by each teacher for the good ordering of the classroom and to provide good instruction. But Bible reading should not be encouraged; even worse would be to require it by law. The reason was twofold. First, such religious practices could potentially violate the consciences of nonbelievers. Consequently, although secular education was "an evil," it was a "necessary" one.[23] Second, inserting religious observances into public spaces hurt religion. "What could be more terrible," Machen wrote, "from the Christian point of view, than the reading of the Lord's Prayer to non-Christian children, as though they could use it without becoming Christians, as though persons who have never been purchased by the blood of Christ could possibly say to God, 'Our Father, which art in Heaven'?"[24] The only way to supplement public schooling with religious education, in Machen's view, was a system of released time during which students, at the discretion of their parents, could receive religious training. But even here, Machen was quick to keep the public and private realms as separate as possible by insisting that the state "refrain both from granting school credit for work done during these hours and from exercising any control whatever either upon attendance or upon the character of the instruction."[25]

Machen's ideas about primary and secondary education reflect the libertarian convictions that surfaced regularly in his writings. As such, public institutions always had the capacity to be intolerant, given the powers of coercion they possessed, such as the ability to punish law breakers. Private organizations of citizens could not pose such a threat because membership in them was voluntary and they lacked the authority and weapons that states legitimately possessed.

Still, Machen's notions about the legitimacy of intolerance in private and its danger in public stemmed as well from a strain of thought among Presbyterian theologians that stressed the church's character as essentially spiritual, as opposed to political or temporal. According to the tradition of the spirituality of the church, the church's task was not social or political. It was simply to care for souls. And the tools it used in this endeavor were as spiritual as was the church's mission. Those tools consisted of preaching, the sacraments, and church discipline, the classic marks of the church in Reformed theology. Machen articulated this doctrine in the following manner:

> You cannot expect from a true Christian Church any official pronouncements upon the political or social questions of the day, and you cannot expect cooperation with the state in anything involving the use of force. Important are the functions of the police, and members of the Church, either individually or in such special associations as they may choose to form, should aid the police in every lawful way in the exercise of those functions. But the function of the Church in its corporate capacity is of an entirely different kind. Its weapons against evil are spiritual, not carnal; and by becoming a political lobby, through the advocacy of political measures whether good or bad, the Church is turning aside from its proper mission.[26]

Ecclesiastical intolerance, of the kind Machen prescribed for Presbyterians, then, was not a threat to political liberty because the church was not part of the political establishment. The First Amendment to the United States' Constitution not only gave churches the right to organize but also prevented those churches from meddling in political affairs. As long as the church remained a separate organization, almost like a sect, its coercion of belief among ministers and members was not only a requirement (how else do you tell a Presbyterian from a Baptist?) but also a natural outgrowth of political liberalism.

Protestant liberals, however, did not hear Machen, the orthodox Presbyterian, as a political liberal.[27] For instance, in his infamous sermon "Shall the Fundamentalists Win?" Harry Emerson Fosdick made fundamentalism virtually synonymous with intolerance of an illegitimate sort, and liberalism with a generous and charitable outlook. The fact that fundamentalists wanted to throw liberals out of the church, a group of Christians "intellectually hospitable, open-minded, liberty-loving, fair, [and] tolerant," was a supreme instance of "immeasurable folly!"[28] So, too, the responses to *Christianity and Liberalism* gave the impression that Machen's plea for exclusive churches was tantamount to a form of authoritarianism commonly associated with the pope. Here a book designed as a reply to Machen's by William P. Merrill, a prominent Presbyterian minister in New York City, is instructive. To defend liberal Protestantism, Merrill thought it necessary to contrast it with other types of Christianity. The sharpest contrast, he asserted, was between liberalism and a form of Protestantism "as completely authoritarian in spirit as is the Roman church itself." These dogmatic Protestants took "the Bible as the sufficient and sole authority" in matters of religion and then proceeded to "define Bible teaching in authoritative terms" by establishing a "set of doctrines which one questions at his peril." Even though authoritarian Protestantism and Roman Catholics disagreed over the authority of the Bible in relation to the church, Merrill concluded that at "heart their position is the same."[29] Indeed, so intolerant did Machen's polemic strike Protestant liberals that Gerald Birney Smith, who taught theology at the University of Chicago Divinity School, compared Machen's methods to those of Pope Pius X. "Having defined Christianity as he wished it to be defined, and having shown that modernists did not concur in this definition," the pope had the authority to expel those "who did not agree with him." Machen's only difference on this score was that he had "no such ecclesiastical authority behind him."[30]

The reason for this reaction to Machen stemmed in part from an understanding of Protestantism that had guided its adherents in the United States since the nation's founding. Unlike the European expressions of the

Enlightenment in which the new science and philosophy were decidedly anticlerical, the Enlightenment ideals that fueled America's war for independence and political settlement received vigorous support from Protestant clergy. This had a lot to do with differences between the moderation of the Scottish Enlightenment, which Calvinistic clergy embraced, and the radicalism of the French philosophes.[31] Still, Protestant support for American independence had an important effect on Protestant self-understanding in the United States. Not only did the mainstream Protestant view put Christianity on the side of freedom, progress, and democracy, but the scientific norms that validated modern political philosophy also became the criteria for religious truth. Science vindicated the ideal of liberty as well as the Bible, so many Protestant clergy believed. This led to the conviction that just as all right thinking people accepted the self-evident truth that democracy was superior to monarchy, so common sense inevitably underwrote Christianity as the only reasonable faith.[32]

The assumptions of American Protestants about the scientific and public character of their faith, combined with the social activism inherent in pietism, made the United States a very foreign place for Roman Catholics. The 1840s witnessed riots and the formation of political parties that were directed against Catholicism as an un-American religion. The chief difference between Protestants and Catholics, according to the former, concerned the matter of freedom. The Catholic hierarchy opposed freedom of thought, restricted access to the Bible, and made the laity dependent on the clergy. It was, from the American Protestant perspective, a religion of tyranny, bigotry, and superstition. Protestantism was its opposite, a religion that encouraged freedom of conscience, a well educated laity who did not simply repeat the opinions of clergy but could think and act for themselves. This outlook that associated Protestantism with modernity, what some have called the Whig cultural ideal, identified the Anglo-American Protestant denominations "with the advances of civilization and the cause of freedom." As George M. Marsden has helpfully explained, "Freedom in this outlook meant not only political freedom and personal liberties derived from higher moral law but also the free inquiry necessary for modern science." Catholicism, in contrast, was the very incarnation of "absolutism."[33]

Reactions to Machen that derided him as an authoritarian were completely understandable given the main lines of American Protestant development. By emphasizing the creedal and, therefore, exclusive character of the Protestant churches, Machen was proposing that Protestantism's liberal and public exterior was really a facade. Even in its efforts to be progressive and public spirited, Machen believed, American Protestantism could not help but be intolerant. The debates about language education in primary schools revealed, in his estimate, just how exclusive Protestant paternalism could be. To provide unity and a national culture, Machen wrote, "we have attacked [the immigrants] by oppressive legislation or proposals of legislation." But when these measures proved ineffective in overcoming the immigrants' "perverse attachment to the language that they learned at their mother's knee," public officials turned to religion. The result was a program of "Christian Americanization" in which Protestants "proceed against the immigrants now with a Bible in one hand and a club in the other offering them the blessing of liberty."[34]

Machen's solution, then, was to make Protestantism explicitly intolerant by emphasizing the confessional nature of church membership and ordination, while also privatizing the faith by keeping it out of public life. This is why he thought confessionalists were actually more liberal, in a political sense, than liberal Protestants. Uniformity in the religious sphere of the church did not require uniformity in public life. Confessional intolerance, in Machen's mind, went hand in hand with cultural diversity and intellectual freedom. The bargain was that churches, schools, and other private organizations could be as ideologically pure as they wanted, as long as they kept their views private. This was, however, a bargain that mainstream Protestantism could not accept because it would have sacrificed the achievement of almost 150 years. Machen was asking Protestants to be something they believed they were not—namely, intolerant and sectarian. But his argument also showed what Protestants had sacrificed by refusing this deal; by making their faith the one that gave coherence to the nation, they had to jettison vast swaths of Christian teaching, such as the deity of Christ, hell, and original sin, doctrines that would have been obviously intolerant in a public setting. What Machen did not see was that pietism had allowed Protestants to abandon their creedal statements in favor of experience and morality. For that reason, a noncreedal Protestant faith continued to look like the genuine article as well as a publicly useful religion until the 1960s when Protestant piety and ethics no longer appeared to be benign.

Machen himself would experience firsthand the intolerance that he believed to be implicit in a noncreedal religion that took pride in religious flexibility. After a series of episodes in which Presbyterian officials denied the existence of liberalism in the church and blamed conservatives like Machen for the controversy in the denomination, in 1935 they finally brought him to trial for spearheading a rump missions agency that threatened to divert power from the official denominational board. In what still ranks as one of the most blatant forms of authoritarianism, the Presbyterian commission that tried Machen in the Presbytery of New Brunswick (New Jersey) ruled, just before he was about to defend himself, that they would receive no evidence that questioned the legality of church proceedings to that point. What made this decision remarkable was that there was no widespread support for Machen in the denomination. He had become so identified with the forces of intolerance and authoritarianism that the conviction by the Presbytery was as sure as the church's relief to be rid of a man many regarded as temperamentally deficient.[35]

Equally remarkable was that Machen's Presbyterian peers ended up proving his point. Churches were indeed intolerant places with rules and standards for how to be a member or an officer; they were not public institutions open to any ordinary citizen without passing the right tests. The problem for American Protestantism was that its criteria for admission and leadership had become so blurred with the norms of civil society that they lacked definition. As Machen argued, the Protestant churches were creedal; each affirmed some sort of doctrinal statement that defined boundaries for admission and ministry. But the churches no longer played by those rules. Consequently, when dissenters like Machen ran afoul of Presbyterian law, the decision to ban criticism of the church could look incredibly arbitrary and tyrannical, the very antithesis of how a noncreedal, tolerant faith was supposed to function. A southern Presbyterian put Machen's predicament strikingly when he pointed out that at the same General Assembly that had condemned Machen's actions as illegal had also pledged its support to Protestants, led by Karl Barth, who opposed the Nazi dominance of Germany's churches. But the irony of opposing tyranny in Europe while also inflicting it much closer to home was lost on most northern Presbyterians thanks to an American Protestant myopia that was blind to the aspects of Christianity, such as creeds, ordination vows, and supernatural revelation, that make the churches it inspires intolerant.[36]

Scientific Protestantism

As much as Machen's appeal to the creedal nature of Protestantism was an odd perspective in his time, his understanding of the church's intolerance did not include an abandonment of all efforts to make Christianity reasonable. In fact, another component of his response to the criticism that ecclesiastical dogmatism was at odds with modern culture's recognition of science as the primary arbiter of truth (as opposed to tradition or revelation) was the tried and true mainstream Protestant approach that said all truth was God's, and so true religion could not contradict true science. Machen specifically attacked liberal Protestants as the party of anti-intellectualism because of their dichotomous view of truth, as if a proposition like God created the world *ex nihilo* could be religiously true but scientifically questionable (few clergy had the nerve to use the word *false*). "We shall have to reject," he insisted, "the easy apologetic for Christianity which simply declares that religion and science belong in independent spheres and that science can never conceivably contradict religion." Indeed, Christianity would be an inferior religion if it abandoned "to science the whole realm of objective truth, in order to reserve for itself merely a realm of ideals."[37]

As other historians have argued, this point about the harmonization of science and theology was one of the few defects in the confessional Presbyterian mind, a holdover from the way Protestants had earlier appropriated science and Enlightenment thought.[38] For all of his rigor in keeping the public and private separate, Machen still clung to the notion that Christianity, a private faith, was publicly verifiable. Consequently, he repeatedly defended older arguments for the existence of God, as well as the historical reliability of the Bible. Confessional Calvinists less enamored of the Enlightenment than American Presbyterians regarded any attempt to prove Christianity by scientific criteria as an inappropriate transfer of authority in religion from special revelation to autonomous human reason. What is more, Machen's statement that Christianity was compatible with science appeared to contradict his forthright admission of his religion's intolerance. He actually defined science, in part, as being open-minded and broad, a posture that did not readily fit with the restraints imposed by the *Westminster Confession of Faith*.[39]

Machen's intellectual predicament became a concrete reality when in 1925 William Jennings Bryan invited him to testify on behalf of the prosecution at the Scopes trial. The Great Commoner from Nebraska had already raised the issue of evolution at the General Assembly of the northern Presbyterian Church at a time when Machen thought it hurt the case he and other confessionalists were trying to make about the creedal nature of their church. Consequently, he was well aware of the anti-intellectual reputation conservative Presbyterianism was gaining even before he received this invitation from Bryan. But this letter put Machen clearly on the spot. If he testified, he would open himself up to the kind of ridicule that greeted Bryan during the proceedings. If he did not go to Dayton, Tennessee, Machen's decision could be interpreted as that of a faux conservative. As it turned out, he was able to avoid Dayton because of a previous commitment, along with the explanation to Bryan that he was unsure how an expert on the New Testament helped the court understand an Old Testament text.[40] Even so, Machen's brief for intolerance in other settings opened him up to the charge that he favored a return to the Dark Ages when dogma prevented the unfettered pursuit of scientific truth.

Here it is helpful to recognize a distinction that confessionalism permitted Machen to make in the negotiations he conducted between dogma and science. He had little hesitation throughout the Presbyterian controversy in affirming the infallibility and truthfulness of the Bible, interpreted in a more or less literal manner (he used the term *grammatico-historical*), as opposed to a mythological or figurative sense. Scripture, accordingly, was the word of God and functioned as the supreme authority in the life of Christians and the church. The Bible's authority, however, did not mean that it taught science, especially in the way that anti-evolutionists thought. Machen admitted that the "assertion that the Bible is not intended to teach science does contain an element of truth." The reason was that the Bible said nothing about "many departments of science." He also conceded that academic specialization—that is, the isolation of certain studies from other areas of knowledge for the sake of greater precision—was "advantageous" as long as a "real synthesis of truth" was the ultimate goal.[41] A high view of the Bible as an inerrant book, as well as a firm commitment to confessional boundaries for the church, did not require, therefore, a definite position on the mechanics of human origins, although many fundamentalists and liberals assumed it did (and still do). In other words, theological intolerance and hostility to modern science did not necessarily go hand in hand.

Evidence of confessional Presbyterian flexibility on science comes from Machen's own quirky views on evolution. Unlike most who approached this problem, Machen used the example of Christ's miraculous birth to defend a traditional understanding of humankind's creation. In the same way that Christ's birth involved both natural (i.e., developments in the womb) and supernatural (i.e., born of a virgin) aspects, so the creation of the first man and woman relied on natural phenomena and God's miraculous intervention. Machen did not spell out what the natural development in the origin of the human form might look like. Nor was he clear about the nature of divine intervention into the creation process. What was clear, however, was that Machen was using categories he learned from Benjamin B. Warfield at Princeton Seminary, another confessional Presbyterian, who considered himself to be an evolutionist of the "purest water."[42] The latter's teaching distinguished carefully between divine power that created from nothing and the providential control of the created order through secondary causes. This distinction between creation and providence allowed Warfield to argue that although divine creation was necessary to account for the beginning of the human soul, the human body could well have evolved from lower forms of life through providence. Although Machen departed from Warfield's effort to accommodate evolution, he did rely on the same distinction between creation and providence made by his teacher.[43]

More important, however, is what confessional Presbyterian responses to Darwinism reveal about the mental dexterity of confessionalism more generally. A sharp distinction between matters specially revealed in holy writ and the more general truths contained in the book of nature leads to related distinctions that imposed real restraints on the kind of dogmatic intolerance confessional Presbyterians championed. Two of these distinctions concern the object of investigation. First, confessionalists did not believe that the creeds to which they and their clerical peers subscribed were a summary of all that the Bible taught, but they were under the impression that confessions and catechisms like those written by the Westminster divines came pretty close. In other words, confessionalists believed that the Bible's teaching was primarily concerned with the large themes of sin and grace, the meaning of history, and the nature of the Christian life; it was not a textbook of biology any more than it was a manual of psychology. Consequently, although confessionalism reserved for Scripture an authoritative status altogether above other legitimate authorities, it narrowed the scope of biblical instruction to the theological disciplines.

This recognition of the Bible's limited scope led to a second distinction that enabled confessionalists to adapt their intolerance to the new standards of modern learning. This one tapped differences between theology and other academic disciplines. To be sure, confessionalism ranked theological investigation as the queen of the sciences, but it also sequestered this scholarly monarch in her own department. Theologians could not, by virtue of their status, pontificate about any field of study. Their expertise was divine revelation, not the workings of the market, the dynamics of nation-states, or even the meaning of classical literature and history. In sum, intolerance in the field of theology did not give license to theological dogmatism in other fields of investigation.

A second set of distinctions stemming from the differences between special and general revelation involved the persons producing scholarship and their location. First, because of the Bible's narrow concern with salvation and Christian devotion, it was properly a book for the church, not for the secular academy. Indeed, the effort to teach the Bible outside a churchly setting inevitably compromised the book's message. The academic impulse in confessionalism, then, ran usually toward creating parochial institutions and structures that would reflect the Bible's specific purpose and restrict the teaching and study of Scripture to settings overseen by appropriate church authorities.[44] Second, such institutional differentiation between church and academy led to a further distinction between believers and nonbelievers. In effect, the limited nature of biblical teaching meant that only one area of study qualified as believing science or Christian scholarship—namely, the theological disciplines. Consequently, confessionalism reserved theology for the faithful since the insight necessary for understanding the Bible belonged to Christians. But as exclusive as this restriction might seem, it also implied an openness to the scholarship of non-Christians because the investigation of general revelation, whether the created order, human nature, or the organization of society, did not require Christian belief. Confessionalism, thus, offered the possibility of removing the antagonism between believers and nonbelievers in fields of study outside the theological disciplines because matters of faith were not explicitly at stake.

To be sure, confessionalists were not a cohort of intellectual doormats, offering no resistance to the findings of modern learning. But as Machen's own scholarship on the New Testament showed, confessionalism provided clear guidelines for determining when science was a real threat. Evolution, for instance, was not such a threat because, narrowly understood, the mechanics involved in the development of the human form did not necessarily require a denial of God's existence. Certain forms of evolutionary theory could be compatible with the Christian view of providence. But if evolution involved an understanding of the universe that denied the possibility of any and all miracles, then the challenge to Christianity was even greater than fundamentalists thought because it would require a repudiation of all the miraculous events accomplished by Christ. For this reason, Machen insisted that the separation of science and religion into two airtight spheres was not only impossible but scary. Such a compartmentalization undermined the historicity of Christ's death and resurrection, the very foundation of the church's hope for salvation. "At the very centre of the Bible," Machen insisted, "are assertions about events in the external world in Palestine in the first century of our era—events the narrating of which constitutes the 'gospel.'" Specifically, "the emergence or nonemergence of Jesus from the tomb—a question upon which the very existence of Christianity depends"—was a phenomenon subject to historical investigation and, therefore, a potential site of hostility between church and academy.[45] Still, Machen's reasoning here illustrates the nature of confessional intolerance; when things clearly revealed in the Bible were under attack, the church had no option but to oppose modern scholarship. But in areas less clear, especially if they had less to do with the salvation of souls, the church and its theologians possessed a measure of freedom.

Machen's position stands in significant contrast to that of his pietist Presbyterian peer, William Jennings Bryan. What is more, the latter's opposition to evolution demonstrates well how pietism, with its stress on conversion and personal and social morality, missed the subtleties fostered by creeds, thus resulting in a ham-fisted approach to intellectual matters. As Bryan's testimony at Dayton revealed, his grasp of Hebrew narratives in the Old Testament was less keen than his sense of democratic politics and the interests of ordinary citizens. Even so, his effort to show evolution's threat depended less on his interpretation of Genesis than that of recent events in Europe. Bryan blamed German aggression in World War I on evolutionary theory, thereby establishing a utilitarian criterion for evaluating new ideas. Evolution undermined Christianity, he believed, because it led inevitably to immorality. And because Bryan understood Christianity as primarily the basis for morality, both individual and national, in contrast to Machen's stress on human sin and divine grace, each man drew the lines of intolerance at different places. In fact, Bryan approached the intellectual controversies of the 1920s precisely in reverse fashion from Machen. While the pietist was flexible on the issue most pressing to the confessionalist—namely, Presbyterian theology—Bryan opposed a matter on which Machen believed Christians could legitimately disagree. This difference reflected the fundamental tension between pietism and confessionalism—whether Christianity is a parochial and churchly or a public and experiential religion.

Creeds and Anti-Intellectualism

According to observers and historians of the conflict, the Protestant controversies of the 1920s were generally a variation on the theme of the extent to which the Bible was authoritative. Accordingly, conservatives like Bryan and Machen, who believed the Bible literally revealed divine (and hence authoritative) truth, opposed liberal interpreters, such as Harry Emerson Fosdick, for whom the Bible was a collection of classic Jewish and Christian inspirational literature that figuratively revealed moral and religious truths. In the words of Garry Wills, the question that evangelicals asked at the beginning of the twentieth century when faced with interpretations of the Bible that accommodated Darwinism was this: "If the Bible is just another piece of profound literature, on which an Augustine can play brilliant variations, why is it any more 'revealed' than the writings of Tolstoy or of William Blake?" To be sure, the conflicts in denominations like the northern Presbyterian Church involved such doctrines as the virgin birth and the resurrection of Christ. But these lists of doctrinal affirmations are usually regarded, again in Wills's words, as "rallying points for those who still took the Bible as inspired in a special way."[46]

This way of reading the Presbyterian controversy, however, misses a significant event in the memory of confessional Presbyterians. In 1923, liberal ministers and seminary professors put together a statement that questioned what Wills called the "rallying points" of the fundamentalists. The *Auburn Affirmation* declared that the doctrines of biblical inspiration, the virgin birth, the vicarious atonement, the resurrection of Christ, and the persistence of miracles were capable of a variety of interpretations, and so the Presbyterian Church should not adopt any one particular understanding of each article of faith.[47] J. Gresham Machen responded with a "Counter-

Affirmation" that objected to the *Auburn Affirmation*, not because it denied a literal reading of the Bible but because it "really advocates the destruction of the confessional witness of the Church." For if the church allowed a variety of interpretations of the doctrines contained in the *Westminster Confession of Faith* the way the *Affirmation* advocated, it would be in exactly the same position "as to have no confession at all."[48] Machen's conservative colleagues advised him not to publish his response. They would later rue this decision as they saw signers of the *Auburn Affirmation* appointed to positions of power within the church.[49] The reason for their regret was that once the battle with liberalism became simply a debate over the meaning of the Bible, conservatives were reduced to the same status as liberals, with each side claiming its views were biblical. This is why for confessionalists like Machen, the conflict was really one over creeds, not the Bible. Confessions established the boundaries for permissible views in the church. Without them, any view could conceivably be permitted.[50]

Although Machen made the most plausible case to intellectuals of his day—Walter Lippmann called it the "best popular argument" by either side—the defense of creedalism continues to run against the grain of American notions of intellectual life.[51] Not only has theology as an academic enterprise failed to produce works of distinction, but the process of drawing lines between heresy and orthodoxy, implicit in the theological enterprise, does not encourage the kind of openness and curiosity necessary for serious reflection.[52] According to R. Laurence Moore, thanks to their defeats of the 1920s, theological conservatives suffered "a defensive reaction to intellectual insecurity. In America's best-known centers of learning, they were losing a battle of prestige."[53] More recently, Alan Wolfe has written of evangelical scholars that as long as they "insist on drawing up statements of faith that shut them off from genuine intellectual exchange, they will find it difficult to [develop] the kind of intellectually exciting institutions they hope to [have]."[54] American associations of creedalism with anti-intellectualism may help explain why Machen actually charged liberalism Protestantism with being dangerous to the life of the mind; his reason had to do with liberalism's stress on feelings in opposition to doctrine. One way to defend your own sins is to show that your foes' sins are even worse.

The common prejudice against creeds and dogma, however, misconstrues the character of statements of faith. To be sure, as Machen himself argued, creeds limit who may and who may not be a Presbyterian minister;

in this sense they are intolerant. But as someone like Alan Wolfe also admits, this is not necessarily more intolerant than a department of philosophy that refuses to hire Continental philosophers or a department of economics that subscribes to rational-choice theory.[55] Intellectual life and exclusion are not by nature opposites since the former often requires conclusions about the inferiority and superiority of specific arguments or ideas, and these conclusions are intolerant. What is more, creeds and confessions are forms of systematic thinking that have actually encouraged reflection in most places where they have been implemented. American higher education provides examples of Roman Catholic, Lutheran, and Reformed universities and colleges where the tradition of confessionalism provided a better climate for intellectual endeavor than evangelical Protestant schools that relied on a short list of doctrinal affirmations.[56] A further important point to recognize about confessions is how little they have to say about many of the topics and theories on which most intellectuals think and write. The *Westminster Confession of Faith* has a detailed affirmation of the doctrine of the Trinity but not much on the study of birds. In other words, as efforts to summarize the Bible and define a church's confession of faith, creeds narrow the scope of the Christian message, not necessarily the range of human inquiry.

However, the idea of confessionalism's anti-intellectual ways persists. And the persistence of this idea may well be further proof of pietism's triumph in American religion and culture. To be sure, the pietist insistence on the Bible as the only authority bears little resemblance to a secular academic's insistence on freedom of thought. Even so, the secularist and pietist share a similar distrust of clerics, the one's who write, enforce, and subscribe to creeds. In the case of academics, this suspicion is ironic since it ignores the formal similarities between the kind of study and peer review involved in the process of writing creeds for the church and the kind of procedures that scholars follow in learned societies. If the parallels between confessionalism and intellectual inquiry were more closely observed, then it might be easier to understand and appreciate Machen's reading of the Presbyterian controversy of the 1920s. The issue before Presbyterians was not the Bible as much as it was the creed. That way of putting the matter alienated both liberals, who regarded creeds as oppressive products of a backward Protestant age, and fundamentalists, for whom the Bible was the only reliable standard. Yet the confessionalist take on the Presbyterian controversy also managed to steer clear of the debate over Darwin, thereby demonstrating that creedalism may in fact be more intellectually supple than its detractors think.

The downside of confessions is that they may be wrong. That was certainly the perception of H. L. Mencken when contemplating the confession of Machen's Presbyterian Church. "Calvinism," according to the Baltimore journalist, "occupies a place, in my cabinet of private horrors, but little removed from that of cannibalism." Nevertheless, Mencken recognized Machen's scholarly attainments and did not regard them as anti-intellectual. This was not the case with Bryan. "Bryan," Mencken wrote,

> was a fundamentalist of the barnyard school. His theological ideas were those of a somewhat backward child of 8, and his defense of Holy Writ at Dayton during the Scopes Trial was so ignorant and stupid that it must have given Dr. Machen a great deal of pain. Dr. Machen himself was to Bryan as the Matterhorn is to a wart. His Biblical studies had been wide and deep, and he was familiar with the almost interminable literature of the subject. Moreover, he was an adept theologian, and had a wealth of professional knowledge to support his ideas. Bryan could only bawl.[57]

Of course, Mencken may have been wrong about Machen and his scholarship. Still, Mencken's ability to see a connection between Machen's Calvinist theology and his intellectual achievement, though by no means a proof, suggests that the kind of intolerance that confessions encourage is not the chief source of anti-intellectualism. In fact, if Mencken's comparison of the two Presbyterian conservatives, Bryan and Machen, is any indication, the pietist faith of the former may be the greatest danger to responsible reflection. If so, the irony is that the intolerance of confessionalism might have spared mainstream American Protestantism the embarrassments of both fundamentalism's simple-mindedness and liberalism's intellectual evasiveness.

Notes

1. Will quoted in R. Laurence Moore, *Religious Outsiders and the Making of Americans* (New York: Oxford University Press, 1986), 43.

2. On these developments, see Thomas G. Alexander, *Mormonism in Transition: A History of the Latter-Day Saints, 1890–1930* (Urbana: University of Illinois Press, 1986),

chap. I; and Robert T. Handy, *Undermined Establishment: Church-State Relations in America, 1880–1920* (Princeton, N.J.: Princeton University Press, 1991), 30–36.

3. *Proceedings before the Committee on Privileges and Elections of the United States Senate* . . . (Washington, D.C.: Government Printing Office, 1906), I: 25, 663.

4. On differences between opposition to a Catholic presidential candidate in 1928 and 1960, see Martin E. Marty, *Modern American Religion, Volume 2: The Noise of Conflict, 1919–1941* (Chicago: University of Chicago Press, 1991), 240–46; and Martin E. Marty, *Modern American Religion, Volume 3: Under God, Indivisible, 1941–1960* (Chicago: University of Chicago Press, 1996), 456–69.

5. For a good overview of the United States' presidency and American religion, see Richard V. Pierard and Robert D. Linder, *Civil Religion and the Presidency* (Grand Rapids, Mich.: Academic Books, 1988).

6. On Wilson's religiosity, see Arthur S. Link, "Woodrow Wilson and His Presbyterian Heritage," in *The Higher Realism of Woodrow Wilson and Other Essays* (Nashville, Tenn.: Vanderbilt University Press, 1971), 3–20; and John M. Mulder, *Woodrow Wilson: The Years of Preparation* (Princeton, N.J.: Princeton University Press, 1978), 33–38.

7. On Protestant developments in the 1960s, see Sydney E. Ahlstrom, "The Radical Turn in Theology and Ethics: Why It Occurred in the 1960s," *Annals of the American Academy of Political and Social Science* 387 (1970): 1–13.

8. See Edward J. Larson, *Summer for the Gods: The Scopes Trial and America's Continuing Debate over Science and Religion* (New York: Basic Books, 1997).

9. On Machen, see Ned Bernard Stonehouse, *J. Gresham Machen: A Biographical Memoir* (Grand Rapids: Mich.: Eerdmans, 1954); and D. G. Hart, *Defending the Faith: J. Gresham Machen and the Crisis of Conservative Protestantism in Modern America* (Baltimore: Johns Hopkins University Press, 1994).

10. Richard Hofstadter, *Anti-Intellectualism in American Life* (New York: Vintage, 1962), 123, n. 1.

11. J. Gresham Machen, *Christianity and Liberalism* (New York: Macmillan, 1923), 162, 164.

12. Machen, *Christianity and Liberalism*, 163.

13. Machen, *Christianity and Liberalism*, 169.

14. H. L. Mencken, "Doctor Fundamentalis," *Baltimore Evening Sun*, January 18, 1937.

15. Machen, *Christianity and Liberalism*, 22–23, quotation from 23.

16. Machen, *Christianity and Liberalism*, 165.

17. Machen, *Christianity and Liberalism*, 6.

18. Machen, *Christianity and Liberalism*, 167–68.

19. Machen, *Christianity and Liberalism*, 10.

20. Machen, *Christianity and Liberalism*, 14, n. 1.

21. Machen, *Christianity and Liberalism*, 15.

22. Machen, "The Necessity of the Christian School," in *Education, Christianity, and the State: Essays by J. Gresham Machen*, ed. John W. Robbins (Jefferson, Md.: Trinity Press, 1987), 81.

23. Machen, "Reforming the Government Schools," in Robbins, ed., *Education*, 63.

24. Machen, "The Necessity," 79.

25. Machen, "Reforming," 65.

26. Machen, "The Responsibility of the Church in the New Age," in *What Is Christianity?* ed. Ned Bernard Stonehouse (Grand Rapids, Mich.: Eerdmans, 1951), 286.

27. For Presbyterian reactions to Machen's arguments, see Hart, *Defending the Faith*, chap. 5.

28. Harry Emerson Fosdick, "Shall the Fundamentalists Win?" in *American Protestant Thought in the Liberal Era*, ed. William R. Hutchison (Lanham, Md.: University Press of America, 1968), 181, 182.

29. William P. Merrill, *Liberal Christianity* (New York: Macmillan, 1925), 74–76.

30. Gerald Birney Smith, "A Short and Easy Way of Dealing with Liberals," [review of *Christianity and Liberalism*] *Journal of Religion* 3 (1923): 542.

31. Henry F. May, *The Enlightenment in America* (New York: Oxford University Press, 1976), remains a reliable guide to the various shades of Enlightenment thought.

32. See Mark A. Noll, "The Rise and Long Life of the Protestant Enlightenment in America," in *Knowledge and Belief in American: Enlightenment Traditions and Modern Religious Thought*, ed. William M. Shea and Peter A. Huff (Cambridge: Cambridge University Press, 1995), chap. 3.

33. George M. Marsden, *The Soul of the American University: From Protestant Establishment to Established Nonbelief* (New York: Oxford University Press, 1994), 84.

34. Machen, *Christianity and Liberalism*, 149.

35. On these developments, see Hart, *Defending the Faith*, chap. 6.

36. William Childs Robinson, "Which Is the Rule of Faith and Life: The Word of God or the Voice of the Church?" *Christianity Today* 6 (June 1935): 6, pointed out the irony of the PCUSA's condemnation of Machen and its simultaneous siding with Karl Barth's resistance to the Nazi usurpation of the German churches' authority.

37. J. Gresham Machen, *What Is Faith?* (New York: Macmillan, 1925), 241–42.

38. See George M. Marsden, "The Collapse of American Evangelical Academia," in *Faith and Rationality: Reason and Belief in God*, ed. Alvin Plantinga and Nicholas Wolterstorff (Notre Dame, Ind.: University of Notre Dame Press, 1983),

219–64; Noll, "Rise and Long Life"; Theodore Dwight Bozeman, *Protestants in an Age of Science: The Baconian Ideal and Antebellum American Religious Thought* (Chapel Hill: University of North Carolina Press, 1977); and Herbert Hovenkamp, *Science and Religion in America, 1800–1860* (Philadelphia: University of Pennsylvania Press, 1978).

39. Machen, *What Is Faith?* 240.

40. See Hart, *Defending the Faith*, 84–85.

41. Machen, *What Is Faith?* 241.

42. For Warfield's views on science and evolution, see Benjamin B. Warfield, *Evolution, Scripture, and Science: Selected Writings*, ed. Mark A. Noll and David N. Livingstone (Grand Rapids, Mich.: Baker Book House, 2000).

43. On Machen's understanding of evolution, see *The Christian View of Man* (New York: Macmillan, 1937), 145.

44. On the implications of confessional Presbyterians for education, see Charles L. Glenn Jr., *The Myth of the Common School* (Amherst: University of Massachusetts Press, 1987), 182*ff.*, 213*ff.*

45. Machen, *What Is Faith?* 241.

46. Garry Wills, *Under God: Religion and American Politics* (New York: Simon & Schuster, 1990), 132, 133.

47. *An Affirmation Designed to Safeguard the Unity and Liberty of the Presbyterian Church in the United States of America* is reprinted in the first appendix of Edwin H. Rian, *The Presbyterian Conflict* (Grand Rapids, Mich.: Eerdmans, 1940), 291–97.

48. "Counter Affirmation," reprinted in Stonehouse, *J. Gresham Machen*, 367.

49. See Rian, *Presbyterian Conflict*, 59*ff.*

50. For debates about the place of confessions in the Presbyterian Controversy, see Bradley J. Longfield, *The Presbyterian Controversy: Fundamentalists, Modernists and Moderates* (New York: Oxford University Press, 1991); William J. Weston, *Presbyterian Pluralism: Competition in a Protestant House* (Knoxville: University of Tennessee Press, 1997); and Hart, *Defending the Faith: J. Gresham Machen and the Crisis of Conservative Protestantism in Modern America.* (Grand Rapids, Mich: Baker Books).

51. Walter Lippmann, *Preface to Morals* (New York: Macmillan, 1929), 32.

52. On the difficulties of theology in the twentieth century, see Bruce Kuklick, *Churchmen and Philosophers: From Jonathan Edwards to John Dewey* (New Haven, Conn.: Yale University Press, 1985), 221–29; and Van A. Harvey, "On the Intellectual Marginality of American Theology," in *Religion & Twentieth-Century American Intellectual Life*, ed. Michael J. Lacey (New York: Cambridge University Press, 1989), 172–92.

53. Moore, *Religious Outsiders*, 165.

54. Alan Wolfe, "The Opening of the Evangelical Mind," *The Atlantic Monthly* 286, no. 4 (October 2000): 76.

55. Wolfe, "The Opening of the Evangelical Mind," 74.

56. See James Tunstead Burtchaell, *The Dying of the Light: The Disengagement of Colleges and Universities from Their Christian Churches* (Grand Rapids, Mich.: Eerdmans, 1998), for a comparison between confessional Protestant and evangelical educational institutions.

57. H. L. Mencken, "Dr. Fundamentalis," *Baltimore Evening Sun* (January 18, 1937).

The Sectarianism of Reformed Polity   5

hen some Christians refuse to join other Christians in professing allegiance to their Lord, accusations of bad form usually follow. A good illustration of this principle was the *Christian Century*'s reaction to the formation in 1942 of the National Association of Evangelicals (NAE). The headline to the editorial read: "Sectarianism Receives New Lease on Life." The single-paragraph explanation that followed accused the new effort for interdenominational cooperation among "representatives of sects which hitherto have refused to cooperate with their fellow Protestants on anything" of "the worst form of atomistic sectarianism." The one element that united "these self-styled 'Evangelicals'" was opposition to the Federal Council of Churches (FCC). But their refusal to join with the genuine embodiment of Protestant ecumenism—that is, the Federal Council—made these conservatives guilty of the perennial scandal of Protestant Christianity—namely, the inability to unite. Although it had been almost two decades since the most acrimonious episodes of the fundamentalist controversy, the *Century*'s editorial proved that those old wounds had still not healed.[1]

Aside from the irony of the leading voice of liberal Protestantism sounding decidedly illiberal, the *Century*'s reaction to the NAE was also puzzling because the new evangelical organization was designed to overcome the perception that conservative Protestants were inherently sectarian. Yet, from the perspective of the Protestant mainline, which in the *Century*'s case was situated in Chicago's Loop (downtown), the new evangelical attempt at ecumenism was in fact a charade. In another editorial, written five years later, the *Century* blasted the NAE's claim of offering a "valid alternative" to the FCC. The reasons were obvious. The FCC was forty years old; the NAE was young and unproven. The FCC consisted of official representatives from twenty-five "national denominations," the membership of which totaled over 27,000,000; the NAE was a "loose association" that represented a "few small fundamentalist sects" along with some local churches, youth groups, radio evangelists, and independent missionary societies. The FCC made the confession of Christ as Lord the sole criteria for membership; the NAE had a "detailed creedal statement. The FCC was recognized as the "voice through which the priceless heritage which comes to Protestantism through the Reformation speaks to America"; the NAE "is not and can never become so recognized."[2]

To some churches, however, the inferiority of the NAE was not so obvious. One of the reasons for the *Century's* cheerleading in 1948 for mainstream Protestantism's ecumenical option was that three denominations—the Reformed Church in America, the United Presbyterian Church, and the Presbyterian Church in the United States (southern)—were reevaluating their membership in the FCC while also considering the NAE as an alternative. It is not clear whether the latter association looked so promising or the former was growing more liberal in the eyes of these respective church leaders. But the formation of the NAE, and its efforts to duplicate the services provided by the FCC, meant that churches had a choice in demonstrating their commitment to Christian unity. Either they could join the upstart NAE, which was decidedly conservative but not in a fundamentalist mean-spirited way, or they could join forces with the considerable resources of America's largest denominations in the FCC. Although a technicality allowed for membership in each ecumenical body, chances were that any denomination that identified with mainline Protestantism would never consider the NAE or vice versa. In a word, the existence of interdenominational Protestant organizations, one broad in the American Protestant sense of ecumenical and the other broad in a revivalistic way of interchurch cooperation, meant that the effort to demonstrate the unity of the body of Christ had taken a sectarian turn; ironically, Protestant unity resulted in division.

Confessional Protestant communions outside the Anglo-American Protestant mainstream and looking for some interdenominational outlet were hard-pressed to know whether to choose the liberal FCC or the evangelical NAE, since these appeared to be the only ecumenical options in the United States. The experience of the Christian Reformed Church (CRC) during the first half of the twentieth century only proves this point. An ethnic communion made up primarily of Dutch Reformed immigrants to the United States and Canada, from the latter third of the nineteenth century down to the middle of the twentieth, the CRC faced the dilemma common to many denominations with close and strong ties to the old world when considering friends and allies in the wider world of American Protestantism. Neither the mainstream Protestant organization nor evangelical cooperative endeavors were adequate for churches that tried to maintain historic Protestant forms of ecclesiology and piety. The former was theologically lax, while the latter were often doctrinally reductionistic and devotionally indecent. Consequently, the CRC joined each ecumenical body, first the Federal Council during World War I for the sake of its ministers serving as chaplains, and then roughly two decades later the NAE in order to be a part of conservative Protestant links to federal agencies that regulated military chaplains and religious broadcasting. In each case, however, the CRC's ecumenical partnering was short-lived because confessional Protestantism was a poor fit with the dominant forms of American Protestantism.

Yet as much as the CRC's ecumenical relations during the middle decades of the twentieth century illustrate the way that confessional Protestantism eludes the categories supplied by evangelical and mainstream Protestants, more important, it reveals the shaky foundation on which Protestant ecumenism in the United States has rested. As CRC leaders and officials discovered, the prevailing orientation of both evangelical and mainstream Protestant ecumenism was more national and political than it was churchly and spiritual. To be sure, the need for denominations to coordinate their agencies and religious activities with a federal government that was growing in its regulatory powers made very attractive the efficiency provided by the offices of one interdenominational association, such as the FCC or the NAE. Still, the social agenda of both bodies tapped the reform heritage of pietistic Protestantism, a legacy that often exchanged the admirable desire for the unity of Christ's followers into the less lofty concern to preserve the United States' Anglo-American Protestant culture. Confessional Protestants such as the Dutch Reformed turned out to be especially alert to the divisiveness of mainstream Protestant ecumenism thanks not only to their own ethnic identity but also to their understanding of the church. As such, the better ecumenical alternative for the CRC were Reformed Protestants from around the world who fixed the boundaries for church unity more in religious categories than national interest. The CRC thus proves that although faith is never as unifying a force as many American Protestants think, its inherent divisiveness, once stripped of political interest, is never as threatening as the foes of sectarianism allege.

When Ecumenism Is No Virtue

According to historian Robert A. Schneider, the Protestant ecumenical movement in the United States has not received the historical scrutiny it deserves.[3] In fact, the best accounts of interdenominational cooperation and church union efforts have come most often from those who participated in them. Here the writings of Samuel McCrae Cavert, general secretary of the National Council of Churches, stand out as an example of cheerleading masquerading as history. Of his many books, Cavert's studies of the twentieth-century ecumenical movement in the United States are the most complete accounts of Protestant consolidation and church unity. The first, *The American Churches in the Ecumenical Movement: 1900–1968* (1968), is a survey of denominational and social developments that helped the churches "move forward in overcoming the weaknesses of their divided state."[4] The second book, *Church Cooperation and Unity in America, A Historical Review: 1900–1970* (1970), demonstrated Cavert's concern to give a full account of the efforts in which he played a prominent role, concentrating on fifteen key areas of interdenominational cooperation from evangelism to race relations. Through it all, Cavert proved to be more than a historian with decided rooting interests but also something of a religious zealot who could see the guidance of the Holy Spirit in the Protestant pilgrimage "toward a greater unity."[5]

Because Protestant ecumenism has received so little attention from academics, assessing the attitude of religious historians toward church union is a difficult prospect. Still, a reasonable expectation would be for the majority of scholars to regard interdenominational cooperation as a desirable end, since ecumenism reflects a process that breaks down religious antagonisms that have throughout history contributed to social division. In other words, sectarianism, ecumenism's opposite, is a hard position with which to sympathize because of the way it apparently takes neighbors who inhabit the same community during the week and balkanizes them into competing religious camps on the one day set aside for worship. The view of Martin E. Marty may not be representative but does confirm the suspicion about academics' preference for expressions of unity as opposed to those sanctioning division or separation. In a 1981 book, *The Public Church*, on communions "especially sensitive to the . . . public order that surrounds and includes people of faith," Marty tipped his hand, demonstrating strong support for Christian churches that recognized "measures of truth and light" in non-Christian faiths.[6] His reasons for advocating the "public church" were not entirely negative. It had become clear to Marty, for instance, "that billions of non-Christians are not going to disappear or be converted," thus making it necessary to find common ground among churches and religions in "responses to the sacred and the service of humanity." Still, just as important to Marty's argument were recent tendencies among conservative believers that encouraged totalism, tribalism, and privatism.[7] These tribalist religions tended to "huddle together, worship their local deities, and display a kind of solipsism in which they talk in a language they alone can understand because it takes rise from thoughts that cannot belong to any other group than theirs." In a word, believers who cut themselves off from the polis displayed an absence of those virtues that made "interaction, minimal consensus, a public philosophy, or a republic possible."[8]

Fifteen years later when Marty wrote the third volume in his chronicle of twentieth-century American religion, however, he presented plenty of evidence for questioning the sort of public religion that had fueled twentieth-century Protestant ecumenical energies even if his personal convictions about the need for interreligious and interdenominational cooperation had remained the same. The chapter on the 1951 formation of the National Council of Churches (NCC), the successor to the Federal Council of Churches, until then mainstream American Protestantism's chief ecumenical outlet, showed just how public, and therefore political, Protestant cooperation could be. At the first meeting of its board, the council declared that "the churches have special responsibility and a special contribution to make to the world and to the nation in its relations with other nations." It added that the primary concerns of the churches were with "peace, freedom, and justice for all peoples," language that sounded more like a pronouncement from the United Nations than an ecclesiastical body whose mission might reasonably be defined by the language of sin and grace.[9]

Protestant critics of the NCC were no less prone to resort to politics, such as when the evangelical Presbyterian J. Howard Pew chided the politically liberal efforts of council leaders for not being sufficiently supportive of big business or adequately alarmed about communism.[10] Even so, despite opposition to the council from political conservatives, the fusion of national and religious ideals were clearly evident in the remarks of the NCC's first president, Henry Knox Sherrill. According to Marty, Sherrill made clear the NCC's purposes: it "marks a new and great determination that the American way will be increasingly the Christian way, for such is our heritage. . . . Together the Churches can move forward to the goal—a Christian America in a Christian world."[11] The mainline Protestants who championed Christian unity and the churches' responsibility to the needs of the nation and the world were clearly not guilty of the sort of tribalism that withdrew from public life in pursuit of a religiously homogenous ghetto. Still, a Protestant cosmopolitanism that assumed churches in the United States had the world's best interests at heart could appear to be a bit tribal when American Protestant ideals had a direct influence on the policies of one of the world's mightiest and wealthiest governments.

The NCC's political agenda, as high-minded as it might have been, was not an aberration but in fact reflected aptly seventy-five years of developments among the mainstream American Protestant denominations who favored interdenominational cooperation and church union. In fact, the subordination of theological, liturgical, and ecclesiastical concerns to questions of national import had typified American Protestant ecumenism since its origins just after the Civil War when Protestants on both sides of the Mason-Dixon Line discovered that their common endeavors during war could provide a basis for denominational cooperation during a time of peace. One early example of the way Protestants applied the experience of war was the reunion of the northern Old School and New School branches of the Presbyterian Church in the United States of America (PCUSA). In 1837 and 1838, Presbyterians had divided over the revivalist theology of Charles Grandison Finney, cooperation with Congregationalists in home missions, and the nature of church power in parachurch associations. Over the course of these struggles, Old School Presbyterians gained the reputation for being fastidious in matters of doctrine and church polity. Nevertheless, such Presbyterian particulars looked decidedly less important in the wake of civil war and northern Presbyterian support for union. Indeed, pro-union sentiments were crucial pieces in the arguments for reuniting Old and New School Presbyterians. As George M. Marsden put it, "Disputes over moral depravity, limited atonement, and mediate imputation lost much of their urgency in the midst of national crisis."[12]

The reunion of Old and New School Presbyterians was part of a flurry of ecumenical activities that could easily anchor the narrative of American Protestantism between 1865 and 1930, as much as the disputes over Darwinism, biblical criticism, and the Social Gospel that have usually dominated the historiography. Again, to use the Presbyterians as but one example, the trend of late nineteenth- and early twentieth-century developments was as much, if not more, toward denominational mergers as it was a time when conservatives and liberals dug trenches for ecclesiastical combat. In 1877, Presbyterians formed the Presbyterian Alliance, an agency founded to bring the various denominations into areas of common endeavor. That same year, Presbyterian ecumenists tried to do for international heirs of John Calvin what the Presbyterian Alliance had done for American Presbyterians with the forming of the World Alliance of Reformed Churches. Throughout the 1890s, while liberals and conservatives squabbled over biblical infallibility, Presbyterians also debated whether or not to revise the *Westminster Confession of Faith*, a process finally accomplished in 1903, and which paved the way for the 1906 merger of the northern Presbyterian Church (PCUSA) and the Cumberland Presbyterian Church. Instead of regarding the six decades of Protestant history before the Scopes trial as mainly the preliminary rounds in a boxing match between modernists and fundamentalists, just as plausible, if the Presbyterian experience is at all representative, is to view the antagonism between liberals and conservatives as the opening act before the main event of church union.[13]

One reason for thinking Presbyterians were representative of ecumenical trends among American Protestants is the leadership they provided to a number of key interdenominational efforts. The first of these, and perhaps the most important for the period between the Civil War and World War II, was the formation in 1873 of the American Branch of the Evangelical Alliance.[14] Originally founded in 1846 in London, the Evangelical Alliance's purpose was to bring "individual Christians into closer fellowship and cooperation on the basis of the spiritual union which already exists in the vital relation of Christ to the members of his body."[15] Despite such a seemingly innocuous intent, American involvement in the Alliance would have to wait almost three decades. When American clerics did decide to join with the eastern branch of Anglo-American Protestantism, they drew explicitly on nationalistic sentiments generated by the Civil War. According to historian Philip D. Jordan, many Protestants "assumed that America's Christian civilization rested on an evangelical foundation whose pillars were religious and civil liberty."[16] The start of the Evangelical Alliance in the United States and the possibility for interdenominational cooperation it provided, then, was not as much an occasion of spiritual insight into the nature of Christianity or the mission of the church as it was a response of mainstream Protestants to the perils confronting their land.[17]

The specific cultural trends that alarmed Protestant leaders after the Civil War were fairly standard when judged by the perspective of antebellum evangelical reform.[18] Violation of the Sabbath, intemperate consumption of alcoholic beverages, and assaults on the stability of the Christian home were some of the reasons prompting Protestants to join forces under the auspices of the Evangelical Alliance. Protestant desires for what James McCosh called "the moral improvement of mankind" only intensified in the decades after the Civil War as large-scale industrial development and the cheap labor such industry required made urban centers appear to be in even greater need of Christianity's civilizing influences than they had been prior to the war. Furthermore, the Roman Catholic identity of many new immigrants, combined with papal pronouncements against democracy and religious liberty in the *Syllabus of Errors* (1864), fueled American Protestant anti-Catholicism. The papacy's assertion of infallibility along with the unity of the Catholic Church on display during First Vatican Council (1870) reminded American Protestants of their fractured state and the need for maintaining a united front against what they regarded as "the Man of Sin."[19] In sum, the dangers that materialism, skepticism, infidelity, and Catholicism posed to Christian civilization in the United States persuaded Protestants to work toward church unity of some kind.[20]

Leavening the threats to Protestant America was the yeast of eschatological excitement. Anglo-American Protestants in the form of Whig political thought had long connected Christian teachings about liberty of conscience and worship with American principles of civil liberty. But after the Civil War, northern Protestants begged even larger questions about the place of the Union in divine providence.[21] Unlike Europe, where various forms of tyranny still existed, American Protestants believed that the United States embodied the best hope for true religion because of the nation's democratic and republican foundations. For this reason the eradication of slavery during the Civil War loomed especially large in the minds of Protestants advocating the Evangelical Alliance. The United States' stand for orthodoxy and liberty had obviously been compromised by the South's practice of slavery. But with its eradication, according to General Assembly of New School Presbyterians, "not only has our American Christianity been vindicated, our faith and order maintained intact, and our Christian benevolence enhanced," but the Union's victory demonstrated the superiority of evangelical Protestantism and the American form of government.[22] Even the Scotsman James McCosh, newly inaugurated as president of the College of New Jersey, read postbellum America and its place in the world order in providential terms. The United States was "the land of the future" because evangelical principles were thoroughly incorporated in the life and spirit of the country. The nation embodied for McCosh precisely what the Evangelical Alliance was trying to accomplish—namely, a pervasive unity of evangelical spirit. For that reason McCosh urged fellow Americans to join the alliance to "combine the scattered energies of Christendom all over the world."[23]

Consequently, the Evangelical Alliance reflected Anglo-American Protestant attitudes toward the mission of the church as much as it stimulated a greater awareness of the common culture that Protestants shared and wanted to preserve. Protestant ecumenism, in effect, functioned as a kind of civil religion in which theological concerns, liturgical traditions, or ecclesiastical procedures took a back seat to the apparently more important task of maintaining and promoting Christian (read: Protestant) civilization in the United States. This conclusion is well illustrated in the history of America's ecumenical movement provided by Samuel McCrae Cavert. When he wrote his two volumes in the late 1960s, the anti-American attitude of the National Council of Churches in the last stages of the Cold War had yet to gain ascendancy.[24] So Cavert's decision to organize his narrative around the themes of Americanization and cultural assimilation was more understandable then it would be a decade later. Nevertheless, when he began *The American Churches in the Ecumenical Movement* with the lament that the Protestant churches lacked the "solid political unity" of the nation, some readers could well have questioned whether American Protestant ecumenism was more a reflection of political interest than one of moral zeal or religious devotion. Cavert went on to compare the fractured state of the Protestant denominations to the divisiveness that race, ethnicity, and class bred. "Instead of being a force for understanding and reconciliation" the churches "seemed to be adding one more fragmenting factor" to the life of the nation. In other words, the church's mission was primarily social and temporal, not spiritual and eternal.[25]

Cavert inherited these views from the pietist Protestant tradition that sought to make faith relevant to everyday realities, especially the pressing ones that governed the life of the nation. In turn, that tradition was largely responsible for allowing Protestants of diverse theological, liturgical, and ecclesiastical positions to join together formally in the late nineteenth century around the apparently pious aim of following Jesus Christ's command for his followers to be one. That unity was especially important at a time when American society appeared to be veering away from Christian control, thus making it easier for Protestants to put aside differences over religious teachings and practices that had historically distinguished the denominations and then rally to the nation and its culture as an area of common endeavor and means for preserving Protestant hegemony. Indeed, a telling omission in the histories of and plans for Protestant ecumenical efforts is any systematic treatment of the doctrine of the church and the nature of Christian unity. Instead, the ecumenical movement was premised on vague notions about the unity of those who believed in Christ, closely linked to a recognition of the social good that could be accomplished by Protestant cooperation.[26]

Protestant ecumenism was a form of social gospel, not in the technical sense but in the sense that its primary orientation was civil. What is more, the social function of religion was an outlook that united both would-be liberals and conservatives, even though the former usually received credit for the Social Gospel in its precise meaning. Of course, evangelical Protestants who may have feared the corrosive effects of Darwinism or biblical criticism continued to insist on the necessity of individual conversion while their liberal peers talked more and more about the need for societal regeneration. Even so, in the pietist version of Protestantism, the salvation of individuals was a sure route to moral improvement and, thus, a righteous society through the conversion of many. More important, the areas on which Protestants agreed to cooperate overwhelmingly concerned matters of public morality. Observance of the Sabbath, consumption of alcohol, the plight of the working class, and the dangers of infidelity, materialism, and Roman Catholicism were all issues that had a direct bearing on public life and became the criteria for judging whether the nation was Christian. In other words, public morality and civic righteousness pushed aside word and sacrament. According to Richard W. Reifsnyder, "practical results tended to become the church's measuring stick rather than preservation of precise doctrinal standards."[27] The culmination of this outlook was the founding of the Federal Council of Churches in 1908, an agency that grew from the seeds sown by the Evangelical Alliance and whose first substantial piece of business was a plan for alleviating the antagonism between labor and capital.[28] That fundamentalists did not oppose the council but waited almost fifteen years to contest instead liberal conceptions of the beginning and end of human history reveals as much about so-called conservative Protestant views of the ecumenical movement as it does about the politicization of mainstream American Protestantism through the apparently innocuous goal of getting along.

The Isolation of Reformed Confessionalism

As natural an outlet as the ecumenical movement looked to older Presbyterian and Reformed denominations in the United States, ethnic communions with strong ties to the Old World often found the norms of American Protestant fellowship puzzling. The origins of the Christian Reformed Church illustrate well this point. Nineteenth-century Dutch Calvinist immigrants to the United States originally looked for spiritual sustenance in the Reformed Church in America (RCA), the daughter of Reformed churches in the Netherlands with roots in the seventeenth-century Dutch exploration of the New World.[29] But the new Dutch arrivals found the older Dutch-American denomination to have assimilated not only the English language (quite understandably) but also some of the leniency of Anglo-American Protestantism. The RCA supported public instead of parochial schools, sang the hymns of revivals in worship rather than the psalms of the Old Testament, and neglected the catechetical training of children. Consequently, in 1857, many of the recent Dutch Calvinist immigrants, in a move comparable to the Lutheran Church–Missouri

Synod, which resisted the Americanizing ways of older Lutheran bodies in the United States, formed the CRC as an effort to preserve confessional Reformed ways from the corruptions of American Protestantism. The tension between Dutch Calvinism and American Protestantism would continue to mark the CRC's development.[30]

The Dutch Calvinist sense of being at odds with American norms was heightened as much by theology as ethnicity. According to the editor of *De Gereformeerde Amerikaan*, the denomination's first journal of record, "We are not and will not be a pretty piece of paper upon which America can write whatever it pleases."[31] In other words, acculturation, which CRC leaders desired and knew to be inevitable was not going to be a "one-way street." Instead, the goal of making a home in the United States was to reassert "old values in a new context."[32] Consequently, Dutch Calvinist theologians took aim at the nation's "one-sided materialism, subjectivism, and pragmatism."[33] Antimaterialism became an especially prominent theme among the CRC during the first decades of the twentieth century. As *De Gereformeerde Amerikaan* again had it, "American life today is characterized by a rush after material things. People want gold. They want goods. They want pleasure. . . . For many of our nation the dollar is the idol before which they bow."[34] The difficulties posed by the culture of the United States, even if it may not have been all that different from developments in the old world, added resolution to the Dutch Calvinist desire to remain distinct. A 1907 editorial about the CRC's 1857 founding summarized this resolve well when it asserted:

> Christian isolation therefore was a duty, isolation to develop ourselves quietly and without undue haste, to become firmly settled as to our principles . . . until we are prepared enough, strong enough, to cast us with body and soul and all our precious Calvinism as a world-and-life view as well as a religious system, into the arena of American religious and political and social life.[35]

As such, the Dutch-Americans who worshiped in CRC congregations, like so many other immigrant groups, created a host of separate ethnically homogenous institutions—financial, political, educational, welfare, medical—to preserve cultural identity and resist absorption into the American melting pot.

Such segregation was necessary if Dutch Calvinists were to retain their religious beliefs and practices. Here the experience of the CRC revealed that genuine differences existed among Protestants that ecumenism could not hide. And these significant variations could not be attributed simply to differences between Old World backwardness and provincialism compared to the New World's progressive and cosmopolitan ways. Instead, CRC observers of American Protestantism were quick to spot divergent brands of devotion, religious styles that separated pietistic from confessional Protestants. On the one hand, Dutch Calvinists were flummoxed by American Protestantism's general disregard for theology. As one CRC historian summarized a flurry of editorials in *De Gereformeerde Amerikaan*, American churches had no "real love for theory, for dogmatic truth and for clarity of principle." Instead, "everything was judged by its fruits or results," thus making American Protestantism "more broad than deep." Genuine faith had more to do with Christian living, CRC spokesmen complained, than with doctrinal knowledge, with "feelings rather than with understanding."[36] On the other hand, American Protestant liturgical practices veered sharply from those of the Reformed. Again condensing the editorials of another Dutch-language journal, Henry Zwaanstra writes that CRC leaders found American Protestant worship superficial because it replaced psalms with hymns, exchanged "solemn choral singing with a fast, happy manner of singing," shortened sermons, substituted choir singing for congregational song, neglected catechetical preaching, and was oriented by an "indiscriminate looking for something new."[37]

The word that Dutch Calvinists used to describe the American form of Protestantism was "Methodism," a term not reserved simply for those in Methodist denominations but applied to those communions shaped by the spirit of revivalism (i.e., evangelical Protestantism).[38] Again, CRC critics of American Protestantism faulted Methodism in this generic sense for the American sins of activism and success. Evangelicalism sacrificed principle (read: doctrine) for application (read: self-interest). This was especially apparent in the way that American Protestantism stressed conversion as the only way of becoming a Christian. This emphasis was "forced" and "unnatural" because it located the source of authentic faith in human will rather than divine election. Furthermore, the tradition of revivalism "reduced the church to a mission society," constantly seeking converts but neglecting the edification and spiritual maturity of the faithful. As one CRC churchman observed about Billy Sunday during his 1915 trek through Michigan, the evangelist may have been a good "icebreaker" in the United

States' Arctic of "indifferentism and materialism," but his lack of dignity "made Christianity a laughingstock," his message was "superficial," and his methods were "individualistic." In short, Sunday was "good for America but bad for Christianity."[39]

To be sure, not all Dutch Calvinist leaders were wary of American religious and cultural ideals. According to James D. Bratt, by the early twentieth century, three groups of Dutch Reformed outlook had emerged within the CRC, one of which was decidedly more positive about American institutions. The strength of what Bratt calls these "optimistic" and "outgoing Calvinists" may help to explain the CRC's 1918 decision to join the Federal Council of Churches.[40] On one level this determination was little more than the denomination's concern for its soldiers serving in World War I. In the words of Henry Zwaanstra, joining the FCC "did not arise out of a deepening ecumenical consciousness or a clearer understanding of the implications of the catholicity of the church."[41] The U.S. government had ruled that its chaplains would only come from denominations in the FCC, thus, making membership in the ecumenical body a necessity for any church hoping to place its military chaplains. On another level the CRC's membership in the FCC did reveal a degree of assimilation that would have been foreign to an earlier generation of Dutch-American Calvinists. During its brief time in the Federal Council, the CRC underwent a significant controversy over the doctrine of common grace that led in 1924 to the beginning of another Dutch Reformed denomination, the Protestant Reformed Church. Although the terms of the debate were far removed from those separating the likes of William Jennings Bryan and Harry Emerson Fosdick, some CRC spokesmen could not resist charging those with whom they disagreed as liberals, thus demonstrating that the terms and symbols of mainstream Protestantism were trickling down to the provinces.[42]

Twenty years later, when the CRC once again considered its ecumenical relations to other Protestants in the United States, the denomination showed that it no longer shared the resolve of first generation leaders to remain in isolation from the Anglo-American gentiles. The issue this time was membership in the newly founded National Association of Evangelicals and the lure that drew the CRC in initially was world war and the need again to place ministers in the American military chaplaincy. Part of the rationale for the NAE was to represent conservative churches that were not in the FCC to the federal government in such endeavors as providing military chaplains, securing visas for foreign missionaries, and coordinating religious broadcasts on the nationally syndicated networks. But just as important, even though the NAE's leaders tried to distance themselves from fundamentalism's notorious belligerence, was the perception that the FCC was dominated by theological liberalism, thus necessitating an alternative and orthodox Protestant association.[43]

In 1943, the CRC joined the NAE, partly owing to the efforts of Clarence Bouma, a professor at Calvin Theological Seminary and editor of *The Calvin Forum*, who participated in the discussions and plans that led to the Association's existence. By 1951, however, the CRC withdrew its membership, primarily because of doubts about the purpose and identity of the NAE. The debates that took place during those eight years revealed a Dutch-American denomination moving closer to the dominant expressions of Anglo-American piety but still sufficiently confessional to prevent assimilation.[44]

Little fanfare accompanied the CRC's decision to join the evangelical organization. In 1942, the churches in Muskegon, Michigan, had requested the denomination to inquire about starting a council of American Protestant denominations committed to the cause of orthodoxy. That same year, a California CRC ministers' conference petitioned the denomination to send a representative to meetings where the NAE was being organized. In 1943, the synod not only complied with this request but sent along three observers who were promptly informed at the NAE's preliminary meetings that for these observers and representatives to participate in the discussions they would need to affirm the organization's seven-point doctrinal statement and become "delegates." Although the CRC's observers were assured that their individual actions would not bind their denomination, the CRC in effect became a member of the NAE even before it voted on the matter in a deliberative assembly.[45]

For the next eight years, delegates to the synod regularly heard reports about NAE affairs. And for the first four years, the CRC appeared to be content with the evangelical alternative to the FCC. Reports to the synod repeatedly lauded the NAE's short statement of faith—the inspiration of the Bible, the Trinity, the deity and miracles of Christ, regeneration by the Holy Spirit, godly living, the final resurrection, and the spiritual unity of Christians—as "an excellent doctrinal basis" that left "little to be desired."[46] CRC delegates to the NAE also reported proudly back to the synod about the aggressively anti-modernist posture of the evangelical organization. In fact, the militant theological conservatism of the association emerged as one of the primary reasons early on for the CRC's membership. As the 1945 report to the synod put it, the FCC was "wholly controlled by the Liberals and Moderns," who appeared "on the surface to be declaring the Gospel of our Lord, thus by treacherous deceit posing to the unwary as genuine Christianity." Dissatisfaction with the FCC led to the founding of an alternative and orthodox Protestant organization that would serve as a "clearing-house for Evangelical interests" and "safeguard the privileges and rights of Evangelical Protestants in America."[47] The CRC's initial endorsement of evangelical anti-modernism came through loud and clear when its 1945 delegates to the NAE added that this evangelical body "went forward with undaunted courage, Holy Spirit-generated energy, with heaven-lit vision and a holy passion for the gospel as once for all revealed." [48] One reason for CRC excitement about the initial work of the NAE was a shared concern for Western civilization and the need for American society to recover its religious moorings. This kind of cultural analysis had significant appeal to Dutch Calvinists who were heavily schooled in Abraham Kuyper's thought and its insistence upon the religious basis of politics, art, education, and the like. Indeed, the idea of joining forces with other conservative Protestants as a cultural/political bloc bore some resemblance to the kind of coalition building that Kuyper himself had performed as a politician and prime minister of the Netherlands.[49]

To be sure, the NAE was not a full-blown political lobby, but it did sponsor a series of commissions in specific areas designed to make conservative Protestantism a player alongside the Protestant mainstream and Roman Catholicism.[50] For instance, the commissions on missions, radio, and military chaplains coordinated the work of the churches and other members with the proper authorities in Washington, thus ensuring evangelical voices in these arenas. The commissions on education and church schools provided evangelical educators with a forum to confer, while also sparking learning as a means to withstand the forces of secularism and liberalism. CRC delegates were especially interested in Christian schools and hoped they could wean their evangelical peers away from an unwholesome dependence on public schools. "We as a Reformed people with our heritage and our splendid Christian school system have here a grand contribution to make to the movement and a solemn duty to discharge."[51] Finally, the NAE's commission on war relief to Europe and Asia allowed the CRC a more efficient way to send its designated aid to Holland, while the commission on industrial chaplains facilitated the training of laymen to perform religious services in factories and other workplaces.[52]

In 1947, the wheels began to wobble on the CRC's train of support for the NAE. As early as 1943, one CRC minister from New Jersey, Nicholas J. Monsma, had raised questions about the propriety of the NAE carrying out functions that properly belonged to the institutional church (i.e., preaching and evangelism). He also criticized the association's non-Calvinistic theology; as a body primarily composed of Arminian denominations, the NAE was actually guilty of a doctrinal position that Monsma believed to be a "half-way house to Modernism."[53] Despite Monsma's fears, the NAE received overwhelmingly favorable press in the CRC's official publication, *The Banner*, and in other mainstream CRC publications such as *The Calvin Forum*. These positive reports, however, could not hide Dutch Calvinist discontent which formally surfaced in the 1947 delegates' reports to the synod. So great was the concern that the synod during the remaining years of the CRC's membership in the NAE received majority and minority reports from those representing the denomination to the evangelical body. In 1947 and again the following year, the majority reports sounded familiar themes about coalition building, the opportunity for the Reformed to teach the evangelicals, and the religious and cultural crisis of the hour. But the minority reports made forceful critiques that began to make an impression on CRC leaders and officers.

The 1947 minority report picked up on themes outlined by Monsma four years earlier, while the 1948 minority report developed these themes' implications. First, the NAE was too Arminian not simply to be unsuitable to the CRC but also to do harm to the denomination. Evangelically sponsored interdenominational programs were "bound to have a detrimental influence on our distinctiveness"; "they will help to break down precious walls of doctrinal distinctiveness raised up by our fathers at Dort, walls which should stand and be strengthened." Second, the NAE did perform "a certain amount of practical Gospel work" that was reserved for the church and its officers.[54]

In 1948, delegates inferred from these complaints that the NAE was actually a fundamentalist organization with which the CRC should have nothing to do. According to Peter H. Eldersveld, the voice of the CRC's radio broadcast *The Back to God Hour* who wrote a separate minority report, "the NAE is not merely Arminian, but definitely and predominantly

Fundamentalist in character. The atmosphere of its conventions is indicative of the spirit of these independent, irregular, and heterogeneous elements." Of course, Eldersveld was using fundamentalism as an epithet. But in his mind it also had a precise and ironic meaning:

> As to a united front with others who hold the so-called "fundamentals" of the faith with us, it should be pointed out that such a formal united front before the world becomes exceedingly questionable for Calvinists when those with whom we are joined deny the real fundamentals of the Faith, such as: Total Depravity, Unconditional Election, Limited Atonement, Irresistible Grace, and the Perseverance of the Saints. . . . It is ironical, to say the least, that those who deny these Fundamentals should be called Fundamentalists! What happens to our Reformed witness in the world when, by a formal and official representation, we are silent on these salient points of which our Faith is constructed? Are we then not denying them publicly by such an organizational union which silences them?

Eldersveld also introduced into the debate an older Dutch Reformed idea, that of isolation from the American Protestant mainstream, and recommended that only through isolation could the CRC remain theologically strong, even "the strongest church in all of orthodox Protestantism."[55]

Perhaps Eldersveld's popularity as the radio voice of the denomination gave his report added weight, but whatever the reason, by the 1949 meeting of the synod his argument had carried the day, at least by moving opposition to membership in the CRC from a minority to a majority position among the denomination's delegates to the NAE. The 1949 report to the CRC from four of the six delegates to the NAE ended up borrowing heavily from the terms Eldersveld had used the previous year, not a surprising turn since the *Back to God Hour* minister was a member of the majority. The heart of the majority report was a seven-page (out of thirteen total pages) section that spelled out the NAE's fundamentalist identity. Theologically, philosophically, ethically, and ecclesiastically (in that order), the report asserted, fundamentalism was "anti-Reformed and anti-Calvinist." For instance, the NAE's statement of faith brought the CRC's witness down to "rather insecure ground in our combat against the greater apostasy of our day." Too often as well, the NAE engaged in evangelistic activities that were "the province of the Church." In addition, the NAE's pronouncements on social issues reflected the "typical" fundamentalist "antipathies" rather than a witness governed "by a consistent Christian point of view."[56]

Whether these points proved that the NAE was in fact fundamentalist, a conclusion that the CRC defenders of the NAE questioned, the majority report was unambiguous in its assessment of Protestant fundamentalism. The issue before the CRC was not whether the members of the NAE were Christians or whether the CRC should cooperate with other Christians. Rather, the fundamental question was the character of fundamentalism, a movement that was "a negation of what Calvinism, and in general, the mainstream of Protestant Evangelical Christianity, has stood for."[57] Not surprisingly, the majority report advised the synod to "terminate" its membership in the NAE.

The minority report, coauthored by Clarence Bouma, the original CRC delegate to the NAE, conceded the NAE's fundamentalist identity but regarded fellowship and cooperation with this brand of Protestantism as the duty of genuine Christianity. One of the more poignant admissions by the minority was its recognition of the distance between pietist and confessional Protestant forms of piety: "It is true that at times our sensibilities are hurt by forms of expression used in the NAE meetings. But as far as our observation goes they do not stand out; they occur mostly in smaller gatherings. Insofar as they do we can use our influence by calling attention to them betimes and showing their impropriety." Still, despite the off-putting parts of fundamentalist belief and practice, the minority report recognized the members of the NAE as "fellow-Christians" or "our brethren in the Lord." Furthermore, "we include them in the one, Holy Catholic church, which we confess every Sunday." Continued membership in the NAE, which the minority report recommended, was more than an obligation but also an opportunity to "teach our people both to hold to our Reformed position and to recognize also the wider body of Christians, who are after all part of the fold of our Lord and therefore Spiritually related to us."[58]

In addition to debating the merits of fundamentalism, the 1949 reports to the synod also discussed the issue of isolation, a theme also introduced by Eldersveld the previous year. Unlike an earlier generation of CRC leaders, both sides were unwilling to take pride in Dutch-American Calvinist isolation, a likely function of the denomination's assimilation. Still, if the CRC were no longer going to pursue the course of isolation from American culture and religion, which part of the mainstream was the denomination going to enter? For the minority that supported the NAE, the CRC faced a choice between opposing modernism or being complicit in theological liberalism through indifference. "Withdrawal on our part," the report concluded, "would give satisfaction to those who believe in a policy of extreme isolationism, but it would also give no less satisfaction to the modernist elements in our country, who are filled with dismay at the growth of united action on the part of the truly orthodox forces in this country." Despite the NAE's weaknesses, membership in it did not compromise Reformed distinctiveness since it was a "spurious alternative" to argue that the CRC had to choose between cooperation and maintaining its theological and ecclesiastical identity. "We must do both"—that is, "become ever more distinctive" and stand "shoulder to shoulder wherever needed over against the common enemy with those who are on the Lord's side."[59]

For the majority that wanted to leave the NAE, however, ongoing membership, like the American melting pot, would gradually wear away the CRC's distinctive ways. In fact, the majority compared the NAE's policies to that of the Federal Council when it asserted that the history of interdenominational cooperation in the United States "indicates plainly enough that organization on a minimal doctrinal basis for the sake of concerted action, usually ends up in the assumption that fellowship and organization are more important than truth and loyalty to Christ." The things that inevitably suffered in interchurch efforts were those that kept the "disparate elements apart; distinctive creeds, distinctive practices, distinctive forms of devotion." In sum, "the tendency is always to consider the distinctive things as nonessential."[60] Here the majority turned the tables on the NAE's advocates by arguing that membership in the NAE was really a grosser form of isolation than that of maintaining an identity apart from the association. "We are at this moment," the report affirmed, "emerging from our past isolation," but "have we *emerged* from our isolation only to become *submerged* in the current of sectarian Fundamentalism?" Was it really possible to withstand the perils of mid-twentieth-century American life on the stunted faith of fundamentalism, or was the CRC going to "remain uncompromisingly true to *our peculiar calling* . . . with the full power of the historic faith?"[61]

The CRC's final decision to leave the NAE, though undoubtedly pleasing to the authors of the 1949 majority report, was anything but a bold statement of the denomination's determination to remain "uncompromisingly true." Rather than adopting either the majority or minority reports, the synod appointed a committee in 1949 to study the issue of "interchurch affiliation." This report, received the following year, was subsequently sent to CRC congregations for evaluation and instruction. All the while, the CRC continued as a member of the NAE, insisting once again that the association avoid any evangelistic or churchly activities. Then in 1951, with almost as little fanfare as the CRC joined the NAE, the synod voted to withdraw. According to church minutes, "After lengthy discussion Synod decides to terminate the membership of the Christian Reformed Church in the NAE by majority vote."[62] No grounds were given, nor was a report rendered. The CRC almost silently slipped outside the NAE's fundamentalist orbit to return to a position of unwanted and undefined isolation.[63]

Reformed Ecumenicity and American Sectarianism

To be fair to the CRC, its relations with the NAE were not the best indication of the denomination's ecumenical vision. During the same time that the denomination debated membership in the NAE, it took the lead in establishing the Reformed Ecumenical Synod (RES), a body founded in 1946 and consisting originally of Dutch Calvinist denominations from the United States, the Netherlands, and South Africa. Its first assembly took place in Grand Rapids, Michigan, the home of CRC headquarters, and by 1950, the RES included other Presbyterian and Reformed denominations from around the world. For almost fifty years the CRC had been discussing the need for such an international ecumenical body of Reformed churches, and as part of those discussions, a CRC synodical committee produced in 1944 a report on ecumenicity and fraternal relations with other denominations.[64] This statement attempted to walk the narrow line between sectarianism and relativism; it recognized non-Reformed churches as legitimate expressions of the Christian faith while also stipulating that the CRC should only affiliate or cooperate with churches that were Reformed in doctrine, polity, and liturgy, "both officially and actually as is evident from their regular ecclesiastical practices."[65]

Oddly, this report had little bearing on the CRC's deliberations about the NAE. Not even the 1950 study committee on church affiliation that supplied the implicit grounds for the NAE's withdrawal the following year mentioned the 1944 report. The only voice that appeared to connect the dots between the CRC's efforts in forming the RES and its confusion about the NAE was one that appeared almost at the very end of the denomination's membership in the association. George Stob, who taught church history at Calvin Seminary and served on the editorial board of the newly established *Reformed Journal,* seemed to spend most of his time during the spring of 1950 and 1951 writing against the NAE, and he did so by applying the CRC's principles on interchurch relations to his church's relations with evangelicals. Stob noted the irony of the CRC's jealousy in guarding its own autonomy when affiliating with kin as in the case of the Dutch Calvinist denominations in the RES and its granting the NAE, a "motley" group of churches, "the power to 'speak for us,' and the power to make decisions that become our decisions (even when our delegates raise their voices against them)."[66] Part of Stob's reluctance stemmed from worries about the identity, isolation, and assimilation of the CRC. "To be for America what God calls us to be," he wrote, "we must always be our Reformed selves, and speak for ourselves in terms of our Reformed witness." But just as important to Stob was the CRC's understanding of itself as a church. The CRC, he noted, had joined the NAE as a church body yet kept complaining that the NAE should not perform activities that churches normally execute, such as preaching and evangelism. This was "the most distressing instance of a NO-YES that has come out of the whole of our fallible denominational life."[67] But the way out of this inconsistency was to separate the question of whether evangelicals or fundamentalists were part of the "one holy Catholic church" from the more fundamental question of what church polity will allow. According to Stob, the issue was "whether any instituted Church of Christ may unite in a *common witness* and for a *common performance of ecclesiastical functions,* with churches and societies whose conception of the Church and its function and whose conception of the truth of God's Word, differs radically from those which it confesses."[68]

A standard way of parsing the effects of Stob's logic is to note the narrowness, and hence the sectarianism, of this episode in the CRC's history. After all, if a church that forsook membership in the FCC could not even find a home in the right-wing interdenominational body of American evangelicals, then it had taken the principle of separation to an altogether new level.[69] But such interpretations of the CRC and its reckoning with American Protestantism rest on the assumption that liberalism and evangelicalism are the only options and fail to see that considerations about ecumenical relations are much broader than the rather confining categories of the FCC's doctrinal affirmation of Jesus Christ or the NAE's seven-point statement of belief. For confessional Protestants, being a member of a church involves a series of teachings and a host of practices that the reduced versions of Christianity articulated by evangelical and liberal forms of ecumenism do not address. But according to common American notions about religious cooperation and ecumenicity, church bodies that refuse to depart from fuller expressions of the faith practiced by previous generations of saints and clergy are narrow and sectarian. In contrast, from the perspective of confessional Protestantism, as CRC leaders pointed out, the terms of fellowship outlined by mainstream American Protestants, whether evangelical or mainline, were fairly narrow when compared to the breadth of teachings and practices of historic Christianity.

An important factor that helps explain the misunderstanding that attends confessional Protestant forms of ecumenism is the civic purpose that has informed mainstream Protestant notions of church cooperation. Throughout American history, mainstream Protestant church leaders have assumed that the unity of the churches was fundamental to the nation's harmony and well-being. This assumption in turn fed the evangelical and liberal Protestant habit of minimizing doctrinal, liturgical, and ecclesiastical differences for the sake of emphasizing specific personal and social mores that were believed to be in the best interests of cultural uniformity. Accordingly, Protestants who made a priority of their ecclesiastical traditions distinctive teachings and practices were a threat not simply to Protestant unity but also to social harmony.

Yet the development of the CRC's ecumenical relations during the middle of the twentieth century illustrates that the real threat to civic life is a form of ecumenism that merges religious affiliation and national purpose. Mid-twentieth-century evangelical and mainstream Protestant visions of American society did not allow much room for non-Protestants or even for Protestants of the wrong kind. Conversely, the CRC's ecumenical ties to other Reformed denominations in North America, Europe, and Africa could not have been less threatening to the United States since the aim of such church cooperation was not to build a righteous nation but rather to reflect the unity of believers without respect to citizenship. The outlook informing such an ecumenical vision may have been too otherworldly for mainstream American Protestant tastes since it implied that the affairs of twentieth-century political powers were not as important as the struggle between the spiritual armies of darkness and light. But considering the civil religion and national pride that has usually burdened American Protestant ecumenism, a view of Christian fraternity that reduces the importance of the United States and its role in human history may be an attractive alternative.

Notes

1. "Sectarianism Receives New Lease on Life," *Christian Century* 60 (May 19, 1943): 596.

2. "Why the Federal Council?," *Christian Century* 65 (January 28, 1948): 104.

3. Robert A. Schneider, "Voice of Many Waters: Church Federation in the Twentieth Century," in *Between the Times: The Travail of the Protestant Establishment in America, 1900–1960*, William R. Hutchison (New York: Cambridge University Press, 1989), 97.

4. Cavert, *The American Churches in the Ecumenical Movement: 1900–1968* (New York: Association Press, 1968), 8.

5. Cavert, *The American Churches*, 270.

6. Martin E. Marty, *The Public Church: Mainline-Evangelical-Catholic* (New York: Crossroad, 1981), 3, 6.

7. Marty, *The Public Church*, 6, 8–9.

8. Marty, *The Public Church*, 123, 124.

9. Martin E. Marty, *Modern American Religion, Volume 3: Under God, Indivisible, 1941–1960* (Chicago: University of Chicago Press, 1996), 264.

10. Marty, *Modern American Religion, Volume 3*, 268–71.

11. *Christian Faith in Action: Commemorative Volume: The Founding of the National Council of Churches of Christ in the United States of America* (New York: National Council of Churches, 1951), 13, quoted in Marty, *Modern American Religion, Volume 3*, 272.

12. George M. Marsden, *The Evangelical Mind and the New School Presbyterian Experience: Study of Thought and Theology in Nineteenth-Century America* (New Haven, Conn.: Yale University Press, 1970), 211.

13. On Presbyterian developments between 1865 and 1940, see Richard W. Reifsnyder, "Presbyterian Reunion, Reorganization and Expansion in the Late 19th Century," *American Presbyterians* 64 (1986): 27–38; Philip D. Jordan, "The Evangelical Alliance and American Presbyterians, 1867–1873," *Journal of Presbyterian History* 51 (1973): 309–26; J. David Hoeveler Jr., "Evangelical Ecumenism: James McCosh and the Intellectual Origins of the World Alliance of Reformed

Churches," *Journal of Presbyterian History* 55 (1977): 35–56; and James H. Moorhead, "Presbyterians and the Mystique of Organizational Efficiency, 1870–1936," in *Re-Imagining Denominationalism: Interpretive Essays*, ed. Robert Bruce Mullin and Russell E. Richey (New York: Oxford University Press, 1994), 264–87.

14. The following paragraphs are based on material from D. G. Hart, "The Tie That Divides: Presbyterian Ecumenism, Fundamentalism, and the History of Twentieth-Century American Protestantism," *Westminster Theological Journal* 60 (1998): 85–107.

15. Cavert, *American Churches*, 25.

16. Jordan, "Evangelical Alliance," 311.

17. Jordan, "Evangelical Alliance," makes this point. The leaders of the Evangelical Alliance in America included many prominent Presbyterians. In fact, the reunion of the Old and New Schools greatly facilitated support for the Alliance. Henry Boynton Smith, professor at Union Seminary (N.Y.), and James McCosh, president of the College of New Jersey, both supporters of Presbyterian reunion, also argued on behalf of evangelical cooperation. Presbyterians also provided administrative muscle. William E. Dodge Sr., an active New School Presbyterian elder, presided over the American Evangelical Alliance and Samuel Irenaeus Prime, an Old School minister and editor of the influential *New York Observer*, shaped the direction of the alliance.

18. For a recent study of antebellum reform that confirms this point, see Robert H. Abzug, *Cosmos Crumbling: American Reform and the Religious Imagination* (New York: Oxford University Press, 1994).

19. Robert Baird, *The Progress and Prospects of Christianity in the United States of America* (London, 1851), quoted in Jordan, "Evangelical Alliance," 311.

20. See *The Evangelical Alliance for the United States of America, 1847–1900: Ecumenism, Identity and the Religion of the Republic* (New York: Mellen, 1982), chap. 4; Cavert, *The American Churches*, chap. 1.

21. On the connections between Whig politics and American Protestantism, see Mark A. Noll, Nathan O. Hatch, and George M. Marsden, *The Search for Christian America* (Westchester, Ill.: Crossway, 1983), chap. 4.

22. *Minutes* of the General Assembly of the Presbyterian Church in the United States of America (New School), 1866, 263, quoted in Jordan, "Evangelical Alliance," 324.

23. McCosh, "The Religious and Social Conditions of the United States . . . ," *Proceedings of the Evangelical Alliance* (1866), 17, 23, quoted in J. David Hoeveler Jr., "Evangelical Ecumenism: James McCosh and the Intellectual Origins of the World Alliance of Reformed Churches," *Journal of Presbyterian History* 55 (1977): 45, 47.

24. On the NCC's politics, see K. L. Billingsley, *From Mainline to Sideline: The Social Witness of the National Council of Churches* (Washington, D.C.: Ethics and Public Policy Center, 1990).

25. Cavert, *The American Churches*, 15, 32.

26. See Cavert, *The American Churches*; Cavert, *Church Cooperation and Unity in America, 1900–1970* (New York: Association Press, 1970); and Ernst Eldon Gilbert, "The Interchurch World Movement of North America, 1919–1920" (Ph.D. diss., Yale University, 1968).

27. Reifsnyder, "Presbyterian Reunion," 37.

28. See Donald K. Gorrell, *The Age of Social Responsibility: The Social Gospel in the Progressive Era, 1900–1920* (Macon, Ga.: Mercer University Press, 1988).

29. See Randall H. Balmer, *A Perfect Babel of Confusion: Dutch Religion and English Culture in the Middle Colonies* (New York: Oxford University Press, 1989).

30. On the origins of the CRC, see James D. Bratt, *Dutch Calvinism in America: A History of a Conservative Subculture* (Grand Rapids, Mich.: Eerdmans, 1984), 37–40.

31. F. M. Ten Hoor, "Verscheidenheid en Eenheid in de Gereformeerde Kerke en Theologie," *Gereformeerde Amerikaan* I (February 1897): 13, quoted in Bratt, *Dutch Calvinism in America*, 41–42.

32. Ten Hoor, "Verscheidenheid en Eenheid," 42.

33. H. Zwaanstra, *Reformed Thought and Experience in a New World: A Study of the Christian Reformed Church and Its American Environment, 1890–1918* (Kampen: Kok, 1973), 39.

34. S. Eldersveld, "Materialisme," *Gereformeerde Amerikaan* 19 (May 1915): 229, quoted in Bratt, *Dutch Calvinism*, 63.

35. Henry Beets, "Not Ashamed of the Basis of 1857," *Banner* 11 (April 1907): 185, quoted in Bratt, *Dutch Calvinism*, 41.

36. Zwaanstra, *Reformed Thought*, 42.

37. Zwaanstra, *Reformed Thought*.

38. Bratt, *Dutch Calvinism*, 59.

39. John Van Lonkhuyzen, *Billy Sunday: Een Beeld uit het Tegenwoordige Amerikaanische Godsdienstige Leven* (Grand Rapids, Mich.: Eerdmans, 1916), 153, quoted in Bratt, *Dutch Calvinism*, 61.

40. See Bratt, *Dutch Calvinism*, chap. 3.

41. Henry Zwaanstra, *Catholicity and Secession: A Study of Ecumenicity in the Christian Reformed Church* (Grand Rapids, Mich.: Eerdmans, 1991), 21–22.

42. See Zwaanstra, *Catholicity and Secession*, 21–24; Bratt, *Dutch Calvinism*, 112–15; and Joseph H. Hall, "The Controversy over Fundamentalism in the Christian Reformed Church, 1915–1966" (Th.D. diss., Concordia Theological Seminary, 1974), 89–92.

43. On the origins of the NAE and the specific endeavors in which it was involved, see Executive Committee of the NAE, *Evangelical Action! A Report of the Organization of the National Association of Evangelicals for United Action* (Boston: United Action Press, 1942); James DeForest Murch, *Cooperation without Compromise: A History of the National Association of Evangelicals* (Grand Rapids, Mich.: Eerdmans, 1956); and Joel A. Carpenter, *Revive Us Again: The Reawakening of American Fundamentalism* (New York: Oxford University Press, 1997), chap. 8.

44. Hall, "Controversy over Fundamentalism," provides the fullest coverage of these debates.

45. Hall, "Controversy over Fundamentalism," 93–97.

46. Christian Reformed Church, *Acts of Synod* (1944), 326.

47. Christian Reformed Church, *Acts of Synod* (1945), 272.

48. Christian Reformed Church, *Acts of Synod* (1945), 273.

49. On Abraham Kuyper and his influence on the Christian Reformed Church, see Bratt, *Dutch Calvinism*, chap. 2; James D. Bratt, "Abraham Kuyper: His World and Work," in *Abraham Kuyper: A Centennial Reader*, ed. James D. Bratt (Grand Rapids, Mich.: Eerdmans, 1998), 1–16; and Peter S. Heslam, *Creating a Christian Worldview: Abraham Kuyper's Lectures on Calvinism* (Grand Rapids, Mich.: Eerdmans, 1998).

50. Christian Reformed Church, *Acts of Synod* (1945), 276.

51. Christian Reformed Church, *Acts of Synod* (1945), 279.

52. Christian Reformed Church, *Acts of Synod* (1946), 385, 386.

53. Hall, "Controversy over Fundamentalism," 104–5, quotation on 105.

54. Christian Reformed Church, *Acts of Synod* (1947), 401, 402.

55. Christian Reformed Church, *Acts of Synod* (1948), 410, 411.

56. Christian Reformed Church, *Acts of Synod* (1949), 290, 294–297.

57. Christian Reformed Church, *Acts of Synod* (1949), 290.

58. Christian Reformed Church, *Acts of Synod* (1949), 315–16, 318, 319.

59. Christian Reformed Church, *Acts of Synod* (1949), 320, 322.

60. Christian Reformed Church, *Acts of Synod* (1949), 300.

61. Christian Reformed Church, *Acts of Synod* (1949), 301.

62. Christian Reformed Church, *Acts of Synod* (1951), 77–79, quotation on 79.

63. On these debates as they played out in the CRC press, see Hall, "Controversy over Fundamentalism," 89–118.

64. See Henry Zwaanstra, *Catholicity and Secession: A Study in the History of the Christian Reformed Church* (Grand Rapids, Mich.: Eerdmans, 1991); and Paul G. Schrotenboer, "The Christian Reformed Church and the Reformed Ecumenical Synod," in *Perspectives on the Christian Reformed Church: Studies in Its History, Theology, and Ecumenicity*, ed. Peter De Klerk and Richard R. De Ridder (Grand Rapids, Mich.: Baker Books, 1983), 345–62.

65. Christian Reformed Church, *Acts of Synod* (1944), 358.

66. George Stob, "The Christian Reformed Church in the American World," *Reformed Journal* 1.4 (June 1951): 2–3.

67. Stob, "The Christian Reformed Church," 2.

68. George Stob, "That Decision on the NAE," *Reformed Journal* 2.6 (June 1952): 5.

69. See, for instance, Carpenter, *Revive Us Again*, chap. 2; and George M. Marsden, *Reforming Fundamentalism: Fuller Seminary and the New Evangelicalism* (Grand Rapids, Mich.: Eerdmans, 1987), 6–7, 37–38.

The Irrelevance of Lutheran Liturgy   6

To the untrained eye, the Lutheran Church–Missouri Synod (LCMS) would appear to be an evangelical denomination in the sense that it is on the conservative side of the major division within American Protestantism. As a communion that forbids women's ordination, refuses to tolerate homosexuality as a legitimate practice for its members, and has endorsed the doctrine of biblical inerrancy, the LCMS has all the marks that characterize those Protestants on the right—an unambiguous understanding of the Bible's infallible teaching on specific moral and social topics. Thanks to these stands, students of American religion place the LCMS in the orthodox camp of the culture war that divides Protestants between traditionalist and progressive expressions. According to James Davison Hunter, whose book *Culture Wars* made the best and most sustained case for a realignment within American Protestantism according to cultural as opposed to denominational loyalties, the 1970s struggle within the LCMS that led to its endorsing the doctrine of inerrancy mirrored similar developments in mainline denominations where conservatives "repudiated a humanistic and liberally politicized position" in favor of traditional biblical teaching.[1] Nancy T. Ammerman also recognizes the conservatives in the LCMS controversy of the 1970s as fundamentalists because of their insistence "that the inerrancy of Scripture is the foundation of all other beliefs, including the historic Christian creeds."[2]

Part of what complicates such a rendering of the LCMS or its disputes is that American Lutherans themselves, going back to the nineteenth century, are not comfortable using the labels stitched by Anglo-American

Protestants or the scholars of mainstream American Protestantism. Mark Ellingsen writes, for instance, that contrary to the impression that Lutheranism "represents a paradigmatic example of evangelicalism," no Lutheran communion in the United States, not even the LCMS, "the champion of theologically conservative Lutheran orthodoxy," identifies "officially" with evangelical interdenominational organizations such as the National Association of Evangelicals.[3] David P. Scaer, a professor of theology at the LCMS's Concordia Seminary in Fort Wayne, Indiana, even questions whether his denomination's endorsement of inerrancy means the same thing as it does in evangelical and fundamentalist circles. The evangelical quest for "biblical principles" that give guidance about health, wealth, marriage, families, and psychological well-being, he argues, are a long way from the Lutheran approach to Scripture in which the good news of salvation is primary and advice about daily life "belongs to natural knowledge."[4] Scaer's point does not mean that individual Lutherans or their pastors have no interest in evangelical ways of reading or defending the Bible. But it does highlight the way in which Lutheran teachings and practices do not fit neatly the categories supplied by the mainstream Protestant divide between liberals and evangelicals. According to historian Mark Granquist, the LCMS's adoption of the language of inerrancy did not "mean that these confessional Lutherans had substantially adopted the agenda of fundamentalism" or even that they were "deeply influenced by" or "substantially agreed with" fundamentalists. "It is impossible," he adds, "to call these exclusive confessionalists 'fundamentalists' either in doctrine or approach."[5]

In fact, below the surface of disputes about the Bible and how it applies to the personal matters that antagonize the progressive and orthodox cultural warriors is a trend within American Lutheranism that may not explain the outcome of political elections or the formation of special interest groups but does affect significantly the shape of Lutheran piety and identity. This development is the change in worship that has occurred over the last thirty years under the heading of liturgical renewal. In an article for the Lutheran publication *Dialog*, Leigh Jordahl, an emeritus professor of religion and classics at Luther College in Decorah, Iowa, after visiting several Lutheran congregations from different denominations, complained "how freewheelingly the liturgical forms are doctored up, how the least significant ceremonial forms are picked up, and how frantic the search for 'relevance' appears to be."

What Jordahl was observing was the triumph of contemporary forms of worship over historic Lutheran liturgy, with "subjective religious songs" replacing "singable, time-tested hymns," "autobiographical anecdotes or moral social action talks" substituting for a "proclamatory sermon," and the "social science language of therapy" supplanting "kerygmatic preaching." He did more than complain, however. Jordahl also blamed the changes in Lutheran worship on the beguiling advice of church experts, "whether of the 'church-growth' or 'contemporary' variety." The experts on the far left were using the liturgy to "push a particular form of political correctness"; in other words, they were using the church for an "essentially secular purpose." The more evangelistically minded experts were using worship to attract larger congregations, thereby transforming the regular parish into a "megachurch." Jordahl did not put all of the Lutheran denominations in the same camp. The smallish Wisconsin Evangelical Lutheran Synod was doing the best to hold on to classic Lutheran forms, the more ecumenical Evangelical Lutheran Church of America showed the greatest variety—and thus the worst excess—and the LCMS was somewhere in the middle, still using traditional Lutheran liturgy while experimenting with church growth techniques. But for Jordahl, the worship wars in Lutheran circles were every bit as serious as the battle liberals and evangelicals regularly fought over the Bible. Sometimes in conflicts over the forms of the faith "the gospel itself is at stake."[6]

Jordahl's perspective on liturgical innovations among Lutherans is yet another reminder not only that Lutheran concerns elude the common ways of interpreting American Protestantism but also that the standard interpretations fail to account for some of the most significant developments within churches in the United States. One of the most vigorous lines of research in the last twenty years on American religion has been the rise and influence of the religious right (formerly New Christian Right). Indeed, the prominence of such religious figures as Jerry Falwell and Pat Robertson in American politics has given historians and sociologists a sufficient rationale to recover the story of fundamentalists and evangelicals. These lines of inquiry have generally confirmed the notion that the religious contests of the 1920s that separated liberals and fundamentalists are continuing to play themselves out in recent political and cultural contests and that the evangelicals and fundamentalists comprise the right-wing party in these struggles.[7] In the words of George M. Marsden, "an American fundamentalist is an evangelical who is militant in opposition to liberal theology in the churches or to changes in cultural values or mores, such as those associated with secular humanism."[8] Whether or not this is an adequate definition of contemporary fundamentalism, it highlights the links widely assumed between conservative religion and conservative politics in the United States.

Such assumptions, however, miss an important irony in the recent history of American Protestantism. At the same time that scholars have noticed a polarization between conservative and liberal religion and its consequences for American politics, they have not seen that the most vocal defenders of traditional family values are also the most active proponents of liturgical innovation. The conservative party in the culture war, the evangelicals, are liberal when it comes to historic forms of Christian worship. To be sure, one of the reasons for missing this inconsistency is that the history of worship has not figured prominently in the scholarly literature on American religion. But just as important is the way that the debate between soul winning and the Social Gospel continues to dominate treatments of American Protestant identity. Lutheran debates about worship reveal the inadequacy of the standard ways of interpreting the recent American Protestant past. They also yield a markedly different side of the culture wars, one in which the pietistic Protestant quest for relevant religion leads to political and social antagonism, and the otherworldliness of confessional Protestant piety results in a wholesome irrelevance.

Public Religion

Among the many episodes in recent U.S. politics that have hardened the positions separating cultural conservatives and liberals, the removal of prayer and Bible reading from public schools is one development that apparently crystallizes the differences between each party. For liberals, the Supreme Court's rulings to prohibit religious exercises at the beginning of each school day fully accords with the First Amendment's disestablishment clause, thus maintaining a clear separation between the powers of the state and those of the churches. For conservatives, in contrast, those rulings represent an early phase of the courts' usurpation of the legislative branch's powers. They also account for the overwhelming moral decay of the last three decades in the United States. According to Concerned Women for America, "removing prayer and the acknowledgment of God from our classrooms has been the *primary cause* of the devastatingly serious decline in the lives of students, their families, the schools, and our nation." This conservative organization even cites statistics, such as the 200 percent increase in premarital sexual activity, as evidence for its claim about the importance of public school prayer.[9] Although religious exercises in public education are not solely responsible for the culture wars—abortion, feminism, gay rights, and segregation all played a part—prayer and Bible reading function as an important symbol in the lines dividing the left and the right.

This is not the first time in American history, however, that prayer and Bible reading in public schools emerged as a front in a larger battle for national identity. With a firm commitment to Christian morality as the bedrock for American civic life and with the difficulty of maintaining established churches in individual states, public education in the United States assumed the burden of inculcating the basic tenets of shared ideals and it did so often through the means of prayer and Bible reading.[10] The presence of religion in common schools sparked controversy when Roman Catholics objected to the Protestant bias inherent in these religious exercises. Court rulings in the nineteenth century forced school officials to curtail some of the explicitness of Protestant piety, but not sufficiently to prevent Catholics from establishing a large parochial school system to counter the Protestant tone of public schooling. The lesson taught by the nineteenth-century school wars did not include the point that mixing religion and public life was a questionable practice because by the early decades of the twentieth century the legislatures of many states stipulated that the school day begin with prayer and Bible reading. In the 1920s, these religious exercises took on greater significance as white Anglo-Saxon Protestants of both the liberal and fundamentalist variety feared what the immigrants crowding urban areas and coming from questionable religious and political backgrounds would do to the character of the United States.[11]

One gauge to the cultural and political importance of prayer and Bible reading was the number of books written by Protestants who argued that a religious presence in public schools was necessary for the health of the nation. Harold S. Tuttle, a professor of educational sociology who taught at the University of Oregon, wrote one such book. His *Character Education by State and Church* (1930) displayed precisely the sort of WASP distrust of foreign elements in America that demanded religion in public education. Tuttle described his purpose as one simply of describing the ways in which the state may "cooperate in the cultivation of the religious life of the church and the ways in which the church may stimulate and utilize such assistance," all without violating the American principle of the separation of church and state. The notion of the child's religious life was synonymous with "character," which is why many progressives in the educational world advocated character education. The logic was simple: if you have a religious dimension, you have good character; if you didn't have faith, it was hard to see how you could possibly have character. Evidence of this logic came out in the foreword where Tuttle began with the following postulate: "not the criminal acts of the few, but the moral unenlightenment of the masses, constitutes the chief danger to our civilization."[12]

From there it was a fairly straightforward route to recognizing the necessity of religion in forming good and ethical citizens. Tuttle devoted only one chapter to religion in public schools and welcomed the practice of reading the Bible at the beginning of the school day. He also observed that in some school systems daily worship was being conducted, such as singing hymns, prayer, and performing religious ceremonies. Curiously, the author did not think worship an infringement on religious freedom or a violation of the separation between church and state. In no sense did such worship "constitute sectarian instruction."[13] In fact, Tuttle, like many of his Protestant peers, thought it possible to separate worship and ethical conduct from beliefs and dogma. Promoting acts of Christian worship in a public setting like government-run schools was simply a "frank acknowledgment that our present civilization rests on a foundation of Christian ethics."[14] Although the author was not a fundamentalist, his perspective on religion in public schools was one widely shared by conservative and liberal Protestants of Anglo-American heritage.

Of course, Protestant convictions about religion and public schools came in for serious revision during the two decades after World War II when the U.S. Supreme Court issued a series of rulings that resulted ultimately in prayer and Bible reading being declared unconstitutional. The two cases that ended Protestant hegemony in public education were the 1962 decision in *Engel v. Vitale* and *Abington v. Schempp* the following year. In the former case, the Supreme Court found that a generic prayer, from the New York state legislators handbook *Moral and Spiritual Training in the Schools*, constituted an illegitimate establishment of religion even though school officials believed that all "men and women of good will" could pray it.[15] With prayer removed, the Supreme Court eliminated Bible reading in *Abington v.*

Schempp by invalidating a Pennsylvania law that required ten verses to be read without comment at the beginning of each school day and threatened non-compliant teachers with termination of their employment. Justice Tom C. Clark, who wrote the majority opinion in *Schempp*, came to the heart of the matter when he asked whether the practice of Bible reading conflicted with the kind of neutrality that American governmental institutions were supposed to show toward religion. What made his answer particularly complicated was his acknowledgment that public school students needed moral instruction and that secularism did not provide an adequate moral foundation for national life. In other words, this case wasn't simply an issue about whether the Bible was sectarian but whether its sectarian character compromised its ethical function. Clark's opinion overturned almost 150 years of Protestant assumptions about religion and public morality when it granted implicitly that American citizens could be moral in some sense without believing the Bible and recognized that Protestant morality could not be separated from Protestant beliefs and practices.

Reactions to the Court's decisions that culminated in the *Schempp* decision confirm this interpretation. Ever since the late 1940s when the justices began to eliminate religion's place in public education, mainline Protestant leaders became increasingly alarmed over the apparent secularization of America's schools. One Presbyterian pastor from Champaign, Illinois, complained that the Court had committed the nation to "a definite irreligious attitude" that was out of step with United States' history.[16] The *New York Times* reported that various Protestant clergy were "shocked," "scandalized," and "frightened." Billy Graham said that the Court's decisions represented "another step toward secularism," "a most dangerous trend."[17] Even Reinhold Niebuhr led an impressive group of Protestant theologians in drafting a statement that called one of the Supreme Court's rulings on religion in public schools a serious step in secularizing American culture. As late as 1962, Niebuhr asserted that the notion of a "wall" of separation between church and state was misleading and that the Court's decision in *Engel* would "work so consistently in the direction of a secularization of the school system as to amount to the suppression of religion and to give the impression that government must be anti-religion."[18]

Not all Protestants reacted negatively to these defeats for religion in public education. Lutherans in the Missouri Synod, for instance, as early as 1948 after *McCollum v. Board of Education*, asserted that to teach religion in public schools was "unbiblical and unAmerican." The reason was that the state could not teach a "'common core of religious and ethical ideas that goes beyond acknowledgment of the existence of God and man's obligations to the Moral Law." Public schools could teach about religion and such instruction was preferable to atheism. But a positive religious influence was beyond the proper responsibilities of public education.[19] A decade later, the LCMS clarified its understanding of public schools by recognizing the legitimacy of state-sponsored education and the church's duty to teach its children to be Christian "disciples." The church and the state were not at odds in education, and the LCMS encouraged its members to "support and uphold" public schools. Even so, although parochial schools were not in competition with public ones, the former were "established to provide a specifically Christian education," which the latter "cannot supply."[20] LCMS resolve may have softened after the *Schempp* ruling, such as when Arthur C. Stellhorn sounded a more vigorous note that Lutherans had a duty "to see that the Bible is not banished from public schools." Nevertheless, Stellhorn was clear about the limits that Christianity and American law placed upon public educators. Public schools were not "permitted to teach either the Lutheran or any other specific religion." Bible reading may have been permissible but it was hardly a substitute for "a thorough course of religious instruction in a Lutheran school." Prayers were particularly "dangerous" to believing children because such petitions were "formulated by unorthodox persons or by unbelievers." The best alternative, then, was for Lutheran parents to send their children to parochial schools.[21]

Reasons for the lack of alarm among Missouri Synod Lutherans over Supreme Court rulings on religion in public schools stemmed from Lutheran educational philosophy and Lutheran teaching about church and state. As Walter H. Beck observed, Lutheran denominations that "offered little beyond Sunday school for the religious education of their youth" were generally much more supportive of prayer and Bible reading in public schools, demanding that public school officials "cultivate the spiritual life of pupils through devotional exercises."[22] Conversely, those denominations that had a strong tradition of parochial school education, such as the LCMS, opposed religious exercises in public schools and so displayed less dismay about the Supreme Court's reversal of a long accepted form of religious behavior in public life. Clearly, Lutheran parents and church officials active in a local Lutheran day school had much less at stake in the Court's decisions. What is more, Lutheran teaching on the two kingdoms—that is, that a fundamental difference exists between the kingdom of man (the state) and the kingdom of God (the church)—also contributed to a degree of nonchalance among Lutherans regarding religion in public education. Since public schools were institutions of the state, the idea of practicing religion in them was, from the Lutheran perspective, a clear instance of confusing the nature and purposes of each kingdom.[23]

Nevertheless, as important as Lutheran educational and political reflection are for understanding the differences between Lutherans and Anglo-American Protestants regarding religion in public schools, even more significant are divergent views about the purpose and character of worship. Sometimes lost in the debates about prayer and Bible reading in public schools was a recognition that these activities were in fact elements of worship; that is, prayer and Bible reading have historically been two of the chief elements in the liturgy of Christian churches. In his book on character education, for instance, Tuttle conceded that prayer and Bible reading, along with the older convention of singing hymns, were forms of worship, but he still construed their effects along educational, as opposed to liturgical, lines. As such, these religious activities functioned as a form of moral education as students learned, somehow, by reciting Psalm 23 or hearing a generic prayer, how to distinguish good from evil. Even in the arguments before the Supreme Court in the *Abington v. Schempp* case, Luther A. Weigel, who testified for the state, located the value of Pennsylvania's law largely in the Bible's moral, historical, and literary excellence. Solomon Grayzel, who testified for the Schempps, could not understand the Protestant regard for mere Bible reading since in Judaism the value of Scripture came through study, not simply hearing the text read.[24] In its decision, however, the Supreme Court saw through the practices' didactic intent and recognized them for their liturgical significance.

The inconsistency in Anglo-American Protestant expectations for religion in public schools becomes more apparent when contrasted with the sorts of religious exercises promoted in Lutheran day schools. The LCMS supplied pastors and teachers with devotional guides, complete with specific Bible readings that followed the liturgical calendar and covered the sweep of biblical history, along with prayers and hymns appropriate to the biblical passage. For instance, after the reading from Genesis on the fall of Adam and Eve, teachers could say the following prayer:

> Dear Father in heaven, we are sinners like our first parents, Adam and Eve. We have often listened to the devil and been disobedient, lazy, unkind, or wicked in other ways. We have done many things that Thou and our parents did not want us to do. Forgive all the wrong we have done. We want to serve Thee, and not the devil. Help us to live as Christians. When the devil tries to make us do wrong, drive him away, and help us to do what is right; for the sake of Jesus Christ, our Savior. Amen.[25]

Obviously, this was a very different prayer from the sort that in 1962 the Supreme Court ruled unconstitutional: "Almighty God, we acknowledge our dependence upon Thee, and we beg Thy blessings upon us, our parents, our teachers, and our Country."[26]

It was equally obvious that the Lutheran prayer was much more appropriate for a parochial school setting where worship was part of the program. But this was the point. The expectation of parochial school officials was that students in their charge shared a common faith, thus preventing the sort of bind that occurs when religion is inserted into religiously mixed settings. Lutherans could engage in a candid expression of their convictions in a Lutheran school without having to fear that nonbelievers were being forced to participate. In the public schools, however, Protestants were forced to make religion as inoffensive as possible, by removing overt language and reducing the faith to the acquisition of moral guidance. In sum, worship in parochial schools could flourish and be a part of a program of Christian nurture; in public schools religion had to follow a clandestine route in the pursuit of its goal of moral transformation. It is no wonder that prayer and Bible reading in public education were not going to propel Lutherans to become cultural warriors because, in the case of the LCMS, they knew religion's place; acts of public worship were not legitimate in genuinely public spaces.

Parochial Worship

If prayer and Bible reading were illegitimate in the public school classroom, both according to Lutheran theology and United States' legal logic, questions about what kind of activities were appropriate in Lutheran church

buildings were not so easily answered. During the 1970s and 1980s, the
LCMS confronted liturgical issues along two fronts, first in the creation of
a joint Lutheran hymnal, and second in responding to the desire from pastors for the denomination to be more aggressively evangelistic. Throughout
these developments the LCMS showed all the marks of an ethnic confessional communion going through the difficulties of Americanization. At
the same time, it displayed a marked attachment to Old World liturgical
forms and devotion that has been at the heart of confessional Lutheranism.

Until the LCMS in 1982 produced its own denominational hymnal,
Lutheran Worship, the 1941 liturgical resource, *The Lutheran Hymnal*, had served
as the hymn book used by most Missouri Synod congregations as well as
other Lutheran denominations. The earlier hymnal was a cooperative endeavor among several Lutheran communions, under the umbrella of the Intersynodical Committee on Hymnology and Liturgics for the Evangelical
Synodical Conference of North America. In addition, the 1941 hymnal re-
stored some order to what the editor of *Lutheran Witness*, Theodore Graebner, called the "liturgical chaos" of Lutheranism in North America. According to the *American Lutheran*, "it is beyond gainsaying that especially our
English-speaking Lutheran Church has permitted much of Lutheranism's
liturgical heritage to fall into disuse and to be replaced by ecclesiastical cru-
dities and vulgarities and by insipid sentimentalities borrowed from the hip,
hip, hurrah meeting house 'services' of the American sects."[27] *The Lutheran
Hymnal* was able to supply some order to the worship of American Lutherans because it was more than simply a hymnal. The first 169 pages functioned more or less as a book of prayer, complete with an order of service,
prayers for set times in the service along with those to be said at different
days in the church calendar, a psalter, and lectionary.[28] By 1941, W. G. Polack, who chaired the hymnal committee believed that the older liturgical
chaos was "definitely on its way out."[29]

By the late 1950s, plans for a revised hymnal began. Some of the revisions included minor adjustments, such as pocket-sized editions or ones
that could be used more successfully by organists. But Missouri Lutherans
were also raising more substantial issues, such as antiquated language that
left modern lay people cold. Even so, a report requested by the LCMS in
1956 and completed three years later indicated that an "overwhelming per-
centage" of the congregations valued *The Lutheran Hymnal* and did not want
to change.[30] On the basis of these findings the committee for a revised

hymnal suggested that another hymn book not be published for another ten to twelve years. This recommendation did not mean, however, that revisions would cease. The LCMS Committee on Worship, Liturgy, and Hymnology would continue to work during the intervening years toward updating the language of hymns and prayers in *The Lutheran Hymnal.*

In 1965 these plans for an LCMS revision to the older hymnal were put on hold when the denomination decided at its annual convention to join the Inter-Lutheran Commission on Worship, the task of which was to produce a more contemporary hymnal. Although the LCMS entered this work somewhat reluctantly, it continued to participate for well over another decade until the commission produced the *Lutheran Book of Worship* (1978), the hymnal used by the largest American Lutheran denomination, the Evangelical Lutheran Church in America. Part of the reason for hesitation was that some Missouri Lutherans wondered about the desirability of designing one hymnal for all Lutherans in America. Others questioned how long the process would take since hymnals generally have a shelf life of twenty-five years, and the LCMS would likely need a new one before the commission could complete its work.[31]

Fairly quickly in the process, Missouri Lutherans realized that the hymnal revision process was taking them in liturgical directions they did not want to go. In 1969, the commission came out with *Worship Supplement*, a book designed to meet the "demands of changing times and situations" and to apply "timeless truths to timely needs."[32] The commission followed this attempt for more relevant worship with a series entitled Contemporary Worship, which were ten booklets printed between 1969 and 1976 and designed to be provisional and experimental, a form of testing the waters before making the work permanent in a new hymnal. Although the newer elements offered in Contemporary Worship did not all survive to be included in the *Lutheran Book of Worship*, they did demonstrate the influences of liturgical renewal on American Lutheranism. Here the liturgical changes introduced by the Second Vatican Council—that is, the effort to make the liturgy accessible to the laity (in part by using the vernacular)—ended up having widespread effects on worship in other communions. In the Lutheran case, the commission pressed ahead with liturgical forms, changes in language, and hymns that would make worship "meaningful to the man of today" and enable that man or woman to avoid simply going "through the motions."[33]

LCMS critics of the commission's work believed that some of the material was not doctrinally sound. For instance, a rather extended dispute broke out over the second of the commission's booklets that introduced a prayer into the administration of the Lord's Supper that many regarded as foreign to Lutheran liturgy. Others noticed that the revisions were so contemporary in idiom and tone that a hymnal that incorporated them would be necessarily dated and, thus, make another revision immediately necessary.[34] In fact, these criticisms both from the LCMS and other members of the commission turned the production of the new hymnal, the *Lutheran Book of Worship* back in more conservative directions. As one of the commission's members put it, liturgical experimentation was useful for producing a liturgy that consisted not of "passing experiments" but of "more lasting concerns."[35]

Even so, the avoidance of liturgical novelty in the *Lutheran Book of Worship* could not maintain LCMS support. Concerns about the new hymnal led the denomination in 1975 to pass up a resolution that would have made the *Lutheran Book of Worship* accessible to the entire denomination and thus more likely to be adopted. In 1977, a year before its release, the annual convention of the LCMS appointed a committee to review the new liturgical materials. This Special Hymnal Review Committee reported back to the LCMS annual convention the following year, recommending the acceptance of the new hymnal with minor modifications. When the LCMS heard that these modifications were too late to be included in the final draft, the Special Hymnal Review Committee proceeded with its revisions. The culmination of this process came in 1981 when the LCMS adopted a modified version of the *Lutheran Book of Worship* and gave it its own name—*Lutheran Worship*.[36]

It was not coincidental that at the same time that the LCMS was pulling out of the project for a joint Lutheran hymnal, the denomination was also experiencing a split between conservative and progressive elements in its ranks. The epicenter of the dispute was, in good German-American fashion, St. Louis, Missouri, the home of Concordia Theological Seminary where the school president, John Tietjen, led an effort to open the LCMS to the wider, more cosmopolitan world of American Protestantism through cooperation with other churches and through a refashioned scholarly appropriation of the Lutheran tradition. The leader of the conservatives was the LCMS president, J. A. O. Preus, who came into office in 1969, the same year that Tietjen became president at Concordia. Preus saw Concordia as the leading wedge of theological looseness in the denomination and set out to bring the seminary into line. In 1974, events at Concordia and in the denomination came to a head, with conservative pressure forcing Tietjen, a majority of the seminary faculty, and students to form another school named Seminex—short for seminary in exile. Those who sided with Tietjen and Seminex trickled away from the LCMS into the American Lutheran Church and the Lutheran Church in America, two of the denominations that would comprise the Evangelical Lutheran Church in America, a body formed in 1988 of the majority of Lutheran denominations in North America, with two sizeable exceptions, the LCMS and the more conservative and smaller denomination, Wisconsin Evangelical Lutheran Synod.[37]

In many respects the sort of denominational cooperation that led to the publication of the *Lutheran Book of Worship* provided a similar impetus for the merger of Lutheran denominations. At the same time, the reluctance of the LCMS to adopt the joint Lutheran hymnal was symbolic of the denomination's unwillingness to overlook departures from historic Lutheran teaching for the sake of church union. Just as Preus opposed the broadness that Concordia Seminary appeared to be advocating in the early 1970s, so the LCMS's Special Hymnal Review Committee brought to a halt the liturgical breadth that the new hymnal appeared to be introducing into the denomination. According to its report, the hymnal committee judged that the *Lutheran Book of Worship* would represent "quite a departure from all former Lutheran service books." The reason for this departure appeared to be "an ecumenical effort to make this hymnal acceptable not only to a Lutheran constituency, but to an even broader, wider constituency." To keep the Lutheran tradition from being watered down, the LCMS would have to retrench both theologically and liturgically.[38]

The specific liturgical problems in the joint Lutheran hymnal from the LCMS perspective were the sorts of innovations that come from efforts to make Lutheran worship look more like other Christian communions. The Special Hymnal Review Committee took issue with several of the proposed orders for baptism, marriage, and burial. For instance, the service for baptism prescribed that the minister ask, "Do you renounce all forces of evil, the devil and all his empty promises?" But the committee found this question "ambiguous." "What is meant by 'forces of evil'? The traditional form leaves no doubt: 'Do you renounce the devil and all his works and all his ways?'"[39]

Another hotly contested matter was the *Lutheran Book of Worship*'s proposal to add a eucharistic prayer to the liturgy of the Lord's Supper. One of these prayers in particular added words from the Bible typically read by the minister, which in the minds of many reversed the meaning of the sacrament. Instead of the scriptural passage functioning as a form of proclamation and signifying that the Lord's Supper is a divine activity, the proposed prayer gave the impression that "the Lord's Supper is something we do" since a prayer is "an offering to God." What is more, this prayer suggested that the chief function of the sacrament was giving thanks to God rather than, as Luther's Catechism explained it, the shedding of blood "for the remission of sins."[40] LCMS fussiness even extended to selecting a translation of the psalms for inclusion in the hymnal. The *Lutheran Book of Worship* used the psalter translation included in the 1977 edition of the Protestant Episcopal Church's *Book of Common Prayer*. The LCMS hymnal committee was not entirely satisfied with this rendering and adopted instead a new evangelical translation of the Bible, the New International Version.[41] Although these concerns may have looked picky, they were, in the words of John M. Fuchs, "valid" from the perspective of LCMS doctrine. At the same time, the production of the LCMS hymnal *Lutheran Worship*, as an alternative to the ecumenically inspired *Lutheran Book of Worship*, reflected a distrustful mood in the denomination thanks to fears of liberalism in official agencies and publications.[42]

Yet, to interpret the new LCMS hymnal as one of the conservatives' trophies in a battle for control of the denomination is to miss the ways in which these debates revealed the confessional posture of the Missouri Synod. Again, the controversy at Concordia Seminary in the mid-1970s and the place of inerrancy in those arguments has tempted observers and scholars to conclude that, forced with a choice between evangelical and liberal Protestantism, the LCMS chose the former by embracing a non-Lutheran way of interpreting the Bible. But the hymnal that the denomination created, complete with its supporting materials, indicate that at the same time that the LCMS was rejecting the ecumenical liturgy of the Protestant left, it was also avoiding the low-church worship of the evangelical right. This conclusion looks especially obvious in the way that these confessional Lutherans have debated the merits of the church growth movement and its effort to introduce a form of worship that will appeal to people otherwise not inclined to worship.

The origins of the newer style of evangelical worship, to the extent that they have received scholarly scrutiny, appear to be in the work of Donald McGavaran, a professor for many years at Fuller Theological Seminary in Pasadena, California. The Church Growth Movement that he spearheaded owes much of its intellectual force to social scientific studies that analyze the methods and processes by which congregations grow numerically.[43] The thrust of this research has centered on the cultural and linguistic barriers that churches intentionally and, more often, unknowingly, impose on the so-called unchurched. Congregations cannot conceivably expect visitors, the logic goes, to catch on to or feel welcome in a form of devotion where they do not know what is happening or being communicated. Of course, the point of such study is to show churches how to be more evangelistic—that is, how to gain more new church members. Consequently, the Church Growth Movement has been attractive to many old-line Protestant denominations in the United States that since the 1950s have been experiencing significant membership decline while also appealing to evangelical churches always looking for better ways to evangelize.[44]

The implications of this concern for reaching those outside the church are obvious for the way churches conduct their liturgy. A fundamental feature of the Church Growth Movement is the Homogenous Unit Principle. Social scientists have concluded quite commonsensically that people are attracted to churches where they find others like themselves. Accordingly, worship services, from the perspective of church growth experts, need to be redesigned to appeal to a "very specific social-economic-educational portion of society."[45] And one of the most effective strategies for making such an appeal is through music. Worship planners in churches hoping to attract those unfamiliar with the ways of a particular denominational tradition have designed services that not only have music as a prominent element but also feature a form of song heavily influenced by the increasing popularity of rock and roll. Some proponents have referred to this liturgical novelty as "entertainment evangelism." Another phrase commonly used to describe this form or worship is "seeker service." This style of liturgy is one of the basic ingredients in the success of such megachurches as Willow Creek Community Church, located in the suburbs of Chicago. To attract its unchurched neighbors, services rely on musicians and singers who resemble formally the performers in a rock band. Willow Creek has also introduced liturgical drama in which church members perform in skits that are designed to reinforce the sermon. According to James F. White, "in line with the Frontier Tradition, music is half the service. . . . The musical idiom is carefully selected to relate to that homogenous unit being targeted."[46] The major difference between these megachurches and the evangelistic services orchestrated by itinerant evangelists such as George Whitefield, Billy Sunday, and Billy Graham is that the pastors of these large congregations stay in one place. But the design in both cases is remarkably similar. Services use a variety of means that are designed to make an impression on would-be converts that elicits a dramatic, emotional, and, it is assumed, heartfelt response.[47]

The appeal of church growth techniques, however, owes to more than simply the numerical decline of American Protestantism's oldest denominations. It also stems from the stunning growth of the charismatic movement since 1950. An offshoot of Pentecostalism, the charismatic influence has surfaced in practically all Christian traditions in North America, both Protestant and Catholic. Unlike classical Pentecostal piety in which believers demonstrated being moved by the Spirit through speaking in tongues, the charismatic movement has not required such exotic signs of spiritual excitement. But it has made emotional participation an indication of genuine faith. As such, churches under the influence of the charismatic movement have reconfigured worship services to give worshipers an experience of divine encounter. And again, contemporary Christian music has been the most significant means for generating this experience. At the same time, these churches have substituted guitars and drums for organs, overhead projectors or television screens for hymnals, and have been using music that has most often come from song writers and musicians whose backgrounds are in the charismatic movement.[48] As one of the advocates of the newer forms of worship has put it, although ritual can be moving to some Christians, "it goes past many without bringing them into personal engagement." This lack of response among some attending church is the reason for "alternative worship forms." Attendance, he asserts, "is not the point." Instead, the issue is whether worship is "spiritually moving." Church statistics will take care of themselves.[49]

The author of these sentiments about the need for worship to be spiritually exciting was an LCMS pastor, David S. Luecke, whose book *Evangelical Style and Lutheran Substance* (1988) showed that even the liturgically minded and emotionally staid confessional Lutherans who struggled to produce a hymnal faithful to their theological heritage were not immune from charismatic Protestants whom Martin Luther himself might have accused of having swallowed the Holy Ghost, "feathers and all."[50] The title of Luecke's book aptly expressed the author's point: namely, that it is possible to adopt evangelical means of evangelism (i.e., church growth) while retaining core Lutheran beliefs. In Luecke's own words, "style" stands for "dimensions of a church's life and ministry that can be changed," while "substance" signifies "the ingredients of a church's identity that are not open to change." The reason for making this distinction is that inherited styles of Lutheran growth from earlier periods, according to Luecke, are no longer effective. He singled out the LCMS's liturgical worship as part of Lutheran style that is negotiable because Lutheran confessions themselves "recognize considerable latitude in matters of practice and thereby in style."[51] Although the LCMS had just gone through an arduous process of self-definition, part of which involved producing a hymnal that shaped its worship, Luecke wanted the denomination to reconsider its options.

These options involved choosing between the three most successful techniques for building large congregations. The first, according to Luecke, was the "content-oriented approach," typical of fundamentalist churches, in which the emphasis in worship is on the sermon, especially a form of sermonizing that interprets the will of God "in very specific terms for life's situations today." The second was the "relationship-oriented approach," most common in Pentecostal and charismatic circles, in which people go to church to "experience as directly as possible the presence of God in their lives." Finally, the "confrontation-oriented approach," most often associated with evangelists such as Billy Graham, emphasizes conversion and orchestrates religious activities and worship services toward the goal of convincing persons to make a decision for Christ.[52]

Although Luecke advocated a selective borrowing from these three strategies, his preference appeared to be the second option because he believed Lutherans needed to recover a sense of God's presence in worship. Here he appealed to the sacrament of the Lord's Supper as the basis for Lutheran affinity to the Pentecostal style of worship with its stress on experiencing divine presence. According to Luecke, "this style can show how sacramental thinking might be extended . . . how God's presence can be recognized through other forms of combining the Word of His promises with what believers can touch, feel, and experience."[53] But more than Lutheran sacramental teaching provided a way for Lutherans to connect with church growth strategies. For Luecke, the tradition of pietism was the greatest source of commonality between Lutheran and evangelical style. Lutheran pietism, he admitted, had been "driven out" of the LCMS "by more formalized liturgical emphases." Luecke would not, however, recognize an inherent tension between confessional and pietist Lutherans and so concluded that the LCMS experienced its greatest growth when "orthodoxy and piety were cultivated together."[54]

Luecke's critics immediately made up for his naïveté about American Lutheran history and particularly the both-and-approach to confessionalism and pietism. For David A. Gustafson, Luecke was a twentieth-century version of Samuel Schmucker who was guilty of trying once again to Americanize Lutheranism, thereby robbing the tradition of its vitality and identity. "Luecke's proposals," Gustafson wrote, "undermine Lutheran confessional and liturgical integrity." Luecke had called into question Lutheran teaching and practice in matters regarding salvation, the sacraments, and worship. The book was so destructive, wrote Gustafson, that it contained "the potential for the collapse of all Lutheran doctrinal and liturgical substance and the destruction of the Office of the Ministry."[55]

As definitive as Gustafson's assessment may have been, it was not as sharp as David G. Truemper's because of the latter's extended critique of what the Church Growth Movement would mean for Lutheran worship. In Truemper's analysis the issue of liturgy crystallized the differences between confessionalism and pietism. The fundamental expression of the church's existence, he argued, is "the liturgical assembly around gospel and sacrament." In other words, "our confessional tradition is . . . at bottom, liturgical." The reason was straightforward. Unlike the Church Growth Movement that worships in order to gain converts, confessional Lutherans "evangelize in order to gain worshipers." The point of worship—accordingly, the goal of preaching the word and administering the sacraments—was "to worship God," not "to worship so as to recruit new members." Through such theocentric worship, Truemper concluded, believers would become stronger in faith so that they could endure the hardships of life and still trust in God. Instead of facing three options for growth, then, Truemper, echoing John Williamson Nevin 150 years earlier, believed the LCMS faced a choice between a "marketplace mentality" and a catechetical view of the church that emphasized the "nurture of the faithful into that 'assembly of believers.'"[56]

Luecke and his confessional Lutheran critics were much more polemical in their reading of the issues before the LCMS than the denomination's official position papers would be, thus illustrating the differences between statements written individually and collectively. Nevertheless, in a series of pamphlets that addressed the charismatic and Church Growth movements, the LCMS appeared to arrive at an understanding of the leading late twentieth-century forms of evangelical (and pietistic) Protestantism that preserved the integrity of the Lutheran liturgical tradition that *Lutheran Worship* was designed to maintain. The denomination responded to Pentecostalism as early as 1972 and followed up with a subsequent statement five years later, well before the charismatic movement achieved a liturgical groundswell in non-Pentecostal churches. In *The Charismatic Movement and Lutheran Theology*, the LCMS, true to its confessional identity, expressed great reservation about the sort of experiential Christianity that Martin Luther himself branded "enthusiasm." Lutherans, the report explained, had always rejected the notion that believers could experience the movement of the Spirit apart from the means of grace—namely, preaching and sacraments. "The emphasis of our Lutheran heritage on the external Word as the instrument of the Holy Spirit helps prevent a subjectivism that seeks divine comfort and strength through an interior experience rather than in the objective word of the Gospel."[57]

Confessional Lutheran suspicion about the arbitrary nature of experiential Protestantism led the same committee responsible for the 1972 report to caution the church in its 1977 study against ever separating the work of the Spirit or the experience of grace from the objectivity of preaching and the sacraments. The Pentecostal idea that baptism in the Holy Spirit was a second experience of grace above and beyond the sacrament of baptism denied the full benefits of the means of grace. Lutherans, consequently, should not look for "power and renewal" for the church in "special signs and miracles" but simply "in the Word and sacraments."[58]

In its 1987 report on the Church Growth Movement, the LCMS showed once again a refusal to depart from the liturgical bearings that held confessional Lutheranism together. The middle section of the study displayed a remarkable objectivity when it described the principles and techniques of church growth in the terms of its greatest proponents. This was undoubtedly a way of trying not to alienate Missourians such as Luecke and keep the denomination from hemorrhaging. Nevertheless, in the concluding section of analysis the LCMS hammered home once again the notion that baptism, the Lord's Supper, and preaching were the only genuine means of growing the church. To be sure, techniques of organization and sociological and psychological investigation could assist a congregation in approaching the unconverted and therefore "serve the Gospel." But such methods were clearly "not the means of grace" and could not of themselves "build the church and cause it to grow." Only through the means of grace and God's blessing through the Spirit did churches increase numerically or spiritually.[59]

Although none of these reports made explicit reference to the process of producing a hymnal or to the shape of Lutheran liturgy, by distancing itself from the two principle engines driving the transformation of American Protestant worship after 1970, the LCMS provided shelter to the position staked out in *Lutheran Worship*. It did so by rejecting the distinction between form and substance, or the idea that Christian devotion can be expressed in any cultural idiom. Specifically, the report on church growth refused to go along with the idea that worship services needed to be structured according to "current cultural patterns." Even though the Bible did not prescribe a "specific order of worship," Lutheran liturgy was designed to "accent the objectivity of the Gospel proclaimed in the Word and communicated in the sacraments, not the subjectivity of the hearers or their emotional response." This is because the one doing the service in the worship service was God, not "us."[60] In other words, the different parts of the Lutheran worship service—the invocation, confession, absolution, hymn of praise, collects and prayers, lessons, creed, the Lord's Supper, and benediction—were all crucial pieces of the way believers appropriated religion. And to turn the liturgy into a way of attracting new members was to neglect the needs of the established members who needed to be reminded of Christian truths and built up in faith.

The LCMS effort to maintain the older liturgical ways of Lutheranism, then, illustrates once more the difference between confessionalism and pietism in American Protestantism. Worship for the latter is most often a means of evangelism that either generates new believers or sends older ones out either in search of other converts or performing good works of a reformist nature. The model saint in pietist devotion is the activist. In contrast, confessionalism understands worship as a means of nurture that edifies the faithful weekly and throughout the various stages of human life, from birth, through to marriage, child rearing, and bread winning, to death. According to this scheme of devotion the Christian is a pilgrim in need of sustenance for the trials and responsibilities of life. Indeed, worship is the best indicator of the differences between the pietist and confessionalist ways of getting religion. For the pietist, it is one among many means for gaining new converts and receiving added motivation for virtuous deeds. For the confessionalist, as the LCMS illustrates, however, it is an end in itself, a time when believers are reminded that the suffering of this life is temporary and encouraged to trust in divine deliverance from such trials in the life to come. As one Lutheran minister put it, "For confessional Lutherans, liturgy is not about human activity, but about the real presence of the Lord. . . . The liturgy does not exist to provide edifying entertainment, motivation for sanctified living or therapy for psychological distresses, but the forgiveness of sins."[61]

Liturgical Irrelevance

As much as confessional Protestantism appears to be alive and well in the LCMS, critics from within the Lutheran fold continue to argue that the denomination sold its confessional birthright during the 1970s debates over inerrancy for a mess of evangelical pottage. According to A. G. Roeber, an accomplished historian of colonial America and a former Lutheran, the LCMS in 1996 looked indistinguishable from "every other Protestant 'evangelical' body." He detected LCMS assimilation particularly in the denomination's "'megachurch' willingness to indulge in the self-delusion that by any means necessary, the only task is to get warm bodies into the church buildings." But the Americanization of the LCMS did not stop there. It is also evident in the way proponents of traditional Lutheran liturgy have been "trumped by those who advocate a more 'relevant' consumer-friendly worship." Although Roeber hesitates to reduce the transformation of the LCMS simply to a religious version of America's culture wars, he does suggest that the split in the 1970s between hard line LCMS leaders and moderates and progressives who left to help found the ELCA reflected the inability of Lutherans to avoid the temptations of the evangelical religious right and the mainline Protestant leftist orientation. In "the debate on what it means to be Lutheran," Roeber concludes, both the LCMS and its rival, the ELCA, are "trapped now in the competing camps of America's culture war."[62]

If Roeber is correct, then for the purposes of this book his point proves yet again the difficulty that confessional Protestants in the United States have historically faced in trying to practice a form of Christianity different from the pietistic forms of devotion that dominate the Protestant mainstream. But even Roeber concedes that to regard the conservatives who came to power during the 1970s in the LCMS as forerunners of "today's conservative cultural warriors" is "deceptively simple." And one reason for making the case that the LCMS *is* distinguishable from every other evangelical Protestant body is the denomination's liturgy. Irrespective of whether all its congregations follow it, *Lutheran Worship* and the official documents accompanying it, along with LCMS studies on church growth and the charismatic movement, reveal a side of the denomination that is foreign to contemporary evangelicalism. As Roeber himself admits, the LCMS hymnal and the supplemental study, *Lutheran Worship: History and Practice* (1993), "signal a belated determination to re-connect biblical and liturgical study in the Synod."[63]

Roeber could have well added to his list of signs another study sponsored by the LCMS' Commission on Theology and Church Relations, this one on the Lutheran understanding of the relation between church and state. What is striking about this 1995 document is that it was not only written in the context of culture war but that it cited in its prologue James Davison Hunter's popular book, *Culture Wars: The Struggle to Define America* (1991), along with two cultural warriors known to be identified with the right—Richard John Neuhaus and Os Guinness. These references could have well laid the groundwork for an effort to push the LCMS precisely in the camp in which Roeber believed it was heading. Yet, after surveying Protestant history since the Reformation and setting out the Lutheran doctrine of the two kingdoms, the most political and cultural resolve the LCMS could muster was this: "The critical questions . . . are not whether church *should* be involved with politics, or whether it can even *avoid* being involved with politics, but '*how*' church and politics are and ought to be re-lated and '*how* each kind of political involvement affects the nature and mission of the church.'"[64]

Interestingly enough, one of the examples cited in this report was the LCMS's Board for Parish Education's statement on prayer in public schools. Because this practice provided "either a coercive force or an embarrassing situation for both Christians and non-Christians," the Board for Parish Education concluded that it was "best for the public school not to engage in prayer or other religious worship exercises."[65] Even though the LCMS never adopted this statement, a fact that allowed the report on church and state's authors to notice that not all LCMS publications or expressions were of an official nature, it did illustrate the kind of caution churches needed to exhibit when addressing public affairs. To be sure, the church was a legal institution and had a right to address the state to protect its own (as well as its members' spiritual) interests, and individual Lutherans were free as citizens to "engage in the many occupations that . . . constitute human communities and meet human needs," including the political process. But the church was such a "precious institution" that it should not "be jeopardized by immersion in secular politics. The "primary" concern of the church was forgiveness of sins. Consequently, the church spoke "most appropriately through the preaching of the Gospel and the administration of the sacraments." This "public" speech was "spiritually persuasive" to believers, not "temporarily coercive" to those outside the church.[66]

In other words, individual members of the LCMS may have been active in the culture war, but the denomination itself, as this report indicated, would have to be a bystander. Of course, the Lutheran doctrine of two kingdoms helps explain such pacificism. But just as important is the liturgical tradition that confessional Lutheranism has maintained. As the LCMS report on church growth stated, "in a sense, the church (including its cultus or worship) is always *counter*-cultural."[67] The oddness of Lutheran worship, then, extended as much to partisan politics as it did to musical tastes because the purpose of the church and its worship was not to save a nation or a culture but to offer forgiveness to sinners. Individual members of the LCMS, like those in other confessional traditions, have clearly been tempted by the American Protestant habit of applying the Christian faith to temporal circumstances and, no doubt, many have fallen. But if the LCMS as a corporate body has resisted that temptation, a large amount of credit must go to the confessional outlook that regards worship as an exercise wholly irrelevant to the warfare of this world, whether cultural, political, or military.

Notes

1. James Davison Hunter, *Culture Wars: The Struggle to Define America* (New York: Basic Books, 1991), 93.

2. Nancy T. Ammerman, "North American Protestant Fundamentalism," in *Fundamentalisms Observed: The Fundamentalist Project*, vol. I, ed. Martin E. Marty and R. Scott Appleby (Chicago: University of Chicago Press, 1991), 48.

3. Mark Ellingsen, "Lutheranism," in *The Variety of American Evangelicalism*, ed. Donald W. Dayton and Robert K. Johnston (Downers Grove, Ill.: InterVarsity, 1991), 222.

4. David P. Scaer, "Missouri at the End of the Century: A Time for Reevaluation," *Logia* 7, no. I (1998): 51.

5. Mark Granquist, "Lutherans in the United States, 1930–1960: Searching for the 'Center,'" in *Re-Forming the Center: American Protestantism, 1900 to the Present*, ed. Douglas Jacobsen and William Vance Trollinger Jr. (Grand Rapids, Mich.: Eerdmans, 1998), 249.

6. Leigh Jordahl, "Contemporary Worship: The Adiaphoristic Controversy Revisited," *Dialog* 33 (Fall 1999): 302–304.

7. See Michael Lienesch, *Redeeming America: Piety and Politics in the New Christian Right* (Chapel Hill: University of North Carolina Press, 1993); Steve Bruce, *The Rise and Fall of the New Christian Right: Conservative Protestant Politics in America, 1978–1988* (New York: Oxford University Press, 1988); William C. Martin, *With God on Our Side: The Rise of the Religious Right in America* (New York: Broadway Books, 1996); Clyde Wilcox, *God's Warriors: The Christian Right in Twentieth-Century America* (Baltimore: Johns Hopkins University Press, 1992); Leo P. Ribuffo, "God and Contemporary Politics," *Journal of American History* 79 (1993): 1515–33; Robert Booth Fowler, *A New Engagement: Christian Evangelical Political Thought, 1966–1976* (Grand Rapids, Mich.: Eerdmans, 1982); and George M. Marsden, "Preachers of Paradox: Fundamentalist Politics in Historical Perspective," in his *Understanding Fundamentalism and Evangelicalism* (Grand Rapids, Mich.: Eerdmans, 1991), 104–9.

8. Marsden, *Understanding Fundamentalism and Evangelicalism*, I.

9. From a direct mail advertisement for *America: To Pray or Not to Pray?* (Washington, D.C.: Concerned Women for America, 1988), quoted in Hunter, *Culture Wars*, 203.

10. See Diane Ravich, *The Great School Wars: A History of the New York City Public Schools* (New York: Basic Books, 1974); and Paul Gutjahr, *An American Bible: A His-*

tory of the Good Book in the United States, 1777–1880 (Stanford, Calif.: Stanford University Press, 1999), chap. 4.

11. See Martin E. Marty, *Modern American Religion. Vol. 2: The Noise of Conflict, 1919–1941* (Chicago: University of Chicago Press, 1991), chap. 3.

12. Harold S. Tuttle, *Character Education by State and Church* (Cincinnati: Abingdon, 1930), 5, 7.

13. Tuttle, *Character Education*, 95.

14. Tuttle, *Character Education*, 147.

15. *Engel v. Vitale* in *Toward Benevolent Neutrality: Church State and the Supreme Court*, rev. ed., ed. Robert T. Miller and Ronald B. Flowers (Waco, Tex.: Markham Press Fund, 1982), 331.

16. Quoted in Robert Michaelsen, *Piety in the Public School: Trends and Issues in the Relationship between Religion and the Public School in the United States* (New York: Macmillan, 1970), 223.

17. Quoted in Michaelsen, *Piety in the Public School*, 225.

18. Quoted in Michaelsen, *Piety in the Public School*, 226, 227.

19. Raymond F. Surburg, "Historical Survey of the Lutheran Philosophy of Education," in *Readings in the Lutheran Philosophy of Education* (1956), quoted in Curtis Brooks Barby, "The Interaction of Church and State for the Lutheran Church Missouri Synod" (Ph.D. diss., St. Louis University, 1972), 140, 141.

20. *Proceedings of the Lutheran Church–Missouri Synod* (1959), 328, quoted in Walter H. Beck, *Lutheran Elementary Schools in the United States* (St. Louis: Concordia, 1965), 471.

21. August C. Stellhorn, *Schools of the Lutheran Church–Missouri Synod* (St. Louis: Concordia, 1963), 117.

22. Beck, *Lutheran Elementary Schools*, 466.

23. For a fuller statement of the two-kingdom view, see Commission on Theology and Church Relations of the LCMS, *Render unto Caesar . . . and unto God: A Lutheran View of Church and State* (St. Louis: Lutheran Church–Missouri Synod, 1995).

24. See *Abington Township School District v. Schempp* in *Toward Benevolent Neutrality*, ed. Miller and Flowers, 340, 341.

25. William. A. Kramer, *Devotions for Lutheran Schools* (St. Louis: Concordia, 1946), 12.

26. *Engel v. Vitale*, 331.

27. "Liturgical Forms," *American Lutheran* 17 (February 1934): 4, quoted in Michael Hinrichs, "Liturgical Uniformity in Missouri," *Logia* 5, no. 2 (1996): 17.

28. Intersynodical Committee on Hymnology and Liturgics for the Evangelical Lutheran Conference of North America, *The Lutheran Hymnal* (St. Louis: Concordia, 1941).

29. W. G. Polack, "A Reply," *Lutheran Witness* 60 (December 9, 1941): 424, quoted in Hinrichs, "Liturgical Uniformity," 22.

30. Lutheran Church–Missouri Synod, *Reports and Memorials*, 1959, 443, quoted in John M. Fuchs, "From *The Lutheran Hymnal* to *Lutheran Worship*: A Paradigm of Lutheran Church—Missouri Synod History," *Concordia Journal* 20 (1994): 132.

31. See Fuchs, "From *The Lutheran Hymnal*," 132–33; and Fred L. Precht, "Worship Resources in Missouri Synod's History," in *Lutheran Worship: History and Practice*, ed. Fred L. Precht (St. Louis: Concordia, 1993), 106–8.

32. *Worship Supplement*, 9, quoted in Fuchs, "From *The Lutheran Hymnal*," 135.

33. Eugene L. Brand, "The ILCW: Dimension of Its Task," *Dialog* 14 (1975): 95; *Worship Supplement*, 9, quoted in Fuchs, "From *The Lutheran Hymnal*," 141.

34. Fuchs, "From *The Lutheran Hymnal*," 136–37.

35. Philip Pfatteicher, *Commentary on the Lutheran Book of Worship* (Minneapolis: Augsburg Fortress, 1990), 11, quoted in Fuchs, "From *The Lutheran Hymnal*," 137.

36. Lutheran Church–Missouri Synod, *Report and Recommendations of the Special Hymnal Review Committee* (St. Louis: Author, 1978); Fuchs, "From *the Lutheran Hymnal*," 138–40; and Robert Sauer, "*Lutheran Worship* (1982): The Special Hymnal Review Committee," in Precht, ed., *Lutheran Worship*, 117–20.

37. On the events at Concordia, see L. DeAne Lagerquist, *The Lutherans* (Westport, Conn.: Greenwood, 1999), 150–53; and Gilbert Meilaender, "How Churches Crack Up: The Case of the Lutheran Church–Missouri Synod," *First Things* (June/July 1991): 38–42.

38. LCMS, Department of Publications News Release, November 21, 1977, quoted in Sauer, "*Lutheran Worship* (1982)," 119.

39. Sauer, "*Lutheran Worship* (1982)," 121.

40. Sauer, "*Lutheran Worship* (1982)," 125.

41. Sauer, "*Lutheran Worship* (1982)," 126.

42. Fuchs, "From *The Lutheran Hymnal*," 145.

43. See, for instance, Donald Anderson McGavran, *Understanding Church Growth* (Grand Rapids, Mich.: Eerdmans, 1970); and Donald Anderson McGavran *How to Grow a Church* (Glendale, Calif.: Regal, 1973).

44. See James F. White, *Christian Worship in North America: A Retrospective, 1955–1995* (Collegeville, Minn.: Liturgical, 1997), 132–33.

45. White, *Christian Worship in North America*.

46. White, *Christian Worship in North America*, 163.

47. On Willow Creek Community Church and congregations like it, see Kimon Howland Sargeant, *Seeker Churches: Promoting Traditional Religion in a Nontraditional Way* (New Brunswick, N.J.: Rutgers University Press, 2000); and Paul Wilkes, *Excellent Protestant Congregations: The Guide to Best Places and Practices* (Louisville, Ky.: Westminster/John Knox, 2001).

48. See Bernhard Lang, *Sacred Games: A History of Christian Worship* (New Haven, Conn.: Yale University Press, 1997), chap. 6, especially 398–409.

49. David S. Luecke, "How Far Can We Go in Recreating Worship? Knowing the Basic Purpose," *Word and World* 17 (1997): 427.

50. Roland H. Bainton, *Here I Stand: A Life of Martin Luther* (New York: Abingdon-Cokesbury, 1950), 261, attributes this phrase to Luther in reference to Thomas Müntzer.

51. David S. Luecke, *Evangelical Style and Lutheran Substance: Facing America's Mission Challenge* (St. Louis: Concordia, 1988), 9–10, 23.

52. Luecke, *Evangelical Style and Lutheran Substance*, 75–78.

53. Luecke, *Evangelical Style and Lutheran Substance*, 85.

54. Luecke, *Evangelical Style and Lutheran Substance*, 91, 92.

55. David A. Gustafson, *Lutherans in Crisis: The Question of Identity in the American Republic* (Minneapolis: Fortress, 1993), 176, 177.

56. David G. Truemper, "Evangelism: Liturgy *versus* Church Growth," *Lutheran Forum* 24 (Advent 1990): 32, 33.

57. Commission on Theology and Church Relations, *The Charismatic Movement and Lutheran Theology* (St. Louis: Lutheran Church–Missouri Synod, 1972), 29.

58. Commission on Theology and Church Relations, *The Lutheran Church and the Charismatic Movement: Guidelines for Congregations and Pastors* (St. Louis: Lutheran Church–Missouri Synod, 1977), 5, 6.

59. Commission on Theology and Church Relations, *Evangelism and Church Growth: With Reference to the Church Growth Movement* (St. Louis: Lutheran Church–Missouri Synod, 1987), 41.

60. Commission on Theology and Church Relations, *Evangelism and Church Growth.*, 41, 42.

61. John T. Pless, "Divine Service: Delivering Forgiveness of Sins," *Logia* 5, no. 4 (Reformation 1996): 23.

62. A. G. Roeber, "Almost Persuaded? The Anguish of Lutheran Identity and America's Culture Wars," *Lutheran Forum* 30, no. 1 (February 1996): 24, 25, 27.

63. Roeber, "Almost Persuaded?" 25.

64. Commission on Theology and Church Relations of the LCMS, *Render unto Caesar*, 63; the report is quoting Robert Benne, "The Church and Politics: Four Possible Connections," *This World* 25 (Spring 1989): 27.

65. Board of Parish Education of the LCMS, "Statement on the Prayer Amendment Proposed by Senator Everett M. Dirksen," July 29, 1966, quoted in Commission on Theology and Church Relations of the LCMS, *Render unto Caesar*, 85.

66. Commission on Theology and Church Relations of the LCMS, *Render unto Caesar*, 91, 92.

67. Elmer L. Towns, *Evangelism and Church Growth* (Ventura, Calif: Regal Books), 42.

Conclusion

Confessional Protestantism and the Making of Hyphenated Americans

An important question hovering over this study is whether confessional Protestantism exists as a self-contained phenomenon beyond or abstracted from the experience of the various ethnic Protestant traditions that have migrated from Europe to the United States. In other words, does this form of Protestant belief and especially practice transcend ethnicity? After all, practically all of the groups used here to illustrate the primary characteristics of confessionalism are immigrant communions for whom religion and ethnicity are inseparable. For Old Side Presbyterians, Scotch-Irishness created what the historian John Higham has called an ethnic groups' "perception of difference from other collectivities," in this case a heritage different from English Puritans in New England.[1] Religion's reinforcement of ethnicity was even more pronounced in the history of German-American Lutherans and Dutch-American Reformed. The one exception covered here is J. Gresham Machen and his fellow confessional Presbyterians, who were for all intents and purposes part of the Anglo-American mainstream. Even in this instance, however, some have argued that Machen's southernness was such a prominent part of his outlook that it functioned something like an ethnic identity that reinforced differences with the northern-dominated Protestant establishment.[2] If, as Higham has also asserted, ethnicity is the "'skeleton,' or supporting framework around which religious traditions cohere,"[3] what happens to confessional Protestantism when its adherents lose their ethnic identity and move from being Dutch, German, or Scotch-Irish, to being "white," American, or evangelical? Can confessional Protestantism exist without the sense of otherness that ethnicity (or regionalism) nurtures? Can confessionalism contribute anything valuable to already-assimilated Protestants?

Behind this set of questions lies an even more poignant one: if confessional Protestantism has historically been tied to ethnicity, then isn't this form of Christianity a barrier to the kind of cohesion and harmony that the United States has displayed in its remarkable history of absorbing diverse races, creeds, and cultures from all over the world? In sum, is confessionalism a threat to American society? This is a question that historian David A. Hollinger asks implicitly in his thoughtful book on multiculturalism in America. For instance, he notes that in recent debates about cultural diversity some religious groups, ironically, evangelical Protestants, have tried to make themselves over in "the contemporary image of ethno-racial minorities," thus allowing believers to claim the "promise of entitlement" usually reserved in the United States for minorities.[4] Highlighting confessionalism's ethnic character, as any accurate account must do, would appear, then, to contribute to the balkanization of American society because it features differences that exist not only between confessional groups and mainstream Protestantism, but also among the diverse confessional traditions themselves over such matters as creed, polity, and liturgy. Confessional Protestantism is seemingly divisive in ways that pietist Protestantism, with its congenital quest for essentials, is not.

Unmeltable Confessionalists

Before addressing the matter of unity and diversity in American religion and culture, it may be valuable for the sake of clarity to make explicit the ethnic character of confessional Protestantism. Confessionalism represents a form of Christianity that is distinct from the predominant patterns of evangelical or mainline Protestantism because of its churchly and corporate form of devotion. In contrast to pietist Protestantism, which stresses the individual's original encounter with the divine in a flash of spiritual intensity, confessionalism marks the beginning of Christian experience typically with infant baptism and the notion that believers inherit the faith of their parents and the larger Christian community. This does not mean that conversion of adolescents or adults is prohibited but only that the experience of children who grow up in the church and learn the ways of the community of faith is more the norm for Christian life than one that makes the radical change of conversion the paradigm for faith.

So, too, in contrast with pietism and the ideal of the lone convert engaging in times of private or small-group prayer and Bible study, confessional Protestantism regards the ministry of clergy and corporate worship as the primary sources of spiritual edification. To be sure, parents in confessional Protestantism play an important role by providing catechetical instruction in the home. But the devotion of families is simply a microcosm of the church's formal teaching and devotion, not an alternative designed to make up for the deficiencies of the church's routines.

For confessional Protestantism, then, the ministry of word and sacrament, catechetical instruction, and the setting apart of ministers to perform formal religious ceremonies as well as provide informal pastoral oversight, are the building blocks of Christian devotion. Creed, liturgy, and polity are not peripheral or even barriers to genuine faith, as pietist Protestants have usually regarded them, but actually define and communicate religious identity, whether to new converts or those who have grown up in the faith.

If confessionalism constitutes a way of getting religion distinct from the patterns that have dominated American Protestantism, its difference can perhaps best be seen in two contrasting types of Christian devotion, that of crusader and that of pilgrim.[5] For pietist Protestantism the ideal believer is one who is constantly active in extending the kingdom of God. The crusader, accordingly, is always on the lookout for ways to gain new converts and make the good deeds of believers more obvious before the watching world, thereby expanding Christian influence. In other words, the conversionist notion of Protestantism not only relies on the work of full-time revivalists and Christian individuals who share their faith with unbelievers but also results in strenuous efforts to realize the righteous ways of the faithful, whether in various crusades to reform public life or in less noticeable endeavors designed to show the difference that faith makes in daily affairs. Pietist Protestantism is inherently activist; for its adherents the Christian life is one of perpetual motion as converts, secure in their salvation, seek to take their faith to all corners of the globe and to all spheres of human existence.

Confessional Protestantism's devotion is characteristically withdrawn and secluded compared to pietism's aggressive and extroverted ways. For confessionalism a good bit of the Christian life includes a recognition of the spiritual dangers that still afflict believers and their consequent need for spiritual help and sustenance that the ministry of the church is designed to provide. Being a Christian, then, means participating in churchly rites and ceremonies, not simply as means of inspiration for evangelism and Christian activism, but primarily to learn dependence on grace and to persevere through life's doubts and temptations. Pietists have typically complained that the confessional Protestant conception of Christian devotion is too passive if not selfish because it is so oriented to believers rather than those outside the faith. Confessionalism, it is said, exhibits a ghetto mentality. But this complaint is based on an assumption about the nature of Christian devotion that confessionalism rejects—namely, that conversion results in strong believers who are so powerful that the true measure of spiritual zeal is what they accomplish either by winning new converts or by performing moral deeds. Confessionalism's understanding of the Christian life as a pilgrimage, however, assumes the weakness and frailty of believers and measures success by the degree to which they continue to trust in God and hope for the world to come despite the trials and suffering of this life. This outlook even extends to the direction and purpose of history; where confessionalists have regarded human history as a cosmic drama that awaits consummation according to the will of God, pietists have swung between optimism and despair in assessing the relative proximity of history's conclusion.[6]

Here it is important to see how confessional Protestant sensibilities dovetail with those that characterize ethnic identity. Unlike pietism, which thrives on the decisions of sovereign individuals who choose to become Christians, confessionalism relies on patterns of inheritance in which the expectation is for believers to come into the faith through birth and Christian nurture. For confessional Protestants the norms of the religious group are passed on from one generation to the next, and church membership presumes following the established beliefs and practices of spiritual ancestors. Even converts are expected to adopt the tradition's ways. To be sure, this understanding of Christian faith has encouraged a kind of ethnocentrism that appears to be at odds with the evangelistic and missionary efforts of the early Christians who established their faith as a world religion. Yet, even the oldest varieties of Christianity—Roman Catholicism and Eastern Orthodoxy—practice a form of piety that is based much more on the idea of inheritance than that of choice. The reason is that these expressions of Christianity stress the importance of participating in the ways of previous generations as embodied in the corporate life and witness of the church. In other words, Roman Catholics and the Eastern Orthodox have historically measured spiritual maturity by the degree to which a believer conforms to the teachings and practices of the tradition, unlike pietist Protestantism, for which zeal and morality are marks of religious health.

Not all Protestants, however, are pietists, even though the scholarly literature on American religion might suggest otherwise. Indeed, many of the earliest Protestants, those who established churches in the Lutheran, Reformed, and Anglican traditions, continued to expect believers to conform to the doctrines and habits of the church, however novel it was. Although not always successful, confessional Protestants have been the bearers of this outlook in the United States, founding churches and building families devoted to passing on an inherited faith.

In many respects, confessional Protestantism fared better in North America more than it did in Europe thanks ironically to one of secularization's basic features—religious freedom. On the surface, the separation of church and state that the American and French Revolutions inaugurated, though in not exactly the same form, would appear to be inimical to churches and religious traditions because it has privatized faith and made religion marginal to everyday public affairs. To be sure, established churches lost political power and cultural clout by virtue of religious disestablishment. But as confessional Protestants in Europe also learned, established churches rarely experienced independence from governmental interference and were more often than not forced to refashion their teaching and practices to accommodate the designs of the monarchy, kaiser, or parliament. For this reason, religious liberty, not simply the peripheral location of immigrant communities, allowed confessional Protestants in America to flesh out the implications of their beliefs in ways the state churches could not. In the nineteenth century especially, the United States provided a shelter for German Lutherans and Dutch Calvinists when the mother church in the homeland was experiencing pressure from ambitious state and church officials.[7]

The other aspects of modernity, as sociologists have observed, have not been as kind to confessional Protestants and so assimilation into the American Protestant mainstream has been a constant source of strain, especially in the twentieth century.[8] Part of the dilemma for confessionalists has been the sheer size and considerable resources of mainstream Protestantism, in both its evangelical and mainline branches. As the Christian Reformed

Church witnessed during the 1940s, forming links with evangelicals appeared to be the sensible option if the denomination were to leave behind the loneliness of ethnoreligious isolation. But a large element of the pull on confessionalists into Protestant mainstream has also been a social and cultural environment that is inherently friendly to pietism's individualist and experiential form of Christianity and inimical to confessionalism's corporate and churchly faith.

According to the sociologist David Martin, the American style of religion is inherently "Methodist" or pietist. He writes that the greatest difference between the United States and England is "the American insistence on sincerity and openness rather than on form and privacy." As a result, "'enthusiasm' of all kinds, religious, cultural, and personal became endemic in America" compared to England, where it remanded "intermittent and the object of some mild curiosity."[9] To be sure, the explanations for America's way of faith are numerous, and in the specific case of a comparison with England, the presence or absence of an ecclesiastical establishment is significant. Nevertheless, the American cultural ideals of popular sovereignty and individual freedom, though not inherently opposed to confessionalism, do make faith chiefly a matter of one's personal expression. Consequently, a conversionist understanding of Christianity, one that emphasizes the centrality of the individual's decision and experience, is more plausible in America than a faith based on inheritance in which a son or daughter becomes a member of the religious community by receiving and adopting the ways of the faithful.

What another sociologist, Steve Bruce, writes about the traditionless character of recent evangelicalism may also be applied to the Anglo-American Protestant tradition more generally: "the culture which conservative Protestants in the USA seek to defend is one which they have chosen and which they advertise as virtuous, independent of any historical connections with a particular ethnic group."[10] As simplistic as it may sound, America came into existence in part to throw off the traditions of the Old World. It is no wonder, then, that its most popular forms of religiosity would be antitraditional. As such, Protestant believers, hoping to perpetuate their religious traditions, have generally been ethnic minorities wary of the Protestant mainstream because of the latter's similar wariness about the apparently authoritarian nature of faiths bound by custom and history.

The Relevance of Otherworldliness

The ethnic character of confessional Protestantism raises obvious questions, mentioned at the outset of the conclusion, about the degree to which this form of faith is a threat to social harmony. Writers that have treated the subject of America's ethnocultural diversity have tended toward two poles, those advocating cultural uniformity as essential to a healthy and strong nation (i.e., the melting pot ideal) and those championing the United States as a tapestry of distinct cultures, races, and creeds (i.e., the ghetto model).[11] Recent debates about multiculturalism have done little to improve American thinking on this subject since both sides have been forced to fudge the tolerance that the United States implicitly grants to all kinds of peoples; those advocating a common culture rarely acknowledge how restrictive cultural uniformity can be while those favoring diversity forget the fundamental antagonism that often exists among specific cultures. Whatever the limitations of these discussions, the obvious point throughout is that accommodating the diversity of traditions and groups that live in the United States is no easy feat. At the same time, many recognize the danger of so emphasizing a particular group's racial, sexual, or ethnic identity that retribalization of America's population is the natural result. According to David A. Hollinger, who summarizes the legacy of multiculturalism, "Our mission, apparently, is not to purge the old universalism of its corruptions but to renounce it as fatally flawed and to perfect instead the local and the particular, to live within the confines of the unique civic, moral, and epistemic communities into which we are born, to devote ourselves to our ethnos."[12] Hollinger in turn is dubious about the ethnocentrism implicit in multiculturalism and argues instead for a postethnic perspective that recognizes the "psychological value and political function of bounded groups of affiliation" but also looks for points of commonality between seemingly diverse particularities.[13]

Hollinger's concern about the balkanization that accompanies an emphasis on the local and provincial, as opposed to the universal and cosmopolitan, is one that proponents of confessional Protestantism should well consider. Not only has confessionalism historically encouraged ethnic identity and the cultural segregation that often accompanies it, but its very understanding of the Christian faith as a set of truths and habits that are different from other Christian expressions nurtures differentiation and polemic. The centrifugal tendencies of confessionalism are most obvious in comparison to the way in which pietism intrinsically facilitates assimilation and unity. The aspects of the Christian religion most dear to confessionalists—creed, polity, and liturgy—are matters formal and peripheral to pietists, thus making it easier for an understanding of Christianity based on personal experience and morality to provide a basis for unity than one that looks for theological, governmental, and liturgical consistency. The history of American Protestantism bears out this point since confessional Protestants have been the ones who most resisted interdenominational cooperation and church unity, while pietism produced ecumenism's most vocal advocates. What good is confessionalism, then, if its marks of religious identity end up breeding division and antagonism? Will not a recovery or perpetuation of confessional Protestant traditions simply add Protestant voices to the chorus already singing on behalf of multiculturalism, thereby undoing one pocket of unity that appears to exist?

One way to answer these questions is to take the offensive and respond that they simply assume a highly debatable position that holds that religion's purpose is a fundamentally harmonious and unifying one. As R. Laurence Moore has observed, this notion flies in the face of human history. He writes that it is an "odd notion" to think that "unfriendly feeling is somehow abnormal in a religiously plural society," as if such animosity were "a psychological disease based on fear and misperception." Instead, "hostility" is "altogether normal" in culturally diverse societies, American exceptionalism to the contrary.[14] Moore's point, then, is that religion is inherently divisive and one need not look far beyond the conciliatory bonds of pietism to find evidence. As much as the religious fervor and moral ideals of revivalist Protestantism wore away the sharp edges that separated America's largest denominations, they were insufficient to unite a nation. Not only were Unitarians, Catholics, Jews, and Mormons beyond the pale, but nonbelievers and skeptics were also excluded from the mainstream Protestant vision of Christian civilization in the United States. Despite pietism's attempt to find an inclusive Protestant faith that reduced Christianity to a few essentials, the universalism it found was still particular and provincial. In other words, the bar for judging confessionalism's apparent divisiveness should not be higher than the one applied to pietist Protestantism. Neither form of Protestantism is adequate to unify a religiously diverse population such as the one living in the United States, a lesson American Protestants should have mastered once they supported a national government that prevented established religion as the basis for citizenship or public office.

Pointing out pietism's faults is not the same thing as arguing for confessionalism's virtues, however. Consequently, a more straightforward answer to the charge that confessional Protestantism unhealthily divides Americans into religious ghettos is to repeat a point made earlier about the nature of confessional devotion ideally construed. This form of Protestantism is not a crusading or activist faith. In fact, a standard complaint against confessionalism is that its devotion is so spiritual that it is little good for remedying the affairs of this world. To a certain degree this criticism contains a measure of plausibility because confessional Protestantism sees the Christian life as a pilgrimage and the ministry of the church through creed, liturgy, and office as the divinely ordained means of preparing saints not to build heaven on earth but to wait and hope for the new heavens and new earth.

One of the better expressions of confessional Protestantism's spiritual devotion came at the conclusion of J. Gresham Machen's polemical book, *Christianity and Liberalism*. Many scholars who have written about this work have appropriately commented on its militant defense of historic Protestantism and its call for a division between liberals and conservatives. But seldom recognized, if Machen's closing plea is any indication, is the confessional Protestant hope for a place of worship that provides rest for weary and troubled souls, a place where the affairs of the world are inconsequential compared to the weight of eternity. He wrote:

> There must be somewhere groups of redeemed men and women who can gather together humbly in the name of Christ, to give thanks to Him for His unspeakable gift and to worship the Father through Him. Such groups alone can satisfy the needs of the soul. At the present time, there is one longing of the human heart which is often forgotten—it is the deep pathetic longing of the Christian for fellowship with his brethren.

Such places were hard to find in Machen's estimation precisely because American Protestants, both liberal and evangelical, had come to regard religion as a means to the greater good of solving the nation's many difficulties. In such cases, "the preacher comes forward, not out of a secret place of meditation and power . . . but with human opinions about the social problems of the hour or easy solutions of the vast problem of sin." The "warfare of the world" displaced Christian worship, and "the heart of the man who has come seeking peace" left church "sad indeed."[15]

Confessional Protestantism, according to Machen's logic, poses a slight threat to social harmony or cultural homogeneity because its aims are fundamentally different from those concerned with alleviating the divisions that separate races, classes, and nations. The church is supposed to be a place, Machen wrote, where believers can "forget for the moment all those things that divide nation from nation and race from race," "forget human pride," "forget the passions of war," "forget the puzzling problems of industrial strife," and "prepare for the battle of life"—namely, the battle with personal sin.[16] This way of understanding Christianity may make faith so spiritual as to make it impractical and therefore unappealing. Confessional Protestantism appears to make the church indifferent to society's woes or to the daily struggles of individuals and families; churches merely offer good news about the world to come, not short-term solutions to physical pain, political oppression, or poverty. But by redirecting the criteria for evaluating religion's usefulness away from temporal affairs to eternal realities, the faith of confessional Protestantism sidesteps responsibility for unifying humankind into a tolerant and agreeable whole. Such a duty is simply irrelevant because the purpose of faith is not to provide a blueprint for national unity or successful, well-adjusted individuals; its purpose has much more to do with the eternal drama between heaven and hell.

To assert that confessional Protestantism's concerns transcend present-day realities is not the same as saying that confessionalism is indifferent or even antagonistic to such earthly matters as a well ordered society or human happiness. Here it is important to see the supporting apparatus for confessional Protestantism's effort to deliver Protestant Christianity from the bondage of satisfying the demand for a socially and personally useful faith. Of the confessional groups studied here, both Lutherans and Calvinists make an important distinction between the religious and secular spheres. This involves no less a functional or practical understanding of faith than pietist Protestantism. But by making this distinction, confessionalists are able to answer the question of what religion is for in ways significantly different from mainstream American Protestantism, thereby extricating faith from arenas in which it can be nothing but divisive no matter how good the intention. Simply put, confessionalists contend that religion is for religious ends, not secular ones, and where they significantly part company with pietists is over definitions of the religious sphere. Whereas pietists believe that all areas of life have virtually equal religious import, confessionalists hold that some areas should be reserved for believers while others are common to both those within and outside the church.

The locus of religious significance for confessional Protestantism is the institutional or corporate church, as opposed to conceiving of the church simply as a collective body of members. For both Calvinists and Lutherans, the church formally considered has specific tasks to perform, most of which are transacted on or revolve around public worship. As such, preaching, the sacraments, and ceremonies of ordination are holy activities that set the church and its officers and members apart from those who do not administer or participate in such endeavors. At the same time, these activities are crucial elements of confessional Protestant devotion since they provide the nurture that the life of pilgrimage requires. By limiting the corporate church to the work of caring for the souls of those under its charge through sacramental and liturgical means, confessional Protestants construe religious activity much more narrowly than pietists. To borrow the words of Missouri Synod Lutherans, religion, according to this scheme, is chiefly concerned with forgiveness of sins.

Such a narrow definition of what is properly religious does not mean that confessionalists believe that other areas of life lack religious significance or that the logical result of such faith is to live the life of a hermit saint. Instead, confessional Lutherans and Calvinists both argue that outside the bounds of the corporate church is a terrain that, although still under providence, is not subject to the same standards as those that apply to the church. The former arrive at this point through the Lutheran doctrine of the two kingdoms that teaches that the kingdom of God (i.e., the church) and the kingdom of man (i.e., the state) are distinct even if church members exist in both and have a duty to work for the good of each through love of God and neighbor.[17] Presbyterians and Reformed make the same point by virtue of the doctrine of the spirituality of the church which teaches that the spiritual mission of the church is different from the temporal duties of the state and that Christians, by virtue of their membership in each, have different sets of responsibilities in the political and spiritual spheres.[18] Rather than advocating withdrawal from the world, the spiritual devotion of confessionalism supplies a different set of priorities to believers as they negotiate life outside the church. Instead of expecting nonchurchly arenas to conform to religious absolutes, as pietists who reject the distinction between sacred and secular often do, confessional

Protestantism actually supplies reasons for demanding less from earthly institutions even while recognizing their provisional importance. For confessionalists, the site of real religious action is in the church. What takes place in government or culture is negotiable and permits a variety of remedies or approaches.

This is not to say that the members of confessional Protestant churches are inherently indifferent to social and political affairs. As citizens, confessional Protestants may participate in a variety of reform and welfare endeavors according to the dictates of their consciences. But confessional Protestantism warns its adherents against looking at political reform, social welfare, or even personal happiness as a manifestation of the kingdom of God. The blessing of this warning is that it provides ammunition against executing tyranny in the name of God; the curse is that it prevents opposition to tyranny from being identified with divine will. Still, by recognizing the fundamental tension between the kingdom of God and the kingdoms of the earth in good Augustinian fashion, confessional Protestantism offers little support for either regarding one's political allies as saints or one's social enemies as villains.

This distinction between the temporal and eternal, or secular and sacred, is what allows the hyphenated Americans produced by confessional Protestantism to escape, at least ideally, the charge that such religious traditionalism contributes to the balkanization and tribalization of American society. In fact, the Lutheran doctrine of the two kingdoms and the Calvinist notion of the spirituality of the church yield precisely the kind of flexibility that David Hollinger says is necessary for cultivating a postethnic perspective on American culture. This outlook, he writes, "recognizes that most individuals live in many circles simultaneously and that the actual living of any individual life entails a shifting division of labor between the several 'we's' of which the individual is a part."[19] Confessionalism yields precisely this recognition when it narrows the religious identity of believers to their participation in the institutional church and their reception of its ministry.

To be sure, confessionalism would not so restrict this circle of identity as to make it equal with other loyalties or responsibilities. Neither, however, does confessionalism make religious commitment the exclusive location of significance for the Christian. The very idea of pilgrim implies that a person is living with some kind of dual identity, one in which he or she lives in a place that is a temporary home and that provides a means of preparing for life in the permanent or ultimate homeland. In such a setting, faith and religious activities function as a foretaste of or glimpse into the final destination. The remainder of the pilgrim's affairs are simply provisional arrangements, some of which are to be endured, others enjoyed. But these temporary affairs have only an implicit bearing on his or her pilgrimage. What explicitly matters to a pilgrim's arrival at home is participating in the circle of activities that remind of faith's ultimate destiny. In the meantime, pilgrims possess various responsibilities, from work to rearing families, that they share with neighbors whether copilgrims or not. Accordingly, by restricting the scope of religion, confessional Protestantism provides a better mechanism than pietism for sorting out the various identities in a believer's life and providing a justification for common endeavor, while also refusing to compromise on the particulars of religious duty and conviction.

This recognition of a Christian's multiple layers of existence is an important factor in assessing the features that make confessional Protestantism look particularly unappealing. In what may strike some readers as an unwise strategy, this book has emphasized the warts of confessionalism under the headings of intolerance, sectarianism, and irrelevance, the things that make the various Protestant traditions studied here look rigid, uncooperative, and otherworldly. Part of the reason for structuring the subject this way is to make the point that all religion, and especially faiths of a traditional kind, are messy and not easily domesticated for the kind of purposes that American Protestants under the influence of pietism have usually thought make religion effective.

A more important reason for structuring the material in this way is to admit the obstacles that confessional Protestantism poses to the dominant American expectations for faith. As confessional Presbyterians argued in the 1920s, theology is not an exercise in toleration but an instance of defining the faith both positively and negatively in order to establish the church's legitimate boundaries. The example of the Christian Reformed Church during the 1940s illustrates one of the implications of such boundary setting; a church committed to a certain understanding of Christianity is not always willing to cooperate with other Christian communions or groups of Christians but in fact may become more isolated the more it makes a priority of its distinctive convictions and practices.

Finally, the Missouri Synod's efforts during the 1970s and 1980s to preserve Lutheran liturgy demonstrate how the one thing all Christians do—worship—not only isolates them according to their understanding of this activity but also cannot be readily accommodated for the various cultural and political struggles that torment societies such as the United States. Liturgy actually is the most irrelevant of religious exercises if its aim is to encourage pilgrims to endure life's hardships and hope for eternal life. Yet, despite confessional Protestantism's apparently rigid attachment to the particularities of its faith, these traditions resist making demands that the theological, governmental, and liturgical norms of the church should guide public life or those outside the church. Indeed, the history of confessional Protestantism shows that one of its most compelling reasons for remaining separate from pietist Protestants who promoted Christian unity was that the path to ecumenical cooperation involved smoothing over the church's distinctive traditions in order to give Christianity a more prominent public presence. Contrary to the perception that the recovery of confessional Protestantism, as a religious form of multiculturalism, contributes to greater fragmentation of society, this form of faith actually reduces the strains that Protestants have historically put on American society by making the church, not the nation, the locus of religious energy and norms.

The Contribution of Confessionalism

By noting the affinities between confessional Protestantism and ethnic identity, readers could well conclude that this book is little more than an exercise in trying to claim for confessional Lutherans, Reformed, and Presbyterians ground already gained by advocates of cultural diversity. Such a conclusion would not be the worst thing if it yielded a greater awareness of the diversity of Protestants in the United States and the basis for such variety. The recent efforts of religious historians, for instance, have laudably increased awareness of the diversity of faiths in the United States, but, unfortunately, white Protestantism remains a religion with little variety beyond the evangelical and mainline labels. Introducing confessional Protestantism as a separate category, while also attending to differences among confessionalists, might actually reinvigorate the study of American Protestantism by moving it beyond the two-party paradigm. This approach to American Protestantism also makes available another way of making sense of Protestant diversity, other than simply cataloging it. The recovery of confessional Protestantism in the historiography of American religion suggests that the central struggle throughout Protestantism's history has been between confessionalism and pietism, not evangelicalism and liberalism.

But the point of the book is to do more than highlight diversity within the Protestant household and suggest ways to get a handle on it. Implicit throughout has been the assertion that the categories scholars use to evaluate religion in America are inadequate because they assess faith in terms foreign at least to confessional Protestantism. Too often the outlook informing the study of religion is one that asks whether a certain religious tradition makes a positive contribution to the making of tolerant, well-behaved, and civic-minded believers, an assumption that uncannily resembles that of pietism about Christianity's practical value. Confessional Protestantism invites a different form of analysis, one that asks not whether faith makes good Americans but whether it nurtures good Christians. This is a question that academics quite understandably shy away from since it lies beyond the scope of the normal lines of scholarly inquiry by adopting a normative perspective. As a confessional Presbyterian who also believes in the necessary—even if at times clumsy separation of church and academy—I have no interest in seeing religious scholars abandon their pose of neutrality or, much worse, pontificate about the tenets of Christianity.

Instead of asking scholars to make normative judgments about better or worse forms of religion, the point of examining what is involved in the making of good Christians is to call attention to particular teachings and practices that may or may not shape religious identity. Again, one assumption informing much American scholarship on religion is that people become religious according to the pietist model of making a decision, whether called a conversion or not, and voluntarily adopting a certain religion or affiliating with a specific church. Such an assumption does not require neglecting family background or religious upbringing, but it does give precedence to the individual and his or her choice. What is more, American religious scholarship reinforces the importance of individualism when it fails to consider whether a professing Baptist or Congregationalist actually believes and practices what his or her respective church teaches and requires. The decision to convert or join a church is sufficient for designating an individual as a particular kind of believer.

Confessional Protestantism invites another way of evaluating the making of believers. Its history demonstrates the importance of inheritance and the way that believers appropriate faith over a lifetime through the sustained ministry and counsel of pastors as opposed to the momentary crisis induced by the itinerant evangelist or the pressures of sitting around a fire at summer camp. In other words, confessional Protestantism raises important considerations about how people get religion, how they remain devout, whether formal religious activities make a difference in such processes, and the degree to which institutional bodies control the meaning of what it means to be religious in a particular tradition. By taking up such questions, religion scholars would not be catering to confessional Protestant interests, as if needing to make up for the pietist perspective that has governed the field. Instead, attention to patterns of inheritance in the making of believers is useful to the study of confessionalists and pietists alike since both groups desire to pass their faith on to their children. Even if parents state that their children need to make up their minds for themselves, they also invariably orchestrate things so that their children will choose to inherit the faith of the home. The study of confessional Protestantism, then, need not be a return to the narrow confines of denominational history but could actually have wider application at least to other Protestant groups in the United States if not to more general questions about inheritance and the formation of individual identity.[20]

As worthwhile as such an approach to the study of American religion may be, perhaps its greatest contribution would be to challenge the universalistic pretensions of American Protestants. To be sure, Christianity, like other world religions, makes claims that are universal in character and so motivates its adherents to seek the conversion of all people. In the United States, the dominant strain of Protestantism has confused this evangelistic impulse that lies deep within the soul of Christianity with the mission to make all Americans Christian, not simply to save their souls but to make the United States look like the kingdom of God. This identification of God's kingdom with the American nation in turn caused Protestants to abandon historic teachings and practices designed to make them and their children Christians, in favor of novel messages and means aimed at securing a righteous society. Ironically, if mainstream American Protestants had been a little more ethnocentric and less universalistic, more concerned with becoming and remaining "we" and less geared to making "them" like "us," the burden that white American Protestantism now bears as a repressive and moralistic faith would arguably be reduced considerably. If they had lived more like immigrants or in biblical categories, like aliens and strangers in the United States, mainstream Protestants might actually have discovered the spiritual resources to endure the trials of this world rather than creating hardships for others by attempting to inaugurate the world to come in this world. In sum, if American Protestants had been more confessional than pietist, their temporary home may have turned more quickly secular, but their churches may also have remained noticeably more religious.

Notes

1. John Higham, "Ethnicity and American Protestants: Collective Identity in the Mainstream," in *New Directions in American Religious History*, ed. Harry S. Stout and D. G. Hart (New York: Oxford University Press, 1997), 243.

2. See Bradley J. Longfield, *The Presbyterian Controversy: Fundamentalists, Modernists, and Moderates* (New York: Oxford University Press, 1991), 49–53.

3. Higham, "Ethnicity and American Protestants," 243.

4. David A. Hollinger, *Postethnic America: Beyond Multiculturalism* (New York: Basic Books, 1995), 122.

5. It is interesting to remember that only recently have such evangelical institutions as Wheaton College and the Billy Graham Evangelistic Association disassociated themselves from the crusader reputation, the former adopting Thunder instead of Crusader for its mascot, the latter switching from Crusade to Mission.

6. For other attempts to describe confessional Protestantism, see Robert P. Swierenga, "Ethnoreligious Political Behavior in the Mid–Nineteenth Century: Voting, Values, Cultures," in *Religion and American Politics: From the Colonial Period to the 1980s*, ed. Mark A. Noll (New York: Oxford University Press, 1990), 151–55; and James D. Bratt, "Protestant Immigrants and the Protestant Mainstream," in *Minority Faiths and the American Protestant Mainstream*, ed. Jonathan D. Sarna (Urbana: University of Illinois Press, 1998), 110–35.

7. See Walter H. Conser Jr., *Church and Confession: Conservative Theologians in Germany, England, and America, 1815–1866* (Macon, Ga.: Mercer University Press, 1984).

8. See Steve Bruce, *Conservative Protestant Politics* (New York: Oxford University Press, 1998), chap. 1.

9. David Martin, *Tongues of Fire: The Explosion of Protestantism in Latin America* (Cambridge, Mass.: Blackwell, 1990), 21.

10. Steve Bruce, *Conservative Protestant Politics* (Oxford: Oxford University Press, 1998), 24. Elsewhere in his book, Bruce attributes this characteristic of evangeli-

calism to the Protestant Reformation (9–12). But I would argue that he read more of evangelicalism back into the Reformation than he has noticed the discontinuities between Protestantism before and after the emergence of revivalism.

11. For some of the debates about ethnic identity, see Philip Gleason, *Keeping the Faith: American Catholicism Past and Present* (Notre Dame, Ind.: University of Notre Dame Press, 1987); Stephen Steinberg, *The Ethnic Myth: Race, Ethnicity, and Class in America* (New York: Athenaeum, 1981); and David A. Hollinger, "Ethnic Diversity, Cosmopolitanism, and the Emergence of the American Liberal Intelligentsia," in *In the American Province: Studies in the History and Historiography of Ideas* (Bloomington: Indiana University Press, 1985), 56–73.

12. Hollinger, *Postethnic America,* 59.

13. Hollinger, *Postethnic America,* 107.

14. R. Laurence Moore, "Learning to Love American Pluralism: A Review Essay," *American Jewish History* 77 (1987): 321.

15. J. Gresham Machen, *Christianity and Liberalism* (New York: Macmillan, 1923), 179, 180.

16. Machen, *Christianity and Liberalism,* 180.

17. See Commission on Theology and Church Relations of the LCMS, *Render unto Caesar . . . and unto God: A Lutheran View of Church and State* (St. Louis: Lutheran Church–Missouri Synod, 1995).

18. See D. G. Hart, "The Spirituality of the Church, the Westminster Standards, and Nineteenth-Century American Presbyterianism," in *The Westminster Confession in Current Thought,* ed. John H. Leith, the Colloquium in Calvin Studies VIII (privately published, 1996), 106–18.

19. Hollinger, *Postethnic America,* 106.

20. One example of such an approach is Dean R. Hoge, Benton Johnson, and Donald A. Luidens, *Vanishing Boundaries: The Religion of Mainline Protestant Baby Boomers* (Louisville, Ky.: Westminster/John Knox, 1994).

Index

Abington v. Schempp, 146–47, 148, 149
abortion, 78
absolution, 50
absolutism, 48, 49, 96
acculturation, 124
activism, xxii, xxviii, 68, 162
Adventists, 5
Ahlstrom, Sydney E., 34, 76
Albanese, Catherine, xxvi
alcohol, 16, 120, 123
Alison, Francis, 34
America, as post-Protestant, xxii
American Council of Christian Churches, 69, 70
American Lutheran, 151
American Lutheran Church, 154
American Mercury, 63
American Protestants, universalistic pretensions, 184
Americanization, 121, 124, 151, 159, 162, 173. *See also* assimilation
Ammerman, Nancy T., 66, 141
Anglican church, xxiii, 40
anti-Catholicism, 96, 120
anticlericalism, 17–19
anticreedalism, xxiii, 17–19
antiritualism, 17–19
anxious bench, 19, 51

The Anxious Bench (Nevin), 30
Apostles' Creed, xxiv, 32, 61, 62
assimilation, 121, 123, 126, 131–33, 134, 173
Auburn Affirmation, 104–5
Augsburg Confession, 44, 46–47, 48
Augustine, 180
Ayer, William Ward, 71

The Back to God Hour, 129–30
Bacon, Leonard Wolsey, 22
Baird, Robert, 4–8, 20
Balmer, Randall, xxvi–xxvii
The Banner, 129
baptism, 19, 47, 49, 160–61
baptismal regeneration, 44
Baptists, 9, 12, 17, 18, 64
Barnhouse, Donald Grey, 72
Barth, Karl, 98, 109n36
Beck, Walter H., 148
Bellah, Robert N., xix
Benevolent Empire, 16–17
Bible: authority, 104, 141–42; as book for church, 102; inerrancy, 62, 66, 100, 155; limited scope, 101–2
Bible reading in public schools, 92, 144–45
biblical criticism, 119, 122

Billy Graham Evangelistic Association, 185n5
Bloesch, Donald, 21
Bloom, Harold, xxii
Book of Common Prayer, 155
Bouma, Clarence, 127, 131
Bratt, James D., 126
Brownson, Orestes, 29
Bruce, Steve, 174, 186n10
Bryan, William Jennings, 62, 64, 73, 78, 87, 99–100, 103–4, 107, 126
Burtchaell, James Tunstead, 21
Bush, George W., xviii
Bushnell, Horace, 29
Butler, Jon, 16

The Calvin Forum, 129
Calvin, John, 18, 30–31
Calvin Seminary, 134
Calvinism, 18, 67, 107
camp meetings, 6, 8, 9
Carpenter, Joel, 72
Carroll, H. K., 4–7, 20, 22
Carter, Stephen L., xvi
catechism, 51
Cathedral of St. John the Divine (New York), 61
Cavert, Samuel McCrae, 116, 121–22
character, xvii, 146
charismatic movement, 157, 158, 160
Christian America, 97, 118, 120, 184
Christian Century, xxvii, 113
Christian Coalition, xvii, 75, 79
Christian day schools, 68, 93, 128, 148, 149–50
Christian Endeavor, 22
Christian isolation, 124
Christian Reformed Church, 115, 123–35, 181; isolation of, 130, 131–33, 134, 173–74, 181; vs. fundamentalism, 67; and National Association of Evangelicals, 126–34

Christianity and Liberalism (Machen), 89–92, 95, 177
Christianity Today, 69
church, xxiii, 60, 67; authority of, 37; catholicity of, 126; Christian Reformed conception of, 134; confessional Protestants on, 177–80; as counter-cultural, 164; dogmatism in, 91 institutional, 16–20, 21; intolerance, 94–95, 97, 98; as primarily social and temporal mission, 122; and public life, 117–18, 164; spirituality of, 94, 179, 180
church growth, 143, 155–60, 161
church office, xxiv, 20, 35, 39, 50, 159
church order, 21, 37–38, 40
church-state separation, 148, 163–64, 173
civic righteousness, 123
civil liberty, 120
civil religion, 135–36
Civil War, 118–19, 120–21
Clark, Tom C., 147
Clay, Henry, 16
clergy. *See* church office
Cole, Stewart G., 65
common grace, 126
communism, 118
Concerned Women for America, 144
Concordia Theological Seminary, 153–54, 155
confessional Protestantism, 49–50, 79; on Christian life, 171–72, 177; on the church, 105, 177–80; and ethnicity, 169–70, 175; forms of ecumenism, 135–36; vs. fundamentalism, 66–68; as intolerance, 88; as otherworldly, 59–60, 136, 144, 177; and pietism, xxiii–xxv, 183; on politics, 180; resemblance to Roman Catholicism, 49, 50; on worship, 159, 162
Congregationalists, 9
Conrad, Arcturus Zodiac, 62

contemporary Christian music, 157
contemporary worship, 143, 152, 156
conversion, xxvi, 13–14, 21, 23, 60, 122,
    183; as born-again experience, xxvii,
    71; and devotional practices, 8;
    mainstream Protestantism on, 7;
    Mencken on, 2; as paradigm for faith,
    125, 170–72, 174; and Presbyterian
    ministers, 40; as regeneration,
    xxxiiin23; Tennent on, 35; Whitefield
    on, 10–14
Cornell University, 63
creation, and providence, 101
creedal churches, 89–91
creeds, xxiii, 20, 21, 88, 105–7
crusader, 171–72
cultural diversity, 97, 175, 182
cultural uniformity, 175
culture wars, 141, 144–45, 162–63, 164
Cumberland Presbyterian Church, 119

Darwin, Charles, 107
Darwinism, 101, 104, 119, 122
Davies, Samuel, 33
democracy, and Christianity, 17–18, 24,
    96
Democratic Party, 77–78
Dickinson, Jonathan, 33
Disciples of Christ, 18, 64
Dobson, James, 75
doctrine: and experience, 42; minimalized
    in ecumenism, 132, 135
Dodge, William E., Sr. 137n17
Dutch Reformed, 10, 115, 123, 125, 169.
    See also Christian Reformed Church

Eastern Orthodox, 172–73
ecumenism, 22, 114–15, 116–23, 182;
    and civil religion, 135–36; confessional
    Protestantism forms, 135–36; and
    pietism, 22–23; and social reform, 122
Edwards, Jonathan, 6, 10
egalitarianism, 18

Eldersveld, Peter H., 129–30
election, 67
Ellingsen, Mark, 142
Elshtain, Jean Bethke, xvi
emotions, 10–11, 39
Engel v. Vitale, 146, 147
Enlightenment, 96, 99
enthusiasm, 160, 174
Episcopalians, 9, 15, 55n48, 61, 155
eschatology, 120
ethnicity, 124, 169–70
ethnocentrism, 172, 184
Evangelical Alliance, 22, 45, 119–21,
    137n17
Evangelical Foreign Missionary
    Association, 69
Evangelical Lutheran Church in America,
    152, 154, 163
evangelicalism, xxvi, 3–5; affinities with
    liberalism, xxviii, 74; as anti-
    communitarian, 15; rivalry with
    fundamentalism, 70; roots in pietism,
    xxix; and social reform, 71–74, 75–76,
    79; as traditionless, 174; worldly
    orientation, 76
evolution, 62, 68, 73, 100–101, 102–3
experience, xxiv, 10–11, 38–39, 40, 46,
    51, 157, 160

faith: based on inheritance, 174; as
    privatized, 97, 99; relevance of,
    xx–xxii, 122
Falwell, Jerry, xvii, 75, 77, 143
family values, 144
Federal Communications Commission, 72
Federal Council of Churches, 22–23, 69,
    70, 72, 113–15, 117, 123; and
    Christian Reformed Church, 126–28,
    132
Finke, Roger, 8–9, 12–13
Finney, Charles G., 9, 12, 19, 30, 32, 50,
    118
First Amendment, 12, 94, 144

First Great Awakening, xxiii, 3, 9–10, 23, 33, 34, 43
First Presbyterian Church (New York City), 61
First Vatican Council, 120
forgiveness, corporate. See absolution
forms, of religion, 12, 37–39, 49, 161
Fosdick, Harry Emerson, 61, 63, 64, 69, 95, 104, 126
Franklin, Benjamin, 11, 14
Franklin and Marshall College, 30
Freylinghuis, Theodore, 10
Fuchs, John M., 155
Fuller, Charles, 72
Fuller Theological Seminary, 69, 156
fundamentalism, xxvi, 61–68, 143–44; as revivalistic and pietistic, 67–68; and social reform, 73–74, 79

Gallup, George P., xv
general revelation, 102
De Gereformeerde Amerikaan, 124, 125
German Reformed Church, 30, 32, 51–52, 60
German-American Lutherans, 169
Gettysburg Seminary, 44
ghetto mentality, 172, 175
Gladden, Washington, 57
Graebner, Theodore, 151
Graham, Billy, 5, 70, 147, 157, 158
Granquist, Mark, 142
Guinness, Os, 163
Gustafson, David A., 159

Hartt, Rollin Lynde, 62
Hatch, Nathan O., 17, 23–24
Hatch, Orrin, 85
heart, religion of, xxi, 21, 27n52
Heidelberg Catechism, 51
Henry, Carl F. H., 72–74, 75, 77
Heyrman, Christine Leigh, 15, 17
high church Protestants, 55n48, 63. See also confessional Protestantism
Higham, John, 169

Hodge, Charles, 29, 32
Hofstadter, Richard, 89
Hollinger, David A., 170, 175, 180
holy, xxi–xxii
Homogeneous Unit Principle, 156–57
homosexuality, 141
Houghton, Will, 70, 72
Howe, Daniel Walker, 13, 16, 77
Hudson, Winthrop S., 8, 33
Hunter, James Davison, 58–59, 141, 163
Hutchison, John A., 23
hymnal revision, in Lutheran Church—Missouri Synod, 151–55

immigrants, 42–43, 45–46, 68, 97, 120, 124, 185
individualism, xix, xxiv, 12–13, 50, 51, 57–58, 60, 63, 76, 172, 183
industrialization, 5, 16, 65, 120
inheritance, 172–73, 174, 184
interdenominational cooperation. See ecumenism
Inter-Lutheran Commission on Worship, 152
intolerance, 100, 181; in academia, 106; in church, 90–92, 94–95, 97, 98; of confessions, 107; of pietistic Protestantism, 103–4
irrelevance, 181–82; of confessional Protestantism, 144; of worship, 165
Isaac, Rhys, 14, 17
itinerant evangelists, xxiii, 3, 36, 43, 50, 157, 184

Jacobsen, Douglas, xxvi
Johns Hopkins University, 88
Jordahl, Leigh, 142–43
Jordan, Philip D., 120

Kennedy, John Fitzgerald, xvi, 86
kingdom of God, 149, 179, 180
Ku Klux Klan, 64
Kuyper, Abraham, 128
labor-capital antagonism, 123
Lagerquist, L. DeAne, 44

Lambert, Franklin, 10
liberal Protestants, xxviii, 22, 70–72,
    89–91, 95; anti-Catholicism, 63; as
    anti-intellectual, 99; as intolerant, 97;
    and evangelicalism, xii; roots in
    pietism, xxix; and social reform, 79
liberty of conscience, 88, 91–92
Lieberman, Joseph, xviii
Lippmann, Walter, 105
liturgy, 143–44, 182
Livingstone, David N., xxx
Log College, 35, 36
Lord's Supper, xxiv, 19, 32, 44, 45, 47,
    49, 155, 161
low church Protestantism, 55n48, 63,
    155. See also pietistic Protestantism
Luecke, David S., 158–60, 161
Luther, Martin, 47, 48, 158, 160
Lutheran Book of Worship, 152–53, 154, 155
Lutheran Church in America, 154
Lutheran Church–Missouri Synod,
    123–24, 182; assimilation, 162–63; on
    charismatic movement, 160; on church
    growth, 155–60; as evangelical, 141–42;
    and fundamentalism, 67, 141–42; on
    religion in public schools, 147–48; on
    worship, 143, 151–55, 163, 164
Lutheran Church–Wisconsin Synod, 143,
    154
The Lutheran Hymnal, 151–52
Lutheran Worship, 151, 153, 155, 160, 161,
    163
Lutherans: Americanization of, 44, 151,
    159; on church and state, 163–64;
    colonial, 42–43; confessionalism,
    46–49, 60; on generic Protestantism,
    48–49; on inerrancy, 155; moderates,
    45–46; pietism, xxi, 43–44, 46, 159

Macartney, Clarence Edward, 62
Machen, J. Gresham, 62, 66–67, 88–107,
    169, 177–78; on Auburn Affirmation,
    104–5; as authoritarian, 95–97; as
    Presbyterian confessionalist, 89–91; on

public education, 92–94; on science,
    99–103; southernness, 169; on
    spirituality of church, 94
mainline Protestantism, xxxn11, 5, 32, 96;
    decline of, xiii–xiv; as evangelical, 7;
    and pietism, xxiii
Mann, William Julius, 46–49
Manning, William T., 61, 62, 66
Marsden, George M., 96, 119, 143
Marshall College, 30
Martin, David, 174
Marty, Martin E., xxiv, 57–58, 117
Mathews, Donald G., 16
Mathews, Shailer, 69
McCollum v. Board of Education, 147
McCosh, James, 120, 121, 137n17
McGavaran, Donald, 156
McIntire, Carl, 69, 70
means of grace, 19, 47, 160–61
megachurches, 157, 162
Melanchthon, Philip, 47
melting pot ideal, 175
Mencken, H. L., xxi, 2–3, 63–64, 90, 107
Mercersburg Review, 30
Mercersburg Theological Seminary,
    29–30, 32, 45
Methodism, as American form of
    Protestantism, 125, 174
Methodists, 8–9, 12, 14, 17, 18, 64
military chaplaincy, 126
millennialism, 78
Miller, Jean. See Schmidt, Jean Miller
miracles, 103
Moberg, David, 75–76, 78
modernists. See liberal Protestants
modernity, 173
Monsma, Nicholas J., 129
Moody Bible Institute, 62, 70
Moody, Dwight L., 1, 12, 21–22
Moore, R. Laurence, xxix, 4, 105, 176
Moral Majority, xvii, 75
moralism, xxx–xxxi
Mormons, 5, 85–87
Muhlenberg, Henry Melchior, 44, 46

Mullins, Robert Bruce, 55n48
multiculturalism, 170, 175–76, 182
music, 156–57

National Association of Christian
    Schools, 69
National Association of Evangelicals,
    69–72, 113–15; as Arminian, 129;
    and Christian Reformed Church,
    126–34; cultural analysis of, 138; as
    fundamentalist, 129–31; and
    Lutherans, 142
National Council of Churches, 116,
    117–18, 121
National Religious Broadcasters, 69
National Sunday School Association, 69
nationalism, 65, 73, 120, 136, 177
"Neo-Lutheran" party, 45–46
neo-Protestants, 80
Neuhaus, Richard John, 163
Nevin, John Williamson, 29–32, 50–51,
    160
new measures, 12, 19, 50
The New Republic, xviii, xxi
New School Presbyterians, 118–19, 120,
    137n17
New Side Presbyterians, 33–42
New York Times, 147
Niebuhr, H. Richard, 65
Niebuhr, Reinhold, 79, 147
Northern Baptist Convention, 65
northern Presbyterians, 22, 88, 98,
    118–19
Nott, Eliphalet, 31
Nybakken, Elizabeth, 34

Ockenga, Harold John, 69, 70, 71
"Old Lutherans", 45–46
Old School Presbyterians, 118–19,
    137n17
Old Side Presbyterians, 33–42, 60, 169
open-air meetings, 11

ordination. See church office
Orthodox Judaism, xviii
otherworldliness, 136, 177

Paine, Stephen W., 70
paleo-Protestants, 80
papacy, 16
parachurch associations, 118
Park Street Church (Boston), 70
Parker, Daniel, 18
Parks, Leighton, 62
parochial schools, 68, 150
pastors. See church office
Pentecostalism, 157, 160
perfectionism, xxiv
Pew, J. Howard, 118
Pierard, Richard V., 75–76
pietistic Protestantism, xxii–xxiii, 8, 40; as
    activistic, 171–72; and church, 21; and
    ecumenism, 22–23, 115; individualism
    of, 60; intolerance of, 103–4; legacy
    of, 20–24; and liturgy, 159; in
    Lutheranism, 43, 159; and mainstream
    Protestantism, xxiv; as provincial, 176;
    public and political side, 59; as
    relevant, 74, 144; on worship, 159,
    162
pilgrim, pilgrimage, 162, 171–72, 177,
    179, 180–81
Pius X, Pope, 95
Pollack, W. G., 151
polygamy, 85
prayer in public schools, 92, 144–45, 164
preaching, 10, 19
Presbyterian Alliance, 119
Presbyterians, 9; Adopting Act, 35;
    authoritarianism among, 98; as
    churchly, 31; creedalism, 88; form of
    government, 40; fundamentalists, 64;
    and Great Awakening, 10; and pietism,
    xxiii. See also New School Presbyterians;
    New Side Presbyterians; northern

Presbyterians; Old School
   Presbyterians; Old Side Presbyterians;
   southern Presbyterians
Presbytery of Donegal, 41
Presbytery of Philadelphia, 34
Preus, J. A. O., 153–54
Prime, Samuel Irenaeus, 137n17
Princeton Seminary, 62, 88
"progressive fundamentalists", 69
progressives, 58, 65, 78
Prohibition, xix, 73, 78
Protestant Reformed Church, 126
Protestantism: and American ideals, 52,
   86–87, 97, 98, 120–21; as benign
   influence, xvii
providence, 101, 103, 179
provincialism, 175, 176
"public church", xx, 117
public morality, 120, 123, 147
public schools, 128, 145–49
Puritans, xx, 6, 31

radio evangelism, 72
Reagan, Ronald, 75
Reed, Ralph, 75, 79
Reformed Church in America, 114, 123
Reformed Ecumenical Synod, 133
Reformed Journal, 134
regeneration, xxxiiin23
Reifsnyder, Richard W., 123
religion: as divisive, 176; free-market
   approach, 12; genuine, 37, 43, 157;
   and public life, xvi–xviii; as relevant,
   xviii, xxi; trivialization of, xviii
religious disestablishment, 12
religious freedom, 173
religious right, 75–77, 143
revivalism, xx, 3, 6–8, 23, 125, 186n10;
   and activism, 68; and anti-Catholicism,
   49; and institutional church, 17–20;
   Nevin on, 29–32; piety of, 39;
   reinforcing of conservative

Protestantism, 41–42; and relevance, 8;
   rugged individualism, 50; as science, 9;
   and social reform, 73; subjectivity of,
   31; vs. Reformation, 186n10
Riley, William Bell, 62, 73
ritual, 21, 157
Robertson, Pat, xvii, 75, 79, 143
Roeber, A. G., 162–63
Roman Catholics, 3, 5, 63, 71, 86; as
   anti-American, 78, 96; and
   authoritarian Protestantism, 95; as
   fundamentalism, 66; Lutherans on, 44,
   47–48; immigration of, 19, 49; piety,
   21, 172–73; on Protestant religious
   exercises, 145. See also anti-Catholicism

Sabbath observance, 16, 44, 59, 120,
   123
sacraments, 19, 47, 50
Saint-Cyran, 21
Salvation Army, 25n17
Scaer, David P., 142
Scandinavia, 46
Schaff, Philip, 4, 45–46, 47
Schmidt, Jean Miller, 58–59
Schmucker, Samuel Simon, 44–45,
   46–48, 159
Schneider, Robert A., 116
school prayer, 78
science, 65, 87, 99–100, 102–3
Scopes trial, 73, 87, 99–100
Scotch-Irish, 32–33, 169
Scottish Enlightenment, 96
Second Great Awakening, 16
Second Vatican Council, 152
sectarianism, 113, 116–17, 134–35, 181
secular/sacred distinction, 178–80
secularism, 65, 66, 71, 147
secularization, 147, 173
"seeker service", 156
self-denial, 77
self-discipline, 14–16

self-righteousness, xxvx–xxxi
Seminex, 154
separatism, 69–70
Sherrill, Henry Knox, 118
slavery, xxi, 16, 120
small groups, xxiv, 50
Smith, Al, 86
Smith, Christian, xvi
Smith, Gerald Birney, 95
Smoot, Reed, 85–86
Social Gospel, 7, 57–58, 60, 72, 79, 122
social reform, 13, 16, 59, 79; and
    ecumenism, 122; in evangelicalism,
    71–74
sociologists, xxvii–xxviii
sola scriptura, 20
southern Presbyterians, xvi, 98, 114
special revelation, 102
Spener, Phillipp Jacob, 43
Stark, Rodney, 8–9
state churches, 173
Stellhorn, Arthur C., 148
Stob, George, 134
subscription, 35, 40
Sunday, Billy, 1–3, 8, 12, 22, 30, 57, 59,
    60, 62, 66, 70, 73, 125–26, 157
Sunday school, 22
Supreme Court, 144, 146–47
Sweet, William Warren, 64–65
Syllabus of Errors (1864), 120

temperance, 59
Tennent, Gilbert, 33, 35–37, 39, 44
Tennent, William, Sr., 35
this-worldly spirituality, 8
Thomson, John, 38–40
Tietjen, John, 153–54
Time magazine, 61–62
tolerance, xv, 175, 183
Torrey, Reuben, 62
tradition, and revivalism, 12, 17
transformation of society, 58, 59
tribalism, 117, 118

Trinterud, Leonard J., 33, 54n30
Trollinger, William Vance, Jr., xxvi, 73
Truemper, David G., 159–60
Tuttle, Harold S., 145–46, 149
two kingdom teaching, 149, 163, 164,
    179–80
two-party paradigm (American
    Protestantism), xxvi–xviii, 58–59, 79,
    182

Union College, 31, 32
Unitarians, 69, 91
United Presbyterian Church, 114
Universalists, 5
urbanization, 5, 65, 119

voluntary associations, 16, 22, 91–92,
    94

Warfield, B. Benjamin, 63, 101
Weigel, Luther A., 149
Westerkamp, Marilyn J., 13
Westminster Confession of Faith, 35, 90, 99,
    105, 106, 119
Wheaton College, 185n5
Whig political thought, 16, 77–78, 96,
    120
White, James F., 157
Whitefield, George, 9–15, 17, 22, 36, 44,
    157
Will, George F., 85
Willow Creek Community Church,
    156–57
Wills, Gary, 104
Wilson, Woodrow, 78, 86–87
Wolfe, Alan, 105
women's ordination, 141
women's societies, 22
Word and sacrament, 160–61, 171. See
    also means of grace
working class, 123
World Alliance of Reformed Churches,
    119

World Christian Fundamentals
    Association, 73
World Relief Commission, 69
World War I, 73
worship, 125, 159, 177, 179; as irrelevant
    to world, 165; Lutherans on, 142–43,
    149, 150–63; as nurture, 162; in
    public schools, 146

Wright, J. Elwin, 70
Wuthnow, Robert, xxvii–xxviii

YMCA, 22, 25n17
YWCA, 22

Zwaanstra, Henry, 125, 126
Zwingli, Ulrich, 47

About the Author

D. G. Hart is academic dean and professor of church history at Westminster Theological Seminary in California. His other books include *Defending the Faith: J.Gresham Machen and the Crisis of Conservative Protestantism in Modern America* (1994), for which he won the Presbyterian Historical Society's Makemie Award and, most recently, *The University Gets Religion: Religious Studies and American Higher Education* (1999). He and his wife, Ann, live in Escondido, California.